Anne Frankland
The First Lady of Secheron House

Navarine Publishing

First published in 2025 by Navarine Publishing
GPO Box 2178, Hobart, Tasmania 7001
www.navarine.net

Copyright © Nicole Mays
Typesetting by Nicole Mays

Printed in Australia by IngramSpark

All rights reserved. No part of this publication may be produced, stored in a retrieval system or transmitted in any form by any means without the prior permission of the copyright owner.

Enquiries should be made to nicmays@gmail.com

ISBN: 978-1-7637259-2-8

A catalogue record for this book is available from the National Library of Australia

Please note that while the author has intended to provide a definitive and accurate history and profile of Anne Mason, George Frankland and their respective families, some events, names, dates and locations may have been unintentionally and/or incorrectly stated or omitted. Additionally, the author has made inferences as to apparent gaps in their history. Please also note that place names have been used as they were in the times of Anne and George Frankland, particularly those based in India, and that though correct at the time of publication, some website addresses may have become outdated. The author apologises for any errors or omissions. Steps have also been taken to contact copyright owners of images used in this book. Please email nicmays@gmail.com with any questions.

COVER IMAGES:

Painting by George Frankland of an immigrant family arriving at Hobart Town (1827). Allport Library and Museum of Fine Arts, State Library of Tasmania (AUTAS001139593552).

Map of the Secheron Estate (April 1837).
Tasmanian Archives (NS596/1/1).

Contents

Introduction	1
Choices and Resolve	3
Part One	5
Marriage and Settlements	7
Cloth and Coventry	17
Merchants and Money	29
Land and Attorneys	45
London and Napoleon	61
Part Two	69
Clergy and Cholera	71
Babies and Voyages	93
Surveys and Society	103
Secheron and Security	117
Distress and Death	139
Part Three	165
England and Legacy	167
Epilogue	187
Family Tree	190
Index	193

Opposite: Pencil sketch adapted from a photo of Secheron House (1970s).
Tasmanian Archives (LPIC1/3/113).

Introduction

I started writing this book on a whim, not knowing where it would lead. I was in the process of finishing a book on the nineteenth century boat and ship builders of Battery Point, regularly coming across press and other references to the occupants of Secheron House, completed in 1832, including the Frankland, Perry, Pedder and Clarke families. I decided to delve a little deeper into these higher-profile members of Hobart Town's society and their occupancy of this vast estate. It proved quite the adventure, particularly with regards to the ladies of Secheron House.

Independent of records related to births, deaths and marriages, it is often quite difficult to piece together the lives, stories, historical context and significance of women born prior to the twentieth century, unless they were involved in something quite extraordinary. For most women, however, their existence in newspapers, statutory records and other sources of information is

largely associated with those of their fathers, husbands, brothers, sons or other male relations. They are somewhat dormant, hidden in the shadows of history, assumed to be taking lesser-realised parts in the myriad of situations, events and opportunities that came their way, whether welcoming or devastating. Regardless of social status or wealth, however, they often endured loveless marriages; the brutality of mediocre medical care, particularly during childbirth and their children's infant years; the loss of husbands, children, parents, siblings and friends to ailments that would today be considered minor; as well as financial hardship and social and legal constraints. Yet despite these obstacles, for the women of Secheron House at least, they had certain predisposed privileges predominantly associated with their upper-class standing, including education, travel, wealth, fashion and household help.

Like the residence itself, just a 15-minute walk from Hobart, the ladies of Secheron House, Battery Point, stand today as a testament to more than just their perceived role in colonial Van Diemen's Land and nineteenth-century British life. Their lives and memories are intertwined with this home. Built by Van Diemen's Lands' first Surveyor General, George Frankland, the Gothic and Georgian-era sandstone house once stood starkly yet proudly overlooking a small, sheltered bay on the edge of the River Derwent. For nearly 100 years it was also surrounded by eight acres of gardens and fields, until the property was subdivided in the 1920s. While Secheron House itself survives, what was originally envisioned as an expansive and romantic enclave for George, his wife Anne, and their children, is rather belittled by neighbouring properties of varying architectural styles and forms. The land it overlooked is now soaked up by flats, houses, roads and footpaths, encroaching almost to the residence's doorstep. Still, it was once a grand estate befitting of the women who lived there.

Relying on a patchwork of primary and secondary sources, this book relays the life and times of the first lady of Secheron House, Anne Frankland (nee Mason), who lived there from its construction until shortly prior to her husband's death in late 1838. Born in Coventry, Warwickshire, England, in 1793, Anne lived a remarkable life up until her own death in 1843, during this period spending time in England, India, South Africa and Australia.

Choices and Resolve

Anne Mason was 26 years old when she first eyeballed the ship *Phoenix* on the River Thames in London. A bobbing structure much smaller than she envisioned, it was to be her home for the next four months. With all the passengers, luggage and supplies still to be taken on board she wondered how they would all fit.

It was with a swirl of emotions that Anne had left her grandmother's London home that morning for the last time: relief, trepidation and resolve. Though rarely discussed and only briefly opined in quiet conversations with her mother Dorothea and grandmother Arabella, Anne knew that she had been pushed into employment through the choices her family had made going back generations. There had been money, lots of money, but it was all but gone. Frivolous transactions had reduced her family into fools. The worst were the investments and mortgages on sugar plantations in the West Indies, sure propositions that were considered sound by her grandfather Nathaniel but were in fact the opposite. The financial losses had been devastating, thousands and thousands of pounds, if not more, but there had also been the human loss of her uncle Nathaniel (Jr) whom she barely remembered from childhood. His death from yellow fever while trying to sort out the family's business dealings in Tobago and Jamaica was still deeply regretted even though it had occurred decades before. And, shockingly, the loss of her grandmother Ann, whom she never met, who died well before her time in Lisbon, Portugal, while trying to recuperate from the ills that plagued her and the loss of a grand fortune that her husband had frittered away. While she knew only snippets of the true circumstances, Anne was poignantly aware of her family's woes. It was only through the kindness and charity of relatives that they had managed to retain a perception of their status. Loans made and forgiven behind closed doors, funds bequeathed through various wills and testaments, and help with finding employment and gaining apprenticeships masked the financial realties of the situation.

A lady of high upbringing and manners, Anne was the product of an upper-class family with a proud history of well-regarded professional and charitable men, including merchants, mercers, headmasters, reverends and attorneys. There had also been land and estates worthy of grand mansions and visiting gentry. But those assets and resources had been recklessly mismanaged, her grandfather and father draining the family's coffers. In recent years, when the situation had become dire, Anne had felt like an impostor amongst her own class. Though extensively educated, fluently speaking French and Italian, Anne and her sisters had become experts in concealing worn and threadbare gloves, bonnets, stockings and shoes. Accustomed to not having the latest fashions, they had learned to improvise as best they could.

While Anne lamented the loss of a life that could have been, she resolved to not feel its shame. It was not her burden to carry. She was the product of past generations but did not need to continue their downward legacy nor hold on to their mantle of destruction. She could make better choices. She would make better choices. There were obviously few options for a single woman like her, just past the age of marriage, but there were some. Thanks to a family rich in educational stewardship, particularly of its women, she could teach. Her eldest sister Arabella had secured a position as a governess for a family based in Ireland. Though this situation was far from ideal, Arabella wrote kind words of encouragement and positive thoughts of the adventure Anne was about to make. How often did single women get the opportunity to travel abroad, to India of all places? Arabella was always trying to see the good of any situation and Anne thanked her for her optimism. Was it a choice though? No. There was no money left, only debt. By necessity she had to support herself, wherever the waves would take her. *Que Sera, Sera.*

Part One

Marriage and Settlements

With Anne Mason about to leave England for India in June 1820, we must rewind a few generations back to set the scene as to why she was a passenger on board the *Phoenix* that day. Choices and decisions made well before she was born had impacted her life profoundly. Our story thus begins with one such transaction: a marriage settlement. A legal contract that promulgated several generations of siblings, particularly women, into a prosperous future, ultimately filtering down to our subject at hand, the yet-to-be-born Anne Mason (later Frankland). Though such settlements are obsolete and considered rather draconian by today's standards, they were once regarded as standard practice for those within the middle and upper classes of Georgian-era Great Britain.

It is almost impossible for anyone in today's Western world of equality to fathom that, despite the overture of immense fortunes, there was minimal power bequeathed to women at the time of their marriage. Instead, the lady in question was the vehicle for the transfer of assets; the primary benefactor being her husband. Land, property, large sums of money, stock, securities and other resources routinely passed from the bride's father to her impending spouse via a formally-negotiated legal document, often punctuated with various clauses, claims and provisions. This 'dowry' was intended to not only secure the bride's immediate future and that of any children produced by the marriage, but to also support her should she be widowed. Given the state of healthcare in Britain during the 1700s, as well as the fact that wives were often much younger than their husbands, it was quite common for women to outlive their partners, often by several decades.

In rather callous circumstances belittling the true state of the union, marriage settlements were undoubtedly also an arrangement to further business, status and/or political interests and aspirations as opposed to the standard of today: emotional connections. It was not uncommon for patriarchs of the family to select their daughter's potential husband with the goal of benefitting commercial or other enterprises and interests. Though Jane Austen has memorialised Georgian-era England with her tales of kinship, compatibility and romance in several of her books, including *Pride and Prejudice,* her second novel published in 1813 which is centred around the five Bennet sisters, specifically Jane and Elizabeth, the harsh reality facing most middle and upper class brides during this period was something quite different to a 'love match'. Young ladies were rarely fortunate to find their own potential suitors. While there were eligible bachelors in the rotation, none were quite akin to the fictionalised Mr Bingley and Mr Darcy, both handsome and well resourced, with Mr Darcy in particular said to be worth at least £10,000 a year.[1]

It is in this context that we turn our attention to the marriage of Anne Mason's great-grandmother, Ann Fletcher, born in London around 1714. While there are very few records regarding the specifics of Ann Fletcher's marriage settlement to Thomas Hunt, which was negotiated in London in September 1736, the newspaper report of the union itself clearly states her pedigree, i.e., that she was the '*second daughter of the late Mr. Thomas Fletcher, an eminent Haberdasher in Cheapside*'. In standard publishing practices of the day, however, it further noted that Ann was '*a very agreeable young Lady with a fortune of 5000 l* [i.e., £5,000]'. How convenient for her new husband that she was both well-liked and wealthy.

> Yesterday Thomas Hunt, Esq; Mayor of the City of Coventry, and Receiver General of the Land Tax for the same City and County of Warwick, was married to Miss Fletcher, second Daughter of the late Mr. Thomas Fletcher, an eminent Haberdasher in Cheapside, a very agreeable young Lady, with a Fortune of 5000 l.

Daily Journal, 10 September 1736.

---

[1] J. Austen (1813). *Pride and Prejudice.*

Cheapside at the time of Ann Fletcher's marriage was a thriving and populous commercial precinct of London, known for its high-end wares and goldsmiths. Despite being decimated by the Great Fire which had occurred in early September 1666, much of the area had been rebuilt, predominantly made up of multi-storey buildings housing shops and other businesses on the ground floor with residences and lodgings for business owners, their families and their workers located above. While utilised by the British peerage for shopping and commercial activities, Cheapside was considered rather below their station to live. Instead, their grand townhouses within the bounds of London, as opposed to their vast country estates, were situated nearby in newly minted and elite districts such as the West End, including Mayfair. Cheapside's commerce thrived on their patronage, however, along with that of the ever-expanding middle class, eager consumers of goods and fashion. This demand, combined with the spurts of an industrial revolution catalysing rapid economic, technological and social change, meant that many of Cheapside's enterprising merchants soon became wealthy, in the process becoming building blocks of a new society: the upper-middle class. With shrewd and savvy business skills some saw their class status improved in only one or two generations, in the process buying their own country properties and accumulating other assets. This appears to have been the case for Ann Fletcher's father Thomas.

Rising up in society's ranks, helped by a strategic marriage on his own part to Jane Huckell, the daughter of a draper and leather seller, with the ceremony taking place at the Collegiate Church of St Katherine By the Tower, London, in July 1706, Thomas Fletcher had undoubtedly undertaken a seven-year apprenticeship with his father, a master haberdasher, beginning in his teenage years.[2] This qualification then allowed him to acquire the Freedom of the City of London, a status not only associated with social prestige but commercial privileges, including rights of franchise, rights to office, rights to charitable maintenance in old age and, perhaps most importantly, the right to trade or open a shop within the city.[3] He achieved this landmark position in December 1711.[4]

[2] London, England, Wills and Probate, 1507-1858 for Thomas Fletcher (1715); England & Wales, Prerogative Court of Canterbury Wills, 1384-1858 for Thomas Huckell (1738); London, England, Church of England Baptisms, Marriages and Burials, 1538-1812.
[3] P. Earle (1989). *The Making of the English Middle Class: Business, Society and Family Life in London, 1660-1730.*
[4] London, England, Freedom o the City Admission Papers, 1681-1930 for Thomas Fletcher.

Though start-up costs would have been in the realms of hundreds and hundreds of pounds to purchase stock to trade alone, indicating that he was likely helped by family, Thomas Fletcher managed to not only establish a haberdashery business in Cheapside but to nurture it into prosperity. Due to this commercial success, he was 59 years of age at the time of his death and during his lifetime had amassed a small fortune, equivalent to more than £3.6 million in today's money, in addition to owning estates and other properties in Buckingham and Lincoln counties.[5] Given the difference in purchasing power in the 1730s compared to nowadays, whereby the average house cost £10 to rent per year, with annual wages of most lower class workers, including labourers and servants, less than £30, it was quite a considerable amount.[6] In comparison, the perceived minimum yearly income to be considered middle class at the time was around £50. This sum was apparently enough to provide a family with comfortable housing, more than ample food and clothes, as well as pay for household servants.[7]

Indicative of his status within the upper bounds of this burgeoning class, the *London Daily Post and General Advertiser* on 11 February 1736 reported on Thomas' death. '*Yesterday about Two in the Afternoon died Mr. Thomas Fletcher, an eminent Haberdasher of Small Wares, in Cheapside, reputed to have died worth upwards of 20,000l. all of which he acquired with a very fair character.*'

Thomas Fletcher's last will and testament is a fascinating though long read with a level of detail and forethought expressive of his care and concern for his family, particularly his '*dear wife*' Jane and their three daughters, Mary, Ann and Jane (Jr). Given the eighteenth-century handwriting and use of now antiquated terms, the document is also quite difficult to decipher and interpret in certain parts, which spans seven pages, particularly owing to the tendency of the transcriber to make the letters 'c' and 'h' appear to be an 'r' and 's', respectively. Still, obviously written after the marriage of his oldest daughter Mary to Richard Morhall, which occurred in November 1734, Thomas Fletcher took great pains to not only succinctly detail provisions for his wife and two unmarried daughters but also for Mary. With an apparent disregard for his

---

[5] www.bankofengland.co.uk/monetary-policy/inflation/inflation-calculator;
Thomas Fletcher, National Archives UK: PROB-11-675-401.
[6] P. Langford (1989). *A Polite and Commercial People: England 1727-1783.*
[7] P. Earle (1989). *The Making of the English Middle Class: Business, Society and Family Life in London, 1660-1730.*

Opposite: Page five of Thomas Fletcher's will (1735).
National Archives UK, Probate 11-675-40.

Twenty one years or Day of Marriage with such Consent as aforesaid Then I Will that her said Portion of Three Thousand pounds and the Interest thereof shall be and remain unto and amongst my said Dear Wife Jane Ffletcher and my said Son Thomas Ffletcher and my said Daughters Mary Morhall and Anne Ffletcher and the Survivors or Survivor of them equally to be divided between them if more than One of them shall be liveing at such the decease of my said Daughter Jane share and share alike Item I give and bequeath unto my said two Daughters Anne Ffletcher and Jane Ffletcher the further Sume of One Thousand pounds a peice of like Money upon their respective Marriages but not before or otherwise Provided that such Marriages respectively shall be had with the Consent and Approbation of my said Dear Wife Jane Ffletcher if then liveing But if my said Daughters Anne Ffletcher and Jane Ffletcher or either of them shall marry without such Consent as aforesaid or shall dye before their said Legaryes of One Thousand pounds a peice shall become payable according to this my Will Then and in either of the said Cases I Will that the said last mentioned Legary or Legaryes of her or them so dying or marrying without such Consent as aforesaid shall go and remain to and amongst all my other Children or such One or more of them and in such parts and proportions manner and forme as my said Dear Wife Jane Ffletcher if then liveing shall by any Writing under her hand and seale attested by two or more credible Witnesses direct or appoint the same or any part thereof And in default of such Direction or Appointment as aforesaid Then the same Legary or Legaryes shall go and remain unto and amongst all my other Children or such of them as shall be then surviveing equally to be divided between them (if more than One) share and share alike Provided also and my expresse Mind and Will is that in Case my said Wife and Children or my said Son in Law Richard Morhall or any of them shall not acquiesce and rest satisfyed and contented with the Disposition I have hereby made of my Estate but shall claim any part of my Estate by vertue of the Custom of the City of London whereof I am a freeman or shall give any Trouble Molestation or Disturbance to the others or other of them my said Wife and Children or any of them on that Account or otherwise on Account of this my Will Then and in such Case the Legary or Legaryes Sume or Sumes of Money and Bequests hereby given to or for the benefitt of him her or them who shall make such Claim or give such Trouble Molestation or Interruption as aforesaid shall cease determine and be utterly void And Then also and in such Case such of them my said Wife and Children who shall make any such Claim or give such Trouble or Interruption as aforesaid shall not have or claime any Part or Share of the Testamentary Part of my Estate but the Share or Shares of him her or them shall go over and be equally divided unto and amongst such of them my said Wife and Children who shall acquiesce in and rest satisfyed with the aforesaid Disposition of my Estate and son-in-law, the will intentionally circumvents the legal status of a married woman; at the time (and up until 1882) considered to be under the protection and authority of her husband, with her assets, including her clothes and jewellery, belonging solely to him. However, there were exceptions such that a married woman could be left money or property for her own use if this was specifically written into a will, precisely by inserting the phrase *'for her own and separate use and benefit notwithstanding coverture'*.[8] Thomas Fletcher used this exact expression to establish a trust for Mary Morhall earmarking £1,000 for the purchase of real estate on her behalf with the income generated from the rent being for her sole use. Interestingly, there was a further stipulation in the document that stated *'in case of any such claim or molestation from the said Richard Morhall'*, including concerning the shares, sums of money, estate trusts and limitations intended for his wife Mary and thereby ultimately to be passed down to any children they may have, then these items would *'cease and be void'*. Such specificity in language certainly meant that Mary Morhall was more than adequately provided with independence from her husband, as well as resources.

Thomas Fletcher's will also bequeathed both large and small sums of money to his sister, brothers-in-law, father-in-law and business partner. While most of the estate was left to his wife Jane, their son Thomas (Jr) received £1,500, with the couple's two unmarried daughters, Ann and Jane (Jr), receiving £3,000 each with an additional £1,000 to be paid *'upon their respective marriages but not before or otherwise provided that such marriages respectively shall be had with the consent and appropriation of my said dear wife Jane Fletcher'*.[9]

By reason that Jane Fletcher obviously consented to the union, Ann Fletcher, aged over 21 years, and Thomas Hunt were married at Saint Anne and Saint Agnes, London, on Sunday 9 September 1736. The church, built by Christopher Wren in 1680, had also been the location of Ann's sisters' marriage to Richard Morhall.[10] Despite being one hundred miles from Thomas Hunt's residence in Coventry, Warwickshire, it was a convenient location for the Fletcher family, situated only a few blocks from their home in Wood Street, Cheapside.

---
[8] www.oldbaileyonline.org/about/coinage.
[9] Thomas Fletcher, National Archives UK: PROB-11-675-401.
[10] London, England, Church of England Baptisms, Marriages and Burials, 1538-1812 for Mary Fletcher.

Map of London showing Cheapside (1736).
Homannsche Erben, Wikimedia Commons.

Saint Anne and Saint Agnes Church

Wood Street, Cheapside

The ceremony came at the end of a tumultuous period for Ann and her family. Less than a year before, on 29 November 1735, her 20-year-old brother Samuel, an apprentice linen draper, had died. His death notice, published in the *General Evening Post*, reiterated the family's profile, stating that he was the son of '*Mr. Thomas Fletcher, a considerable Haberdasher of Small Wares, near Wood-Street, Cheapside*'.[11] As mentioned, not two months later Ann's father passed away. Bearing in mind that the customary period of mourning at the time was six months for a parent, the marriage of Ann Fletcher and Thomas Hunt was just within this convention. Still, 34-year-old Thomas made no consideration for his own mourning given his father Samuel had only died three weeks prior, on 18 August 1736, at the age of 78.[12]

---
[11] *General Evening Post*, 4 December 1735.
[12] www.findagrave.com/memorial/202439939/samuel-hunt.

Marriage record of Thomas Hunt and Ann Fletcher (1736).
London, England, Church of England Baptisms, Marriages and Burials, 1538-1812.

Ann and Thomas' wedding ceremony was performed under special licence, as opposed to banns, indicating that the couple intentionally avoided the publicity of having the details of their intended union called in church over a period of three consecutive Sundays. The need for privacy and perhaps, more importantly, a shorter timeframe came at a cost with the price of a licence much more expensive than a ceremony performed by the usual banns.

A mercer by trade, i.e., a dealer in fine and expensive cloth and textiles that could not be produced locally, Thomas' father Samuel had additionally been involved in local politics within his home county of Warwickshire and more specifically within the city of Coventry. Of note, Samuel Hunt had served as City Warden in 1688, Sheriff in 1697 and Mayor of Coventry in 1707.[13] He was also the trustee of several tithes, lands, charities and estates located in and around Coventry, as well as assisted with administration of the still-extant Bond's Hospital.[14]

Samuel Hunt's will, which he signed on 7 May 1735, provides some interesting context to the situation that Thomas Hunt suddenly found himself in immediately upon his father's death.[15] As the third child though only son born to Samuel and his wife

---
[13] L. Fox (1986). *Coventry Constables' Presentments, 1629-1742*.
[14] www.coventrycollections.org/search/details/archive/110193929.
[15] Staffordshire, Dioceses of Lichfield And Coventry Wills And Probate 1521-1860.

Hanna, it was likely that Thomas expected to inherit some money and assets upon his father's death, or even to become an executor of his estate. However, while his two sisters and several nieces and nephews received between £100-£150 each, Thomas Hunt was bequeathed only £10 to purchase mourning attire.[16] The remainder of the estate, including property, chattels, money and securities, was left to his mother Hanna. This may have been the reason why, only a few weeks later, Thomas found himself in London in search of a wife.

Exactly how Ann Fletcher and Thomas Hunt met is not known. Considering London's population was approaching 700,000 at the time, they were perhaps introduced through some sort of mutual association. The city was also the seat of government and the centre of banking, commerce and manufacturing so it would not have been out of the ordinary for Thomas Hunt to regularly visit the metropolis, particularly if he had warehouses in the area. Thomas was a mercer by trade, like his father, and thereby could have been a wholesale supplier of cloth and textiles to the Fletcher family's business. It is thus possible they met one another through Ann's older brother Thomas who would have been in the process of finalising arrangements for the transfer of their late father's haberdashery business, though her mother Jane, as sole executor, would have also been involved in this process. What better way to converge a haberdashery business well-established in London with that of a mercer, similarly well-established but in Coventry.

The marriage contract between Ann Fletcher and Thomas Hunt was likely negotiated by Ann's mother Jane and her older brother Thomas and probably echoed that of her older sister Mary's who had married Richard Morhall of Shrewsbury, Shropshire, in November 1734.[17] Importantly, and again indicative of an arrangement likely intended to capitalise on and fortify commercial relationships and supply chains, Morhall was a haberdasher by trade, having undertaken his seven-year apprenticeship in London beginning in 1720.[18] In addition to thousands of pounds being settled on this couple from Mary's father, this particular marriage contract also resulted in Richard Morhall and his new bride receiving a

---

[16] Staffordshire, Dioceses of Lichfield And Coventry Wills And Probate 1521-1860.
[17] London, England, Church of England Baptisms, Marriages and Burials, 1538-1812.
[18] City Of London, Haberdashers, Apprentices And Freemen 1526-1933.

'*Messuage in Ash Parva and tenement in Shrewsbury called The Stalls*'.[19] This gift was likely from Richard's father Thomas Morhall with the intention of not only showing his assurance for the union, but also seeing the couple settle closer to where he lived instead of in London.

Given Thomas Hunt's own father Samuel had passed away just weeks before his marriage to Ann Fletcher, it is assumed that there was no buffering of the marriage contract from his side of the family; his mother would have still been grieving. Thus Thomas would have taken sole responsibility for the negotiations. Despite very credibly having a vested interest in formalising a business arrangement with the Fletcher family and seeking some financial security, Thomas Hunt would have been considered a worthy catch, at least on paper. He was politically useful, being the current Mayor of the City of Coventry and, in July 1734, had additionally been appointed the Receiver-General of Land Tax for the County of Warwick.[20] He also had his own fortune and property portfolio, albeit presumed to be much less than that of his new bride Ann, and only available pending the death of his mother Hanna.

Whether they were near complete strangers or had known one another previously, Ann Fletcher was likely brought up with a realistic notion of marriage, including that social, economic and religious factors of potential suitors needed to be taken into consideration. She would have feasibly known the practicalities of the situation she was entering.

To once more quote my favourite author, the opening paragraph of *Pride and Prejudice* clearly emphases the situation that Thomas Hunt and Ann Fletcher faced. '*It is a truth universally acknowledged, that a man in possession of a good fortune must be in want of a wife*'.[21] Perhaps, however, it should be countered that a man in need of a good fortune must be in want of a wealthy wife.

---

[19] Shropshire Archives, D3651/B/46/1/18.
[20] *Gloucester Journal*, 30 July 1734.
[21] J. Austen (1813). *Pride and Prejudice*.

Cloth and Coventry

Clothes were expensive in Georgian-era England with the sourcing and manufacturing of the fabric, thread, lace, ribbons, buttons and other adornments accounting for the largeness of the cost, as well as the production of the garments themselves. In fact, it is estimated that one-quarter of a middle class family's annual income could be spent on clothes during eighteenth-century Great Britain, amounting to £60 for a couple with two children to support.[22] Still, this staggering amount would only equate to three to four outfits per person.

The procurement and outlay of clothing was such that provisions were often made in wills as to the outfitting of children. Thomas Fletcher's 1736 will, for example, instructed his wife Jane to use the interest generated from the £3,000 bequeathed to their youngest daughter Jane for *'her maintenance and education and buying her clothes and other necessarys'*.[23] Jane's wardrobe, along with that of her mother and two sisters, however, would obviously have benefitted from the fact that her father had been a haberdasher.

Upon the marriage of Ann Fletcher to Thomas Hunt in 1736, Ann's wardrobe would have come under the proprietorship of her husband. She was more than likely outfitted with a few new items, paid for with her own money or a gift from her mother in the lead-up to the marriage, though given the possibility of a rushed ceremony it could have been that there was not enough time to visit a dressmaker to commission new clothes or a comprehensive

---

[22] P. Earle (1989). *The Making of the English Middle Class: Business, Society and Family Life in London, 1660-1730.*
[23] www.oldbaileyonline.org/about/coinage.

trousseau. The couple also married in an era when honeymoons were not yet thought of or in vogue. Instead, the newlyweds would have partaken in a wedding breakfast straight after the ceremony which would have occurred very early in the morning, as was convention, with perhaps only immediate family members joining them. They then may have stayed in London for a few days or elected to travel directly to Warwickshire.

Regardless of the time frame Thomas Hunt and his new bride Ann left London to begin their married life in Coventry. Travelling via carriage, the couple would have taken two to three days to make the journey to Warwickshire, staying in inns along the way.

What Ann Hunt (nee Fletcher) thought of her new city is not known, though it would have been distinctly different to what she was accustomed to in busy London. With a population of around 10,000 people and 110 miles from her home in Cheapside, Coventry was geographically located in the centre of England and about 20 miles from the much larger city of Birmingham. Despite being far from her family in London, the move did put Ann closer to her older sister Mary, with Shreswbury a further 70 miles to the north-east, though considering that Mary gave birth to a son, Richard Morhall (Jr), in London in mid-1737, it is likely that she had not yet permanently moved to Shropshire with her husband.[24] Still, it is worth noting that Ann and Mary were not the first generation of women in their family to move away from London upon marrying. Two of their maternal aunts, Ann and Sarah Huckell, had moved to Winchester, Hampshire, when they married in 1709 and 1716, respectively.[25]

Situated amongst gently rolling hills and bordered by several rivers and brooks, Coventry was well-known for being the birthplace of the legend of Godiva, the eleventh-century noblewoman who famously rode naked through the streets of the city on horseback to remonstrate the oppressive taxation her husband had cast on the local townsfolk. It was additionally a famously walled city harking back to medieval times, though by the 1730s the walls and gates were beginning to be taken down to allow for expansion. Coventry for many centuries had also been an important transportation hub for those travelling to Worcester, Holyhead, Leicester and

---

[24] England, Select Marriages, 1538-1973 for Richard Morhall.
[25] England, Select Marriages, 1538-1973 for Sarah Huckle; London, England, Church of England Baptisms, Marriages and Burials, 1538-1812 for Ann Huckle.

Partial map of England with Cheapside, Coventry and Shrewsbury circled (1842).
Library of Congress (lccn.loc.gov/2021668664).

London. Thirty years after Ann Hunt's arrival in the city, efforts were also underway to connect Coventry to Birmingham, London, Liverpool, Manchester and other important commercial centres via a network of canals.

In terms of trade and the local economy, Coventry had been a major player in England's clothmaking industry for several centuries, helped by the availability of local wool and dye.[26] The city was renowned for a type of woollen cloth dyed a particular shade of blue, colloquially referred to as 'Coventry Blue'. It was also an important locus for the manufacture of leather products, clocks and watches, as well as the weaving of silk and ribbons. Merchants and craftsmen were organised into guilds, thus operating under a charter. Apprenticeships were widely encouraged with those serving out their indenture period, usually seven years, then eligible to take an oath before the mayor to gain the Freedom of the City. As a corporation, the City of Coventry thus required all of its aldermen to be freemen.

A new charter implemented in 1663 required the council responsible for managing and administering the City of Coventry, including its laws, licences, roads, water, lands, tithes, taxes, police, gaols, courts, charities, poor relief, schools, hospitals, trades and apprentices, etc., to consist of a minimum of 21 members and for members to be made up of those who had been sheriffs or were deemed eligible to hold the office of mayor or sheriff, as elected by the council. Six members of the council were additionally tasked with managing the lease, sale or purchase of city lands.[27] Others were responsible for collecting rents from city properties for which they were then accountable for maintaining. Various lands and tithes owned by the city were leased to feoffees, i.e., appointed trustees who were also members of the council, often at low cost. For decades and decades this system had evolved into one plagued by serious corruption with aldermen (and their families and friends) gaining much personal benefit from the city properties and charities under their care and administration.[28] Deliberately deceptive accounting practices were also rife.

As an elected member of the civic body since 1728 and the current Mayor of Coventry, Thomas Hunt would have been a

---

[26] W. B. Stephens (1969). *A History of the County of Warwick: Volume 8, the City of Coventry and Borough of Warwick.*
[27] W. B. Stephens (1969). *A History of the County of Warwick: Volume 8, the City of Coventry and Borough of Warwick.*
[28] W. B. Stephens (1969). *A History of the County of Warwick: Volume 8, the City of Coventry and Borough of Warwick.*

powerful member of the local community with his new bride Ann very much a person that the men and women of the city would have been eager to meet, particularly since she was from London and rather a stranger to the endemic set.[29] After a period of settling in, including meeting her new mother-in-law Hanna, Ann Hunt, formerly Fletcher, would have needed some courage and perhaps a little boldness to assimilate amongst her husband's circle of family and friends. Given her husband's position within the city council, Ann would have also been expected to become involved in local charities and other benevolent activities.

Invitations to dinners, parties and balls, however, would have soon filled her calendar, many of these events attended with her new husband by her side. Ann would have found herself amongst several like-minded young women too, including those who had similarly been transplanted to Coventry by marriage. For example, a local man by the name of Thomas Brownlow, Esq., had married Miss Lowfield of Daventry, Northamphshire, in October 1732 with his new bride noted to be *'an agreeable young lady of 4000l. fortune'*.[30]

Considering Ann and Thomas Hunt were married in September 1736, towards the end of summer, Coventry would have been showcased to her in its prettiest aspect. Quickly, however, the autumn months and then winter would have befallen the city. Ann would certainly have become familiar with Coventry's market days, holidays, fairs, feasts, festivals and other customs. There were also occasional visits by the peerage to celebrate. Though a non-conformist, along with the rest of her family, Ann would have also joined the local parish, attending the Holy Trinity Church which dated back to the twelfth century.[31]

Adapting to her new city, the years went by for Ann Hunt, accentuated by births, marriages, deaths and other significant events, as well as visits from family and friends. It is very likely that Ann travelled too, taking trips with her husband to London and possibly to Shrewsbury to visit with her sister.

Ann and Thomas Hunt also welcomed two children. A son named Thomas (Jr) and a daughter named Ann (Jr) were born in the late 1730s, though no baptism records have yet been found.

---

[29] www.coventrycollections.org/search/details/archive/110299858.
[30] *Gloucester Journal*, 3 October 1732.
[31] www.findagrave.com/memorial/202439941/thomas-hunt;
England & Wales, Non-Conformist and Non-Parochial Registers, 1567-1936 for Ann Hunt.

In terms of Thomas Hunt's professional activities during this period there were many, including that he continued to operate as a mercer dealing in expensive fabrics. With regards to his municipal and political roles, while he was not immediately re-elected Mayor after serving in this position in 1735-1736, Thomas continued to be an Alderman and involved in the Coventry City Council.[32] He additionally served as City Treasurer during the 1730s and 1740s, principally as the Receiver-General for assets such as land tax, houses, windows and lights.[33] Further, Thomas Hunt helped administer charities, including as a trustee of Sir Thomas White's Charity which provided interest-free loans to local businessmen, as well as Baker's and Billing's charities.[34] He was also a corporation tenant of Cross Cheaping premises; a Justice of the Peace; a lender of money for mortgages associated with properties located in Cross Cheaping, Bishop Street and Smithford Street; and a buyer of mortgage loans.

Thomas Hunt's real estate portfolio was quite substantial, steadily growing commensurate with his roles and responsibilities within the city of Coventry. Of note, his holdings included a property known as Little Pudding Croft, land in Hill Street, land at Hearsall, closes outside the Cook Street Gate, a house at Broadgate, the Cranes Inn in Bishop Street, and land around Bishopgate Green and Radford.[35] These latter three properties were likely acquired using funds provided from his marriage settlement to Ann Fletcher in 1736.

In October 1741 Thomas Hunt was once again elected Mayor of Coventry.[36] Just over a year later, on 6 November 1742, his mother Hanna died. She was purportedly 82 years of age.[37] Her will, unlike that of her late husband's, bequeathed the bulk of her estate, including real and personal assets, chattels, goods, ready money and securities, etc., and all of her testamentary estate and effects, to her only son Thomas.[38] Hanna also left £200 to her daughters Hannah (wife of George Porter, a watchmaker of Coventry) and Ann (wife of Thomas Oldham, an alderman of Coventry),

---

[32] www.coventrycollections.org/search/details/archive/110299858.
[33] National Archives UK, PA 309/1.
[34] www.coventrycollections.org/search/details/archive/110299858.
[35] www.coventrycollections.org/search/details/archive/110299858.
[36] *Aris's Birmingham Gazette*, 18 October 1742.
[37] www.findagrave.com/memorial/202439941/thomas-hunt.
[38] Will of Hannah Hunt, National Archives UK: PROB-11-721-438.

and £50-£100 to her grandchildren: Ann Porter, Hannah Porter, Elizabeth Porter, Hannah Oldham, Thomas Oldham and Samuel Oldham. Thomas and Ann Hunt's two children, Thomas (Jr) and Ann (Jr), were bequeathed £100 each, to be given to them upon reaching the age of 21.[39]

While both of his parents had lived long lives, Thomas Hunt died in Coventry on 20 February 1752 at the age of 50. He was buried at the Holy Trinity Church in Coventry where a memorial was erected in memory of him as well as his parents, Samuel and Hanna. The plaque is still in existence, more than 270 years following Thomas Hunt's death.

Memorial for Samuel, Hanna and Thomas Hunt, Holy Trinity Church, Coventry.
www.findagrave.com/memorial/262439941/thomas-hunt.

---

[39] Will of Hannah Hunt, National Archives UK: PROB-11-721-438.

With probate granted on 6 March 1752, a few weeks after Thomas Hunt's death, his will is another interesting though long read.[40] First, to his *'dearly beloved wife Ann'*, which as custom in eighteenth-century wills was an intentional and meaningful term of endearment, he gave the sum of *'fifteen hundred pounds of useful money of Great Britain in performance of my agreement in that behalf contained in my marriage articles'*. He also gave her all of his household goods, furniture, plate and jewels. In addition he directed that the sum of £2,000 be invested by his executors in either real security or parliamentary funds in trust with the dividends to be used by Ann during her lifetime. Following her death, it was to be given to their two children, assuming that they were both still living at the time.

The will additionally bequeathed a farm and tenements in the vicinity of Foleshill near Coventry, then under the tenancy of William Drifters, as well as *'Bull Fields, Marry Close and Crow Meadows'* with their appurtenances, to his wife Ann on the direction that the last three properties not be *'plowed, tilled, dug up or reverted into gardening or tillage'*. After her decease the properties were to pass to their children, Thomas (Jr) and Ann (Jr), and their heirs. If they were both deceased, the properties were to be given to his nephew Thomas Oldham and his heirs.

Thomas Hunt's will also gave very specific settlement instructions and limitations on many additional properties, including those named Pit Fields, Dorky Field and Crab Tree Field, as well as the Crane Inn, Allens Gardens, several houses situated in Cross Cheaping, a warehouse, an estate in Broadgate, a stable in Gray Fryars Lane, and a tenement in Dead Lane. All of these properties were to go to his son Thomas (Jr) and his heirs. If Thomas (Jr) died without issue then they were to go to his daughter Ann (Jr) and her heirs. Various nieces and nephews were then mentioned as alternative recipients should Ann (Jr) also die without issue. What is interesting about these specific clauses in Thomas Hunt's will, from hindsight, is that the second son of his daughter Ann (Jr) would be the one to benefit the most from them, as we shall see in the following chapters.

Aside from these properties, there was more money to distribute with the sums not as substantial as initially intended. The will

---

[40] England & Wales, Prerogative Court of Canterbury Wills, 1384–1858 for Thomas Hunt.

stated, '*And whereas the sum of five thousand pounds was at the time of making my* [marriage] *articles deposited in the hands of Thomas Fletcher and John Grant on trust to be by them laid out in the purchase of lands which sum was afterwards with the consent of all partys laid out in the purchase of Old South Sea Annuity Stock and which stock by reason of the variation of the market price thereof when the same was afterwards sold out was reduced or decreased in value two hundred and thirty pounds or thereabouts to the end therefore that the provision made by the said marriage articles may fully answer in value the said sum of five thousand pounds in settlement to my said wife I do hereby give and devise unto her for her life all that my close above mentioned called Crabtree Field*'.

A further £5,000 was bequeathed to Thomas Hunt (Jr) to be paid when he reached the age of 21. Thomas Hunt provided the same amount to his daughter Ann (Jr) to be paid when she reached 21 years of age or on the day of her marriage, on the condition that she married with the consent of her mother. With regards to the maintenance of his two children, Thomas directed that his wife Ann be given £70 and £50 annually with the interest generated from these two sums of money to be used for the maintenance of their son and daughter, respectively. She was also entrusted with arranging for the tuition of Thomas (Jr) with the provision that if he should be '*placed out to a trade or profession*' that the executors were to pay such sum of money for that purpose as Ann thought proper. Authority for the tuition of Ann (Jr) until she reached the age of 21 was also provided. The remainder of Thomas Hunt's estate was to be divided equally amongst his two children upon them reaching the age of 21 years.

With his nephew Samuel Oldham, friend Edward Freeman and brother-in-law Thomas Fletcher appointed executors, the three men soon began the process of implementing Thomas Hunt's requests and provisions. He had certainly amassed a great deal of wealth and property during his lifetime, helped handsomely by his involvement with administration and tax collection on behalf of the City of Coventry, and possibly under somewhat dubious circumstances. Given the specificity of his will, and perhaps an underlying outcome of this alleged corruption, the executors were likely surprised when additional sums of money were discovered in undeclared bank accounts. Two annuities were found deposited

Record of Bank of England annuity deposited by Thomas Hunt in 1747.
Bank Of England Wills Extracts 1717-1845.

in the Bank of England during 1745 and 1747, respectively.[41] The first was for a sum of £500, while the second was for substantially more, i.e., £1,100.

Whereas Thomas Hunt had obviously benefitted personally from his involvement with the City of Coventry, by the time of his death in February 1752 the city was experiencing a general decline, owing to the growth of nearby Birmingham as the industrial, political and economic powerhouse of England's Midlands region. With her two children now in their teenage years and the prospect of Ann Hunt's son Thomas (Jr) having success at entering a trade or profession more likely in a bigger city, the trio moved to London. The return placed Ann much closer to her family, including her brother Thomas, by now a highly regarded stationer, as well as her mother and sister, both named Jane.

Less than a year later, in July 1753, 16-year-old Thomas Hunt (Jr) gained an apprenticeship with John Barton, a merchant of London.[42] Ann Hunt paid a premium of £500 for the prominent opportunity with Thomas (Jr) likely indentured for a period of seven years. Thomas (Jr) would have lived with John Barton and his family during this period. Meanwhile Ann Hunt and her daughter Ann (Jr) very likely moved in with Ann's mother Jane who lived in the vicinity of Charterhouse Square in the London borough of Islington.[43]

While the city of London offered Ann Hunt's two children bountiful opportunities in terms of education, social, professional,

---
[41] Bank of England Wills Extracts 1717-1845 for Thomas Hunt.
[42] Britain, Country Apprentices 1710-1808 for Thomas Hunt in 1753;
UK, Register of Duties Paid for Apprentices' Indentures, 1710-1811 for Thomas Hunt.
[43] England & Wales Non-Conformist Burials for Jane Hunt.

and family connections, it was a rather different environment than what they had been accustomed to in the relatively agricultural region of Coventry. By the 1750s London was considered one of the greatest cities in Europe. Trade, banking and industry had dramatically expanded during the reign of King George II (1727-1760) in particular, bringing more and more groups of people into the middle and upper-class income brackets. This increase in prosperity further fuelled options for leisure activities including shopping, with books, toys, jewellery, music, clothes and accessories in high demand. Moving to the centre of this commercial activity, the Hunt family would likely have welcomed the new opportunities offered to them by their relocation to London. There was also art and culture to explore and enjoy, with theatres, libraries, museums and parks becoming established. Considering their status as non-conformists, London would have also offered more places to worship than what had been available in Coventry. A more liberal attitude towards those seeking alternatives to the Church of England amongst the general populous of London would have been very welcome too, particularly for 'Protestant Dissenters' like the Hunts.

In terms of family events, the years following the Hunt family's settlement in London were generally joyful. Ann Hunt was present for the birth of her nephew William Mount on 3 January 1753, born to her sister Jane and brother-in-law John Mount, a stationer of Paternoster Row.[44] Ann was again present for the birth of Jane and John's third and fourth children, sons named John and Harry born on 27 September 1758 and 8 October 1760, respectively.[45] During the interim, however, Ann Hunt's mother Jane died. She was around 70 years of age and was buried on 10 June 1756 in the family's vault at Bunhill Field's Burial Ground.[46]

Jane Fletcher's will further amplified Ann Hunt's wealth. The document also provides an interesting perspective regarding the life and times of a relatively wealthy widow in 1750s London.[47] For example, the opening statement of the will is a direction to give the Rev Sam Chandler, a high-profile non-conformist minister and pamphleteer, £100 in bank annuities. The next item was a

---

[44] England & Wales, Non-Conformist and Non-Parochial Registers, 1567-1936 for William Mount.
[45] England & Wales, Non-Conformist and Non-Parochial Registers, 1567-1936 for Jane Fletcher.
[46] England & Wales Non-Conformist Burials for Jane Hunt.
[47] England & Wales, Prerogative Court of Canterbury Wills, 1384-1858 for Jane Fletcher.

direction to give £100 to the Presbyterian Fund. Following, Jane Fletcher bequeathed £50 to her cousin Elizabeth Harrison, £50 to her servant John Harris and £4 per year for life to several other servants. Jane's household goods from her Charterhouse Square home were to be given to Ann Hunt whereas her household linens and those goods at a residence she had in Mitcham, just outside of London, were to be given to her son-in-law Richard Morhall. Her plate was to be divided between her three granddaughters: Jane Fletcher, Ann Hunt (Jr) and Jane Mount. In addition, Jane Fletcher gave Richard and Mary Morhall, John and Jane Mount, and Ann Hunt £5,000 apiece in varying combinations of cash, annuities, bonds and stock. Ann Hunt specifically received £600 in bank annuities and £4,400 in cash, bonds and stock. Much smaller sums were provided to immediate family members for mourning attire, as well as to Jane Fletcher's siblings, their spouses, her nieces and nephews. All told, however, the will provided the bulk of the estate to Jane's three daughters, Mary Morhall, Jane Mount and Ann Hunt, and their families. Her son Thomas Fletcher was named sole executor, though having been financially successful in the decades since his father died, appears to have been intentionally side-stepped by the will. Instead Jane saw fit to take the opportunity to adequately provide for the women in her family, her employees and those associated with her religion.

Merchants and Money

The first half of the eighteenth century coincided with many of London's middle and upper-class businessmen marrying their daughters off to men with vast land holdings in predominantly rural counties with the goal of achieving landed status. By the second half of this century, however, London-based family dynasties built on mutual commercial endeavours were becoming more prevalent.

An indication of this sideways trajectory is evident in the next generation of the Hunt family. On 12 June 1759 Ann Hunt (Jr) married Nathaniel Mason at Saint Botolph Aldersgate, London.[48] At 20 years of age Ann (Jr) was considered a minor such that her mother Ann had to consent to the union. The couple were married by licence, as opposed to banns, with one of the witnesses being her uncle Thomas Fletcher. The other was Joseph Paice, a London-based merchant who was Nathaniel Mason's first cousin on his mother's side.[49]

It is an interesting point in time for Joseph Paice, who remained a bachelor his entire life, to enter this scene. Over the decades to come, using funds generated from his many commercial activities, he would become an eminent philanthropist of London, bestowing his wealth on institutions and individuals alike.[50] Yet more intriguing, in a memorial published in 1841, the author relays an apparent love tryst involving Ann Hunt (Jr), Nathaniel Mason and Joseph Paice. '*I have before me, in the feeble characters of*

---
[48] London, England, Church of England Marriages and Banns, 1754–1938 for Ann Hunt.
[49] England & Wales, Prerogative Court of Canterbury Wills, 1384–1858 for Nathaniel Paice.
[50] en.wikipedia.org/wiki/Joseph_Paice.

Marriage record for Nathaniel Mason and Ann Hunt (Jr), London (1759).
London, England, Church of England Marriages and Banns, 1754-1938 for Ann Hunt.

an old man's writing, a memorandum ... enumerating the white days of his life, and thanking the Almighty for them, among which are briefly but emphatically reckoned some of the days spent, doubtless in Miss Hunt's company, at the house of his valued friend [Thomas Fletcher, Ann Hunt's uncle] in the Old Jewry. A growing passion for this interesting young woman was still undeclared for her, though there was reason to believe she would encourage it, when Mr. Paice became painfully aware that his first cousin, Mr. Mason, was in love with the same lady. One of the parties, it was plain, must be sacrificed to the other: the young lady's chance of happiness between the two was the next point, as well as the comparative fortitude with which disappointment was likely to be met by the several rivals. Mr. Paice debated, and decided against himself: he silently withdrew his attentions, and had the distressing trial of witnessing his cousin's success'.[51]

Having been born in London around 1736, Nathaniel Mason was only a few years older than Ann (Jr) at the time of their marriage. He had also not fully completed his apprenticeship with London-based merchant Abraham Henkell, which began in late 1757, though the indenture may have been transferred from another master.[52] Records indicate that a member of Nathaniel's family paid a premium of £550 for the position, albeit his father's name is distinctly missing from the document; he had died during Nathaniel's childhood such that it was another family member that provided the funds.

While Nathaniel Mason obviously came from well-resourced family connections, he also had land. Upon the death of his

[51] E. Littell (1841). *Museum of Foreign Literature, Science and Art, Volume 43*.
[52] Britain, Country Apprentices 1710-1808 for Nathaniel Mason;
UK, Register of Duties Paid for Apprentices' Indentures, 1710-1811 for Nathel Mason.

Portrait of Joseph Paice by John Whessell.
Wikimedia Commons.

maternal uncle Thomas Edwards in January 1757, Nathaniel had been bequeathed a half-share in an estate and farm called Keely End in the parish of Wootton and Kempston in the county of Bedfordshire; a quarter-share in a house at Reigate in the county of Surrey; a quarter-share in an estate and farm in Terrick in the parish of Ellesborough in the county of Buckingham; and a half-share in a house in Bread Street, London, that would become vested following the death of his uncle Nathaniel Paice (Joseph Paice's father).[53] He was also given a half-share in the remainder of Thomas Edwards' estate.[54] Clearly financially endowed from a young age, Nathaniel Mason would continue to expand his real estate and investment portfolios in the decades to come.

Despite Ann Hunt (Jr) being under 21 years of age, Nathaniel Mason certainly had the right connections, religion and fortune for Ann Hunt (Sr) to approve of her daughter's marriage. And this coupling may have in fact been a 'love match', as surmised by Joseph Paice's memoirs.

The couple's assets further benefitted from their marriage articles, whereby the £5,000 bequeathed to Ann (Jr) by her father on the day of her marriage would have been due. More land was also given to Nathaniel in the county of Bedfordshire, specifically in the parish of Sharnbrook, as part of the marriage settlement.[55]

Newlyweds Nathaniel and Ann Mason, formerly Hunt, moved into a residence in Laurence Poultney Lane, an area popular with London's more prominent merchants and only a few blocks from Cheapside. Two children were born to the couple over the next two years. They were a son named Nathaniel, born 5 October 1760, and a daughter named Ann Harriet, born 3 October 1761.[56]

While the two births would have been celebrated, there was much grief when Ann Hunt (Sr) died in early September 1762 at the age of 47. Her death occurred in the town of Epsom, Surrey, a location popular with London's elite due to the therapeutic benefits of a spring containing epsom salts that was located nearby.[57] Situated 12 miles south of London, Ann had moved from Charterhouse Square to the area a few years prior, possibly because of underlying health reasons.

---

[53] England & Wales, Prerogative Court of Canterbury Wills, 1384-1858 for Thomas Edwards.
[54] England & Wales, Prerogative Court of Canterbury Wills, 1384-1858 for Thomas Edwards.
[55] England & Wales, Prerogative Court of Canterbury Wills, 1384-1858 for Nathaniel Mason.
[56] England & Wales Non-Conformist Births And Baptisms for Nathaniel Mason.
[57] England & Wales, Non-Conformist and Non-Parochial Registers, 1567-1936 for Ann Hunt.

Birth records for children born to Nathaniel Mason and Ann Hunt, London (1760-65).
England & Wales Non-Conformist Births And Baptisms.

Ann Hunt was buried in a vault at Bunhill Fields, London, on 7 September 1762.[58] The following day probate was granted. Her will carried on the legacy of the Fletcher and Hunt family fortunes. Of note, she gave another £3,500 pounds to her daughter, as well as an additional sum of £1,000 and an annuity of £50.[59] Her jewels and wearing apparel were also gifted to Ann (Jr). Her son Thomas (Jr), named an executor of the will, along with her brother Thomas Fletcher, received the bulk of the estate, as well as an annuity of £50 each.[60] Additional smaller sums of money went to her servants. Her will, dated before the marriage of Ann (Jr) to Nathaniel Mason, unfortunately provided no stipulation for money or other gifts to be solely for the use and benefit of her daughter. These assets thus became the property of her husband.

[58] England & Wales, Non-Conformist and Non-Parochial Registers, 1567-1936 for Ann Hunt.
[59] England & Wales, Prerogative Court of Canterbury Wills, 1384-1858 for Ann Hunt.
[60] England & Wales, Prerogative Court of Canterbury Wills, 1384-1858 for Ann Hunt.

Though now buoyed by large sums of money, Nathaniel and Ann Mason remained living in Laurence Pountney Lane, expanding their family in the years that followed. A daughter named Jane was born on 17 August 1765 and a son named Thomas was born on 22 July 1766.[61]

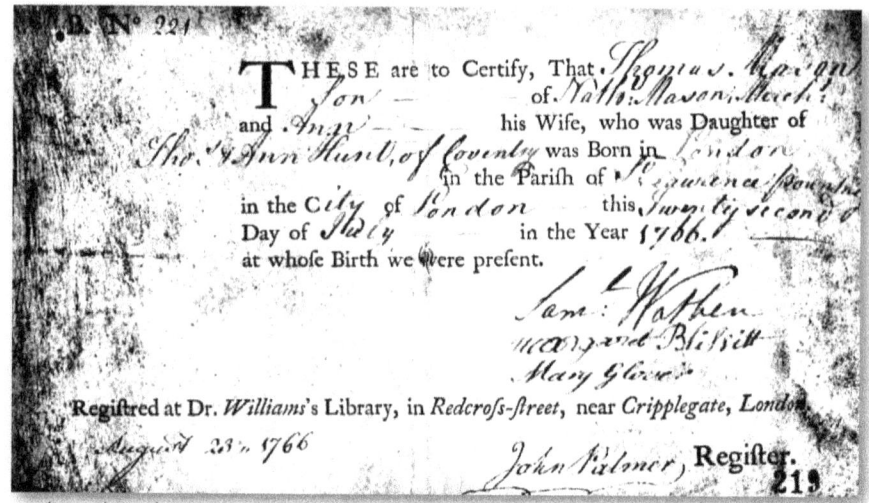

Birth record for Thomas Mason born to Nathaniel Mason and Ann Hunt, London. England & Wales, Non-Conformist and Non-Parochial Registers, 1567-1936.

In terms of professional associations, as well as being a merchant, Nathaniel Mason was appointed a Director of the Royal Exchange Assurance Office in July 1762, a position he maintained for nearly two decades.[62] Also charitable with his time and money, on 13 April 1764 Nathaniel gave a gift of £50 to St Thomas' Hospital, located across the River Thames in nearby Southwark.[63] This legacy allowed him to become a Governor of the institution, a noteworthy position. He remained active on the hospital's board for several decades, making additional donations.[64] Other members of the hospital's board were Thomas Fletcher, i.e., Nathaniel's uncle-in-law, as well as his brother-in-law Thomas Hunt and his cousin Joseph Paice.[65] Another area of interest was the Royal Society of Arts which Nathaniel Mason

---

[61] England & Wales, Non-Conformist and Non-Parochial Registers, 1567-1936 for Jane Mason; England & Wales, Non-Conformist and Non-Parochial Registers, 1567-1936 for Thomas Mason.
[62] London Chronicle, 8 July 1762; London Chronicle, 31 October 1782.
[63] London Lives, Culture & Society 1680-1817 for Nathaniel Mason.
[64] London Lives, Culture & Society 1680-1817 for Nathaniel Mason.
[65] London Lives, Culture & Society 1680-1817 for Thomas Fletcher, Thomas Hunt and Joseph Paice.

joined in mid-1760.[66] In addition, he was a Churchwarden for the parish of St Laurence Pountney between 1766 and 1768.[67]

By the late 1760s Nathaniel Mason, his wife Ann and their four children had moved to Clapham in Surrey, an area quickly becoming popular with London's more wealthy bankers and merchants who sought modern mansions on larger estates in close proximity to their commercial and financial endeavours. Situated just five miles from the centre of London, it was an ideal location for the Mason family to not only grow but be amongst like-minded people, including those considered religious dissenters. Twin boys, Peter and Joseph, were born to the couple in early November 1771.[68] Sadly one of the twins, Peter, would not survive infancy. He was buried at the Holy Trinity Church in Clapham on 25 April 1772.[69] The couple's seventh and final child, a son named Langham, was born at Clapham on 8 July 1773.[70]

It was during this period that Nathaniel Mason, along with his cousin Joseph Paice and his brother-in-law Thomas Hunt, began investing in the island of Tobago in the West Indies. It was an interesting yet extremely ambitious financial gamble on the part of all three men, particularly since the island had been the subject of multiple takeovers by the Dutch, French and English in the centuries prior, to the profound detriment of the local indigenous population.

After a 70-year period of largely being left alone, Britain had regained control of Tobago in 1763 as part of the Treaty of Paris. Two years later the island had been surveyed with commissioners on behalf of the British Government beginning to dispose of the land in allotments between 100 and 500 acres in size. This process remained in place until May 1771 when the sales were completed. There were several stipulations to the purchase of the parcels, including that no single person could acquire more than 500 acres, that the highest bidder for each lot was declared the purchaser, and that a 20 per cent deposit had to be immediately provided, with future instalments made annually in the years to come.

With a view to producing sugar (and thus rum), cocoa and cotton, enterprising speculators purchased the lots, in a few short

---

[66] Royal Society Of Arts Membership Lists And Minute Books.
[67] H. Bristow Wilson (1831). *A History of the Parish of St. Laurence Pountney, London.*
[68] England & Wales, Non-Conformist and Non-Parochial Registers, 1567-1936 for Peter and Joseph Mason.
[69] London, England, Church of England Baptisms, Marriages and Burials, 1538-1819 for Peter Mason.
[70] England & Wales, Non-Conformist and Non-Parochial Registers, 1567-1936 for Langham Mason.

years creating large plantations. Labour was, however, needed to work the land, with thousands and thousands of African men and women forcibly transported to Tobago to become slaves.

Entirely dependent on enslaved workers, the plantations of Tobago soon became cultivated, with sugar, cocoa, cotton and other products, including nutmeg and cloves, transported back to England. In the process, the plantation owners began to fill their pockets. Between 1770 and 1775, for example, the island's sugar output increased from 965 to 4,550 hogsheads and rum from 411 to 3,247 puncheons.[71] Becoming more and more appealing to London's merchants as an investment opportunity, it was not long before they too sought to provide security for those wanting to purchase and develop plantations on the island.

Eager to join in the seemingly profitable financial transactions taking place, Nathaniel Mason became part of a contingent that purchased annuities totalling £18,150 from Captain Archibald Campbell of His Majesty's 26th Regiment of Foot. A complicated legal document, still in existence, details the transaction. With a guaranteed annual income of £1,650, the annuities were secured against three plantations located in the 'Sandy Bay Division' of Tobago, including land, slaves, buildings, stock and produce.

Other parties to the transaction were his relations Joseph Paice and Thomas Hunt. While the latter named duo had each provided £1,500 towards the investment portfolio, Nathaniel had laid out more than £12,000, as well as agreed to act as Captain Campbell's security, thus guaranteeing the annual payments of the annuities via bonds. In case payments were not made, he was thus liable. This made him an essential figure in not only ensuring the financial stability of the annuities, but also protecting the annuity buyers from financial risk.

To safeguard Nathaniel Mason from financial losses, Captain Campbell had assigned the three plantations to Thomas Bennett of London in trust. The agreement also granted Nathaniel the right to profits from the plantations should payments fall in arrears, curiously with the exception of rum, which would have been the most sought after product of the enterprise.

Designated as lots 17, 18 and 32, the three plantations had originally sold on 19 March 1767 for the price of £1 per acre

---

[71] R. B. Sheridan (1774). *Sugar and Slavery: An Economic History of the British West Indies, 1623-1775.*

To all People to whom these Presents shall come Thomas Hunt of the Old Jury London Merchant and Joseph Paice late of Cloak Lane London Merchant but now of Broad Street Hill London Merchant Send greeting Whereas by Indentures of Lease and Release bearing date respectively the fifth and sixth days of September in the year of our Lord one thousand seven hundred and seventy one the Release being Quadrupartite and made between Archbald Campbell then of the Parish of Saint James Westminster in the County of Middlesex Esquire Captain in his Majesty's Twenty sixth Regiment of Foot lately called Archbald Graham Heir at Law and Heir Apparent of John Graham late of Dongalstown in the County of Stirling in that part of Great Britain called Scotland Since of the Island of Grenada in America but then of the Parish of Saint James Westminster aforesaid Esquire of the first part Nathaniel Mason of Lothbury London Merchant of the second part Thomas Bonnett of Lombard Street London Gentleman of the third part and the said Thomas Hunt and Joseph Paice of the fourth part RECITING (among other things) That by Twenty seven several Indentures all bearing date respectively the fourth day of the said Month of September the said Archbald Campbell in Consideration of the several Sums of Money therein respectively mentioned and amounting together in the Whole to the Sum of Eighteen thousand one hundred and fifty Pounds Did grant to the several Persons in such Indentures respectively named the several Twenty seven Annuities yearly Rents Charge or Annual Sums in such respective Indentures mentioned and amounting together in the whole to the yearly Sum of One thousand six hundred and fifty Pounds to be issuing and payable out of and charged and chargeable upon the Plantation Plantation Lots or Parcels of Land in the Island of Tobago therein and hereinafter mentioned And also reciting that the said several Sums of money making together the said Sum of Eighteen thousand one hundred and fifty Pounds were advanced and paid to the said Archbald Campbell for the Purchase of the several Annuities upon Condition that he the said Archbald Campbell should find good and sufficient Personal Security for Payment of the same in the said City of London And that the said Archbald Campbell having prevailed upon the said Nathaniel Mason to become Security for the Payment of the said several Annuities accordingly he the said Nathaniel Mason at the request of the said Archbald Campbell did by Twenty five several Bonds or Obligations bearing date the said fourth Day of the said Month of September become bound with the said Archbald Campbell to each and every of them the said several Purchasers of the said several Annuities in several Penal Sums with Conditions under the said several Bonds respectively written for making Void the same respectively on Payment by the said Archbald Campbell and Nathaniel Mason or either of them his or either of their Heirs Executors or Administrators unto the respective Obligees in the said Bonds respectively named their respective Executors Administrators or Assigns of the several Annuities in the Conditions of the said several Bonds or Obligations respectively mentioned at the times and in the Manner therein mentioned And also reciting that by Indenture bearing Date the said Sixth Day of September and made between the said Archbald Campbell of the first part the several Purchasers of the said several Annuities of the second part and John Willett and Charles Turner therein described of the third part He the said Archbald Campbell for the further and better securing the Payment of the said several Annuities and for the Consideration therein mentioned Did demise unto the said John Willett and Charles Turner their Executors Administrators and Assigns The Plantation Plantation Lots Lands Tenements Negroes Hereditaments and Premises thereinafter mentioned upon the Trusts and for the Ends Intents and Purposes in the said Indenture mentioned and declared And also reciting that by one other Bond or Obligation bearing Date also the said fourth Day of September the said Nathaniel Mason at the request of the said Archbald Campbell became bound unto the said John Graham the Father of the said Archbald Campbell in the Penal Sum of Twelve thousand Pounds with Condition thereunder written for making Void the same on Payment by the said Archbald Campbell and Nathaniel Mason or either of them unto James Duncan then or late of Tobago Esquire of Three thousand Pounds on the   day of   one thousand seven hundred and Seventy six together with Interest for the same of the said Island of Tobago hit paid in Satisfaction and discharge of a certain Bond or Obligation dated the   day of   one thousand seven hundred and seventy and entered into by the said John Graham to the said James Duncan for securing to him the Payment of the said Sum of Three thousand Pounds with Interest on the Day therein mentioned It is by the now reciting Indenture Witnessed that for Enabling the said Nathaniel Mason his Exors Admors and Assigns to pay the said Twenty seven several Annuities yearly Rent Charges or Sums thereinbefore mentioned and for saving harmless and indemnifying the said Nathaniel Mason his Heirs Executors and Administrators against the Payment of the said Twenty seven several Annuities and against the Payment of the said Sum of Three thousand Pounds to the said James Duncan and the interest thereof and against all Costs Charges Damages and Expenses in respect of the said several Annuities and of the said Three thousand Pounds and the Interest thereof and for securing to the said Nathaniel the Consignment of the Sugars and other Produce (except as therein mentioned) of the said Plantation Plantation Lots and Premises and for other the Considerations therein mentioned He the said Archbald Campbell Did grant release and convey unto the said Thomas Bonnett All that Plantation Lot Piece or Parcel of Land situate in Sandy Point Division in the Island of Tobago aforesaid distinguished by the Denomination of Lot No 92 of the said Division containing One hundred Acres of Land or thereabouts And also All that other Plantation Lot or Piece or Parcel of Land situate in Sandy Point Division aforesaid in the said Island of Tobago distinguished by the Denomination of Lot 18. of the said Division containing also One hundred Acres of Land or thereabouts And also all that other Plantation Lot Piece or Parcel of Land situate in Sandy Point Division in the said Island of Tobago containing by Estimation Fifty one Acres of Land or thereabouts And which said three several Plantation Lots are in the said Indenture mentioned to have been theretofore holden into one Plantation and to have been named by the said John Graham and which was then usually called or known by the Name of Scarsfield Plantation and all Messuages Tenements Outhouses Sugar houses and other Works Edifices Erections and Buildings whatsoever on the said Plantation Lots three several Plantation Lots or Parcels of Land erected built standing or being And also all those fifty Negroes or Slaves thereto belonging and in the said Indenture particularly named And also all other Negroes or Slaves upon or belonging to the said Plantation or Plantation Lots together with the issue and increase of all the females of the said Slaves thereafter to be born And also all Mules Horses and other live Stock Mills Coppers Plantation Tools Utensils Implements and other dead Stock upon the said Plantation or any Part thereof being or thereto or to any Part thereof belonging or appertaining And also all Sugars Rum Molasses Coffee and other Product growing or being or to grow or be upon the said Plantation or any Part thereof with the Appurtenances thereto belonging And all that other Plantation Lot or Parcel of Land distinguished by the Denomination of Lot No 17, in Sandy Point Division in the said Island of Tobago containing by Estimation Two hundred Acres of Land with the Appurtenances and all other real and personal Estate whatsoever of the said Archbald Campbell in the said Island of Tobago TO HOLD unto the said Thomas Bonnett his Heirs and Assigns To the several Uses upon the Trusts for the Intents and Purposes and under and subject to the several Provisoes

and comprised 200, 100 and 100 acres, respectively.[72] Since that time, they had been combined into a single plantation known as Jeanfield, though renamed Shirvan after Captain Campbell's estate in Scotland, with the land cleared, houses and other infrastructure built and cultivation of produce well underway. Over 50 slaves were also named in the indenture as working on the plantation.

With the original transaction taking place in September 1771, by September 1774 a credit crisis had tightened its grip on the British economy with many of London's merchants teetering on the brink of bankruptcy or being declared insolvent. Nathaniel Mason was one of many of his cohort looking to recoup missed mortgage payments and other debts from numerous sources, with the annuities from Major Campbell becoming a crucial target. Given payments were in arrears, the agreement stated that Nathaniel had the authority to manage, sell, or mortgage the plantation and its assets to cover the debt. With his relations Thomas Hunt and Joseph Paice also missing payments, Nathaniel sought to remedy the situation. In October 1774 he sailed to Tobago to investigate the matter.[73]

Upon arriving in Tobago Nathaniel Mason would have realised that his investment was not immediately retrievable. He no doubt wrote back to London confessing to the situation with the goal of remaining in Tobago to regain some control of the affairs. Unlike Joseph Paice and Thomas Hunt, he had a great deal more to lose, having not only invested a substantial amount of money in the transaction, but also provided security for the annuities.

Given Nathaniel Mason's trip to Tobago was to take over a year to complete, Thomas Hunt would have taken over the family's affairs. With an immediate need to alleviate large amounts of debt and generate income to help support his sister Ann and her large family, he advertised the Mason's Clapham estate for sale.

The six Mason children then undoubtedly moved in with their uncle Thomas Hunt and his wife Susanna in Ewell near Epsom in Surrey, 10 miles south of Clapham.[74] The couple did not have any children so there was likely ample room to accommodate

---

[72] J. Fowler (1994). *A Summary Account of the Present Flourishing State of the Respectable Colony of Tobago, in the British West Indies.*

[73] 28 Jan. 1775. Thomas Hunt and Joseph Paice to Nathaniel Mason} Special Power of Attorney (docket title), Special Collections Department, Hamilton College, Clinton, New York, United States.

[74] *Gazetteer and New Daily Advertiser*, 11 February 1786; *Morning Post*, 2 May 1786; UK, Poll Books and Electoral Registers, 1538-1893 for Thomas Hunt.

the family. The Mason's Clapham estate was sold at auction on 29 May 1775. That same day all of the household furniture, ornaments, porcelain, drawings, pictures, linen, garden utensils and other effects were sold by auction.

> To be SOLD by AUCTION,
> By Mr. SKINNER,
> On Monday the 29th Inftant, on the Premifes, at Twelve o'Clock,
>
> A Valuable Leafehold Brick Manfion, defirably fituate at Clapham, in Surrey: A Spot much diftinguifh:d and admired; Garden, Shrubberies, Pleafure Grounds, fuitable Offices, and four Fields of rich Pafture Land, containing ten Acres, late in the Poffeffion of
> NATHANIEL MASON, Efq:
> The Manfion contains five Rooms on a Floor, agreeably arranged, elegantly fitted up, and finifhed in true Tafte; the Kitchen and lower Apartments are extenfive and convenient; the out Offices correfpond; built on a moft exquifite Plan, and forms a compleat Refidence.
> To be viewed 10 Days preceding the Sale, by a Ticket from Mr. Skinner; when printed Particulars may be had of him, and on the Premifes.

Public Advertiser, 10 May 1775.

> To be Sold by Auction by Mr. SKINNER,
> On Monday the 29th inftant, and the two following Days, on the Premifes, at Clapham, in Surry, at Twelve,
>
> THE elegant Houfhold Furniture, curious ornamental and ufeful Drefden, Chelfea, and India Porcelain, fine Drawings, Pictures, and Prints, Houfhold Linnen, Garden Utenfils, two fmall Ricks of Hay, and other valuable Effects, the Property of NATHANIEL MASON, Efq.
> To be viewed on Friday and Saturday the 26th and 27th, and Monday Morning till the Sale, when Catalogues may be had on the Premifes, and of Mr. Skinner, Alderfgate Street.

News, 17 May 1775.

Sadly, this is not the end of the family's distressing circumstances. Ann Mason had died a few weeks prior, on 12 May 1775, at the age of 36.[75] She was buried at the Holy Trinity Church in Clapham on 27 June 1775.[76] Another memorial published on Joseph Paice, this one by a distant relation named Anne Manning in 1861, relays the situation, with Paice obviously still reeling from the loss of his first love to his cousin and the life that could have been. In the author's words it begins, '*I am not a sentimentalist, but I feel the tears stealing into my eyes as I go over again the well-known love story. That the grief of the young man amounted to agony, may be learnt from the anguish of the old man, thirty-five years after* [i.e., well after Ann Mason's death],

---

[75] *The Daily Advertiser*, 15 June 1775.
[76] Greater London Burial Index for Ann Mason;
London, England, Church of England Baptisms, Marriages and Burials, 1538-1812 for Holy Trinity, Clapham.

when he knelt before the alter of Aldersgate Church, where the marriage had been celebrated, calling on heaven for support under the extremity of mental suffering. The revival of the subject, so many years afterwards, by the discovery of a paper he knew not to have existed, which he destroyed as being "too distressing for even his executors to endure," brought on an illness endangering his life ... Here was love that deserved the name!'.[77]

Unfortunately the contents of the destroyed paper are not known, though the biographer does provide another snippet of information regarding the tragic circumstances surrounding Nathaniel Mason and his wife Ann during this period. It is told via the optics of the author's grandfather, then a teenager. '"*I was a boy of about sixteen,*" continued my grandfather, "*when Mr. Paice invited me to walk with him to Clapham, one morning, to breakfast with the Masons. It was just at the most painful crisis of their affairs. Mr. Mason was on the point of starting for the West Indies, in the faint hope of retrieving some property; and his wife in a deep decline, almost broken-hearted by their misfortunes, was about to embark for Lisbon* [Portugal]*, which was considered to afford the last chance of her recovery. The husband and wife were to start on their opposite journeys on the same day, and Mr. Paice was about to see them off, and bid them a long farewell. What his thoughts were during that walk, I can perhaps better imagine now than I could then. On reaching the house at Clapham, we found that Mr. and Mrs. Mason had not yet left their bedroom; but the servants were hastily preparing the breakfast table, and one of them, in his hurry, overset the spirit of wine beneath the silver tea-kettle, which set the table-cloth in a flame. How well I remember Mr. Paice's anxiety to have every vestige of the accident removed before Mrs. Mason came down, lest it should add to her more serious sources of trouble! At length, she appeared; harassed and agitated. Though no longer very young, she was still a pretty woman, with blue eyes and fair hair and something very graceful about her. Her thoughtless, good-humoured husband was very little impressed with their approaching separation. My dear, they never met again! Mr. Paice, who defrayed all the expenses of the visit to Lisbon, sent out to the poor invalid every English comfort he thought she would need, but in vain. She died - was sent to his house in a leaden coffin - and, to satisfy her family of her identity, he uncovered her face and looked upon it, with what sensation we may imagine!" Mr. Paice was then forty-eight.*'[78]

---

[77] A. Manning (1861). *Family pictures, by the author of 'Mary Powell'.*
[78] A. Manning (1861). *Family pictures, by the author of 'Mary Powell'.*

While Joseph Paice lamented the devastating loss of his unrequited love, Nathaniel Mason was left with six children in his care, the oldest 14 and the youngest just under two years of age. He was also still in Tobago, over 4,000 miles away by sea, and broke.

In October 1775 Nathaniel Mason transferred power of attorney with regards to the Tobago plantation to Nathan Steward and John Dunnington, both local residents, thereby ensuring that the management of the estate and its assets, as well as the execution of his legal obligations, would continue in his absence. He then left the island en route for England.

Nathaniel Mason returned to London in late 1775 setting up residence at 17 Sherborn Lane, near Cheapside.[79] Borrowing more money from his cousin Joseph Paice and his brother-in-law Thomas Hunt, Nathaniel and his six children managed to maintain their lifestyle. Rather haphazardly, he also appears to have invested in further annuities related to properties in the West Indies, including plantations in Jamaica and Grenada.[80] At the local level, unpaid debt continued to plague him with money invested in annuities to London-based businessmen not being paid, amongst other wayward transactions.[81] Feeling the crunch, by 1779 the Mason family had moved to 27 Bread Street, London, i.e., the house that Joseph Paice occupied and the residence Nathaniel had been left a half-share in by his late uncle Nathaniel Paice.[82]

By the early 1780s Nathaniel Mason and his children had moved to Billericay in Essex, just over 20 miles north-east of London. This move may have been the result of London becoming rather chaotic owing to anti-Catholic riots which rocked the city in June 1780 causing much looting and destruction, as well as the deaths of hundreds of people. With this turmoil came an atmosphere of political crisis, with the Constitution considered under threat, and a general feeling of unease. London had also grown significantly in the decades leading up to this animosity with the city bulging to cope, house and employ the thousands and thousands of new arrivals. Besides political and social change, there was much economic change occurring, as the Industrial Revolution took

---

[79] Nathaniel Mason in the U.K. and U.S. Directories, 1680-1830.
[80] England & Wales, Prerogative Court of Canterbury Wills, 1384-1858 for Nathaniel Mason; enslaved.org/record/person/Q587544.
[81] *The London Evening Post*, 29 March 1777.
[82] Nathaniel Mason in the U.K. and U.S. Directories, 1680-1830.

hold. The American War of Independence was also underway, ultimately resulting in independence for the United States from Britain. With regards to the Mason family in particular, this conflict was to impact them financially, with their plantations in Tobago coming under French control in 1781 and exports thwarted by the war. Another issue impacting operations of their plantations was the potential abolishment of the slave trade, a movement that was gaining much-needed traction in Britain at the time.

Leaving London for the more idyllic Essex, Nathaniel Mason died at his home in Billericay in late October 1782 of an apoplectic fit. He was around 44 years of age and was buried in a vault at Holy Trinity Church, Clapham, on 31 October that had previously belonged to the Langham family.[83] Nathaniel's wife Ann and their infant son Peter were buried within the same vault.

Nathaniel Mason's will offers another interesting read. Whereas previous generations had focused on prioritising their daughter's financial independence and ensuring funds were put aside for their marriage settlements, Nathaniel's will mostly concerned the distribution of landed assets. For example, property located in Sharnbrook and Odell, Bedfordshire, was bequeathed to his oldest son Nathaniel (Jr), while other property in this same county was for the '*use of my six children namely Nathaniel, Ann Harriet, Jane, Thomas, Joseph and Langham, equally*'.[84] Nonetheless, there was very little mention of money, other than a few pounds distributed to various relations for mourning, and to his executors, Nathaniel Mason (Jr), Joseph Paice and Thomas Hunt, for their time in administering the estate. Nathaniel did, however, ensure that his children were taken care of with Joseph Paice and Thomas Hunt being jointly named as '*guardians of all my children both as to their persons and estates until they shall respectively attain the age of twenty one years*'.[85] By this point in time the two eldest, Nathaniel (Jr) and Ann Harriet, were 22 and 21 years of age, respectively.

It obviously took some time to administer Nathaniel Mason's estate. His personal and household effects were not auctioned off until July 1783, including a valuable collection of books numbering 200 in volume.

---

[83] *London Chronicle*, 31 October 1782; Morning Post, 2 November 1782; Greater London Burial Index for Nathaniel Mason.
[84] England & Wales, Prerogative Court of Canterbury Wills, 1384–1858 for Nathaniel Mason.
[85] England & Wales, Prerogative Court of Canterbury Wills, 1384–1858 for Nathaniel Mason.

Though no official paperwork has been found to date, Nathaniel Mason's eldest son and namesake appears to have undertaken a clerkship with a London-based attorney that would have been completed by the time of his father's death. His second eldest son Thomas was 16 years of age when his father passed away. Just over a year later, in November 1783, Thomas also gained a noteworthy clerkship with John Adams, an attorney of Symonds Inn in Chancery Lane, London.[86] The remainder of Nathaniel Mason's children continued to be cared for by Thomas Hunt and his wife Susanna. At this point in time, Ann Harriet was 21 years of age, Jane was 17, Joseph was 10 and Langham was nine.

Unfortunately stability failed to find the Mason family. Their uncle and guardian Thomas Hunt died at his home in Ewell, Surrey, on 10 February 1785.[87] He was 48 years of age. Though married for more than 15 years, he and his wife Susanna did not have any children. Thomas' will thus provided well for the Mason children. With the exception of significant annual payments in the realm of hundreds and hundreds of pounds to be made to his wife during the remainder of her life, and minor payments to other relations and servants, the bulk of Thomas Hunt's real and personal estate was to be put into a trust to be shared amongst the six Mason children equally.[88] This trust was to include the proceeds from the sale of his estate in Ewell, as well as other properties. The Mason children were to receive these payments either at the time of their marriage or upon reaching the age of 21 years.

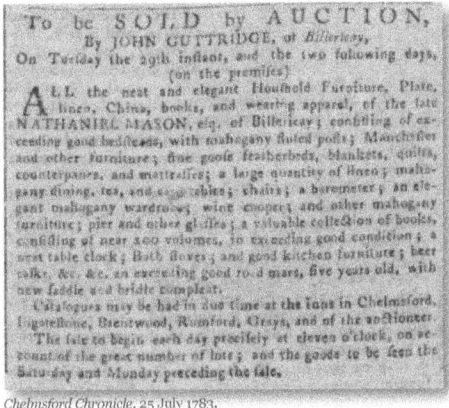

Chelmsford Chronicle, 25 July 1783.

---

[86] UK, Articles of Clerkship, 1756-1874 for Thomas Mason.
[87] *Gazetteer and New Daily Advertiser*, 11 February 1785.
[88] England & Wales, Prerogative Court of Canterbury Wills, 1384-1858 for Thomas Hunt.

In the Kings Bench

George Hatton of Symonds Inn in the County of Middlesex Gentleman and James Joyner of Moulsey in the County of Surry severally make Oath and say and first this Deponent George Hatton for himself says that he was present and did see a certain Indenture of Assignment bearing date the Nineteenth day of July One thousand seven hundred and eighty four and made between Anna Maria Adams of Bedford Row in the County of Middlesex Widow and Administratrix of the Goods and Chattels Rights and Credits which were of John Adams late of Bedford Row aforesaid Gentleman her late husband deceased of the first part Thomas Sturt of Ewell in the County of Surry Esquire and Thomas Mason Nephew of the said Thomas Sturt an Infant under the age of Twenty One years to wit of the Age of Eighteen years or thereabouts of the Second part and Robert Long of Symonds Inn in the County of Middlesex aforesaid Gentleman One of the Attorneys of his Majestys Court of Kings Bench at Westminster and also One of the Sollicitors of his Majestys High Court of Chancery of the third part purporting to be an Assignment of certain Articles of Clerkship bearing date the Eleventh day of November in the year of our Lord One thousand seven hundred and eighty three (and made between the said John Adams of the One part and the said Thomas Sturt for and on the behalf of the said Thomas Mason and also the said Thomas Mason of the other part Whereby the said Thomas Mason became bound to the said John Adams to serve him as his Clerk in the Practice and Profession of an Attorney for and during the space of five years thence next ensuing from the day of the date of the said Articles) from Anna Maria Adams at the request of the said Thomas

Transfer of Thomas Mason's Clerkship to Robert Long (1785).
UK, Articles of Clerkship, 1756-1874 for Thomas Mason.

Land and Attorneys

In order to re-introduce the heroine of our story, the future Mrs Anne Frankland, we must now focus on her father, Thomas Mason, the second eldest son of Nathaniel and Ann Mason (nee Hunt), both by now deceased. Born in London in July 1766, at the age of 17 Thomas commenced a clerkship at one of London's famous Inns of Chancery, Symonds Inn. Here he was notably articled to John Adams, an attorney of His Majesty's Court of the Kings Bench, Westminster, and also one of the solicitors of His Majesty's High Court. The position was for a period of five years, the terms, conditions and payment of which had been negotiated by his uncle Thomas Hunt.[89] With a commencement date of 11 November 1783, it was a prestigious opportunity allowing Thomas Mason to become a fully qualified attorney through a period of indentured service.[90]

Unfortunately for Thomas Mason, less than five months into his clerkship, his employer and mentor John Adams died.[91] Thankfully Thomas was able to take up a similar position with another attorney of Symonds Inn, Robert Long. The paperwork for this transfer took some time to be submitted, however, as it was not filed until August 1785. Still, Thomas Mason was able to complete his period of servitude, by the end of 1788 being a practising attorney.

As the eighteenth century drew to a close, an attorney (later referred to as a solicitor) was quite a handy profession to have in

---
[89] UK, Articles of Clerkship, 1756-1874 for Thomas Mason.
[90] UK, Articles of Clerkship, 1756-1874 for Thomas Mason.
[91] *London Chronicle*, 27 April 1784.

one's family, particularly when it came to the administration and management of multiple estates and properties located outside of London. Merchants and other shrewd businessmen with land holdings acquired only a few generations before obviously needed their assets to generate a profit. Primarily based in London, it was nevertheless challenging for landowners to maintain and supervise these holdings located hundreds and hundreds of miles away. A standard solution to this conundrum was to rent or lease the lands out to short or long-term tenants. With minimal opportunity for oversight, however, contracts often went astray. One way to capitalise and control the power in any legal issue was for their London-born sons to become attorneys specialising in personal, property and bankruptcy management. From merchants and mercers with country estates to attorneys and barristers, the generational jump in professional status was also seen as a strategic move for a family's overall standing. Such professionals would also be knowledgeable in litigation, thereby providing an easier pathway to sue tenants that failed to pay rent on these and other assets. A powerful tool, legalese could also be used as a vehicle for improving wealth.

It was in this situation that the fresh-faced attorney Thomas Mason soon found himself. While monetary assets may have been lacking, there were multiple estates located in Coventry still retained by his family. There was also a multi-generational reputation for the management of lands, tithes and charities within this city that he could draw upon. He soon departed London for the greener hills of Warwickshire.

Accompanying Thomas Mason was his wife Dorothea (nee Mitz). The couple had married on 6 July 1789 at Saint Clement Danes in Westminster, London.[92] Aged 22 years at the time of their union, Dorothea had an equally interesting family background, though it was quite different to that of her new husband.

Born in Switzerland around 1767, Dorothea Mitz was the only daughter of Abel Mitz, a merchant, and his wife Arabella (nee Fountaine).[93] Interestingly, the announcement of this particular couple's marriage, which took place in London in late December 1759, stated that '*Miss Arabella Fountaine* [was the] *Daughter of the Rev. Mr. Fountaine, of Marylebone, a most beautiful young Lady,*

[92] England, Select Marriages, 1538-1973 for Thomas Mason.
[93] *London Evening Post*, 5 January 1760; 1841 England Census for Dorothea Mason.

LONDON Diocese. 4th July 1789

Appeared personally *Thomas Mason* and made Oath, that he is of *the Middle Temple London a Batchelor aged upwards of Twenty one Years*

and intendeth to marry with *Dorothy Mitz of the Parish of Saint Mary le Bone in the County of Middlesex a Spinster aged upwards of Twenty one Years*

and that he knoweth of no lawful Impediment, by Reason of any pre-contract, Consanguinity, Affinity, or any other lawful Means whatever, to hinder the said intended Marriage and prayed a Licence to solemnize the same in *the Parish Church of Saint Clement Danes in the County of Middlesex being the next adjoining Parish to the Middle Temple aforesaid the same being Extra parochial*

Christian

and further made Oath that the usual Place of Abode of *him this Deponent*

hath been in the ~~said Parish of~~ *Middle Temple aforesaid*

for the Space of four Weeks last past.

Thomas Mason

Sworn before me *William Battine Surrogate*

Marriage bond for Thomas Mason and Dorothea Mitz (1789).
London and Surrey, England, Marriage Bonds and Allegations, 1597-1921.

and endowed with every Qualification to make the Marriage State truly happy'.[94] The 'Rev. Mr. Fountaine' was the Rev Dr John Fountaine who in 1735 had married Jane de la Place, daughter of Denis and Katherine de la Place.[95] Denis had operated the prestigious Marylebone School out of the Marylebone Manor House from 1703 until his death in 1734 whereupon it was taken over by his widow.[96] From 1759 up until Katherine de la Place's death in 1767 the school had been jointly run by Rev Dr Fountaine and his mother-in-law.[97] The former died in 1787 such that the institution was then managed by his widow Jane for several years, shortly before her own death in 1791.[98]

A prestigious organisation, several prominent students wrote fondly of their time at the Marylebone School. For example, one pupil, George Hangar, later Lord Coleraine, recollected that *'Mrs. Fountaine ... was the best and most attentive of women to the small boys, and that prior to going into school it was her custom to have them into her own room and coax them to learn their lessons by bribes of biscuits and milk'*.[99] He further affectionately stated that she *'might be considered a mother rather than a schoolmistress to the children under her care'*. Another ex-student, George Colman (the younger), noted that *'the seminary was a fashionable stepping-stone to Westminster and other public schools'*.[100] He also related that *'Dr. Fountaine wore a bush wig, and that Mrs. Fountaine, due to her experimental treatment of hair-dyes, had a head with such a variety of colour that "if Berenice had a right to rank among the stars, Mrs. Fountaine's le chevelure" had as clear a claim to pass for a rainbow'*.[101] With reference to the Fountaine's daughters, including Arabella, Colman noted *'they had no share in the scholastic work, although they enlivened the family drawing-room'*.[102]

Another ex-pupil of the school, the Rev Dr John Trusler, provided further anecdotes of the Fountaine family in his

---

[94] *Public Advertiser*, 8 January 1760.
[95] Huguenot Society of London (1886). *Proceedings of the Huguenot Society of London*, Vol. 11. No. 1-3; A. Miles, N. Powers & R. Wroe-Brown (2008). *St Marylebone Church and Burial Ground in the 18th to 19th Centuries: Excavations at St Marylebone School, 1992 and 2004-6*.
[96] Huguenot Society of London (1886). *Proceedings of the Huguenot Society of London*, Vol. 11. No. 1-3; A. Miles, N. Powers & R. Wroe-Brown (2008). *St Marylebone Church and Burial Ground in the 18th to 19th Centuries: Excavations at St Marylebone School, 1992 and 2004-6*.
[97] Huguenot Society of London (1886). *Proceedings of the Huguenot Society of London*, Vol. 11. No. 1-3.
[98] A. Miles, N. Powers & R. Wroe-Brown (2008). *St Marylebone Church and Burial Ground in the 18th to 19th Centuries: Excavations at St Marylebone School, 1992 and 2004-6*.
[99] Huguenot Society of London (1886). *Proceedings of the Huguenot Society of London*, Vol. 11. No. 1-3.
[100] Huguenot Society of London (1886). *Proceedings of the Huguenot Society of London*, Vol. 11. No. 1-3.
[101] Huguenot Society of London (1886). *Proceedings of the Huguenot Society of London*, Vol. 11. No. 1-3.
[102] Huguenot Society of London (1886). *Proceedings of the Huguenot Society of London*, Vol. 11. No. 1-3.

Painting by Michael Angelo Rooker of the Manor House, Marylebone, when used as a school (1791).
The Fitzwilliam Museum, University of Cambridge.

unfinished memoirs. In particular, he noted '*Dr. Fountaine's school was the nursery of a great part of our young men of fashion, the boys being taken in as soon as breeched, and leaving at the age of twelve or thirteen*'.[103] He further expanded on Mrs Fountaine, describing her as a '*vain, dashing woman, extremely fond of appearing at Court, for which purpose, as was generally known, she borrowed Lady Harrington's jewels. Indeed her passion for display was carried to such an extreme that she kept her carriage ... without the knowledge of her husband*'.[104]

However, Rev Dr Fountaine was apparently well aware of his wife Jane's ostentatiousness and their marriage appears not to have been a happy one. His will, dated 10 July 1781, ruthlessly states that '*as to my worldly possessions what has not been squandered away and consumed by* [my] *most wicked and abandoned wife, I devise and bequeath therein the manner following ... first I bequeath to my ... unmarried daughters Mrs Arabella Mitz, Jane and Elizabeth Fountaine (as being wholly unprovided for) the whole of my remaining fortune lying in the fund of 3 per cent ... after my debts are paid to be equally divided among them .... at the same time ... a fourth of one of the shares to my dear*

---

[103] Huguenot Society of London (1886). *Proceedings of the Huguenot Society of London*, Vol. 11. No. 1-3.
[104] Huguenot Society of London (1886). *Proceedings of the Huguenot Society of London*, Vol. 11. No. 1-3.

Grand Daughter Dorothy [Dorothea] *Mitz'*.[105] Further funds were provided to his *'married'* daughters Frances and Diana and to his son Thomas. He continued to lambaste his wife, however, stating that if had she managed the household affairs well, she could have saved *'five hundred pounds'* per year for the family. Instead, she had been *'most foolish and wanton'*. With additional regards to Arabella and her unmarried sisters Jane and Elizabeth, he devised that all of the furniture, beds, linen and belongings situated in the Marylebone house be fairly appraised and sold with the proceeds to be shared amongst them equally. The will then stated, *'finally if either of my said daughters Jane or Elizabeth Fountaine should marry for my daughter* [Arabella] *Mitz cannot I think by the Laws of God or this Country marry whilst her husband is living … in that case she shall have that share of her fortune as above'*.[106]

It is clearly evident that the Fountaine's daughter Arabella, i.e., Dorothea Mitz's mother, benefitted from her father's will and that she was living separate from her husband by this time. Additional references reveal that Arabella also benefitted from her parents' interest and expertise in education and music, becoming a very accomplished vocalist such that in 1786 she was noted as singing for the Archduke and Duchess of Milan.[107] As 'Mrs Mitz' she was recognised as socialising in the same circle and performing with the celebrated organist and composer Samuel Wesley, i.e., the son of Charles Wesley and the nephew of John Wesley, the founders of the Methodist Church.[108] Another close friend was Frances Maria Sewell Lewis, mother of acclaimed English novelist Matthew Lewis. In a biography written about Lewis' life there is a description of 'Mrs Mitz' which states that she was *'one whose performances, although those of an amateur, made her worthy of being ranked with the most eminent of the profession'*.[109] It continued. *'We allude to the celebrated Mrs. Arabella Mitz, who on one occasion had the honour of being accompanied on the violin by one of the royal dukes. This clever and very vivacious lady was an intimate acquaintance of Mrs. Lewis, and a great patroness of Charles Wesley.'*[110]

---

[105] England & Wales, Prerogative Court of Canterbury Wills, 1384–1858 for John Fountaine.
[106] England & Wales, Prerogative Court of Canterbury Wills, 1384–1858 for John Fountaine.
[107] *London Chronicle*, 30 September 1786;
M. Kassler & P. Olleson (2017). *Samuel Wesley (1766–1837): A Source Book.*
[108] M. Kassler (2017). *Samuel Wesley (1766?837): A Source Book.*
[109] M. G. Lewis & H. Colburn (1839). *The Life and Correspondence of M.G. Lewis: With Many Pieces in Prose and Verse, Never Before Published, Volume 2.*
[110] M. G. Lewis & H. Colburn (1839). *The Life and Correspondence of M.G. Lewis: With Many Pieces in Prose and*

In contrast to the Fountaines, little is known of Dorothea's father, Abel Mitz, though he was apparently born in Switzerland and, as a Huguenot, had immigrated to London in the late 1750s to escape religious persecution. He was naturalised by King George II in March 1760.[111] A few months prior to this event Abel had married Arabella Fountaine with their first child, a son named Abel (Jr), born in London in mid-1761.[112] By 1764 the Mitz family had left London for Switzerland where a son named Lucas was born in Basel. He sadly died in February 1765 at the age of one year.[113] Another death occurred in September 1767 with the loss of Abel and Arabella's son Abel (Jr), aged six years.[114] Their daughter Dorothea was born around this period. Indicative of a strained marriage, however, sometime in the years that followed Arabella returned to London with her only surviving child Dorothea. The pair moved to a residence in Barlow Street, Marylebone, in close proximity to Arabella's parents at the Marylebone Manor House.[115] A few years later, as previously mentioned, Dorothea Mitz married Thomas Mason.

After their marriage in July 1789, Thomas Mason and his bride Dorothea moved to Coventry. This relocation was likely predicated on the fact that Thomas' great-uncle Thomas Fletcher was advancing in age. Since the death of his nephew, Thomas Hunt, several years prior, Thomas Fletcher and Joseph Paice had largely been responsible for administering the Hunt family's properties in Coventry that had been placed in trust for Thomas Mason and his brothers and sisters.[116] Now in his 80s, Thomas Fletcher would have been looking to offload the time and effort needed to ensure that the properties were well managed and tenanted. With his great-nephew Thomas Mason now a qualified attorney, it was a fortuitous time for Thomas Fletcher to hand over the reins.

Given London at the time of Thomas Mason's marriage to Dorothea Mitz was undergoing great economic and social change, they were undoubtedly looking for somewhere more settled, stable and cheaper to raise a family. Coventry offered just that location.

Verse, Never Before Published, Volume 2.
[111] *The Publications of The Huguenot Society of London*, Volume XXVII (1923).
[112] England Births and Christenings, 1538-1975 for Abel Mitz.
[113] Record of Lucas Mitz Burial, Schweiz, Katholische und Reformiert Kirchenbücher, 1418-1996.
[114] Abel Mitz Burial, Schweiz, Katholische und Reformiert Kirchenbücher, 1418-1996.
[115] Arabella Mitz, the corner of Barlow Street in High Street Marybone, widow, Royal and Sun Alliance Insurance Group, City of London Archives.
[116] National Archives UK, PA 184/5/10-11; www.coventrycollections.org/search/details/archive/110046182.

Coinciding with Thomas and Dorothea's marriage, Arabella Mitz had purchased a £400 annuity in land in Coventry known as West Orchard. The holding incorporated a malt house, numerous houses and messuages, as well as gardens, stables and other buildings.[117] While Arabella was to pay the guaranteed annual payment of £40, the rents and other profits were to go to Thomas Mason, thus aiding in the support of his wife, i.e., her daughter.

With some financial backing, Thomas and Dorothea Mason were noted as living in Coventry from at least December 1789, by which time Dorothea was pregnant.[118] Their introduction to a new city, however, would have been far from isolating. They were likely quick to associate with relatives stemming from the Hunt side of the family, including second and third cousins. Thomas Mason's younger brother Joseph would also move to the area in the years to come, operating as a wool stapler.[119]

There was much going on in Coventry at the time. While Birmingham was continuing to be the region's industrial and political powerhouse, there was renewed interest in Coventry when the Oxford Canal officially opened on 1 January 1790.[120] The 78-mile waterway, connecting the River Thames to Coventry via Oxford, was seen as a major trading route, particularly for the shipment of coal from the Midlands to Oxford and London. It was also expected to have a beneficial impact on the local economy which had been in decline for some time owing to its primary source of employment being the silk ribbon weaving industry which at the time was being restructured due to the introduction of more efficient technologies. In terms of culture and entertainment, however, there was progress being made with a library first opened in Coventry in 1791. Balls, assemblies and dinners also continued to be the main social activities for those residents in the upper classes of society, which would have included Thomas Mason and his wife Dorothea.[121]

Establishing themselves in Mill Lane, Thomas Mason became involved in local real estate transactions and contracts, as well as investment opportunities and administration of deceased

---

[117] www.coventrycollections.org/search/details/archive/110289750.
[118] *Coventry Standard*, 21 December 1789.
[119] National Archives UK, PA 184/5/10-11; *Hampshire Chronicle*, 2 June 1798.
[120] en.wikipedia.org/wiki/Oxford_Canal.
[121] www.british-history.ac.uk/vch/warks/vol8/pp222-241.

estates.[122] He also became an attorney for Bond's Hospital and the Southern and Craner's Charity; a feoffee of Baker's, Crow's and Billing's charities; and represented various clients in bankruptcy proceedings.[123] In addition, Thomas was active on the Coventry City Council between 1792-1795, 1796-1797, 1802-1803 and 1805-1806, though there was litigation surrounding his initial eligibility to serve as a councillor given he did not meet the requirements of a sheriff.[124] Thomas successfully appealed the decision.

With regards to their family life, Thomas Mason and his wife Dorothea welcomed their first child. A daughter named Arabella Jane was born on 24 October 1790. She was baptised on 19 February 1791 at the Great Meeting House in Smithford Street, Coventry.[125] Two more daughters soon followed. The couple's second daughter, Harriet Helen, was born on 1 March 1792 and baptised at the same meeting house on 18 June that year.[126] Next came their third daughter Anne, significantly the subject of this book, who was born just over a year after Harriet, on 30 April 1793, and baptised at the meeting house on 23 July 1793.[127]

These births were juxtaposed with several deaths. In November 1792 Thomas Mason's great-uncle Thomas Fletcher, by now a retired stationer, died at his home in Walthamstow, Essex.[128] His wife Martha (nee Stiles) had predeceased him and their only child to reach adulthood, Jane, had died in February 1766 at the age of 24.[129] Thomas Fletcher's will thus bequeathed his estate in multiple parts to various iterations of nieces and nephews (and their offspring) belonging to his three sisters, Mary Morhall, Ann Hunt and Jane Mount, as well as close friends, associates, servants, charities and St Thomas' Hospital.[130] Given his home in Walthamstow near the entrance to Marsh Street was situated on 60 acres of *'rich land'* and was described as *'a commodious brick dwelling house of three and four rooms on a floor, with suitable domestic*

---

[122] *Coventry Standard*, 21 December 1789, 30 August 1790, 17 March 1794; *The World*, 11 February 1791; *Oracle*, 27 October 1791.
[123] *Coventry Standard*, 9 May 1791, 13 May 1793; *Morning Post*, 23 February 1795; *News*, 20 July 1800; www.coventrycollections.org/search/details/archive/110296706.
[124] *Coventry Standard*, 11 February 1793; *Morning Post*, 23 February 1795; *News*, 20 July 1800; www.coventrycollections.org/search/details/archive/110296706.
[125] England & Wales, Non-Conformist and Non-Parochial Registers, 1567-1936 for Arabella Jane Mason.
[126] England & Wales, Non-Conformist and Non-Parochial Registers, 1567-1936 for Harriet Helen Mason.
[127] England & Wales, Non-Conformist and Non-Parochial Registers, 1567-1936 for Ann Mason.
[128] *London Chronicle*, 17 November 1792.
[129] *St. James's Chronicle or the British Evening Post*, 13 February 1766.
[130] England & Wales, Prerogative Court of Canterbury Wills, 1384-1858 for Thomas Fletcher.

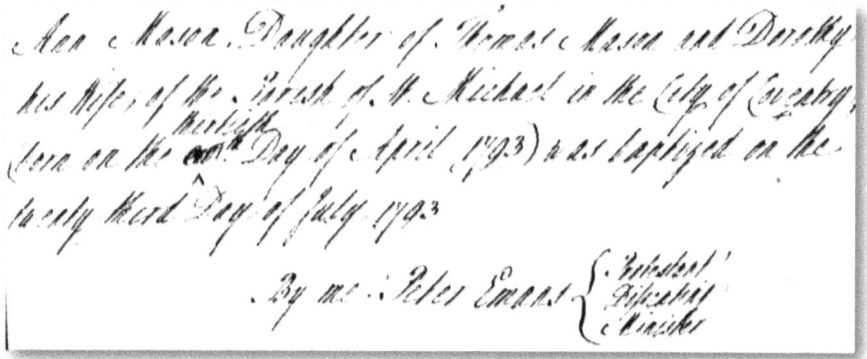

Baptism record of Anne Mason (1793).
England & Wales, Non-Conformist and Non-Parochial Registers, 1567-1936 for Ann Mason.

offices, coachhouses, stabling, pleasure grounds, garden, fishponds, hermitage, and paddocks', one can assume that he was quite wealthy at the time of his death at the age of 85.[131] Moreover, Thomas Fletcher's holdings also included £5,000 worth of shares in a lead mine producing 7.5 per cent interest annually, £1,100 of stock in the Royal Exchange Assurance producing 5.5 per cent interest annually, over 100 shares in London Assurances, 100 shares in the English Copper Company, 30 acres of land known as the Parsonage Closes in the town of Buckingham generating an income of £70 per year, and 152 acres of meadows and grazing land situated at Marton in Lincolnshire on the road from Lincoln to Gainsborough.[132]

In terms of specific allocations, Thomas Fletcher's will instructed his executors to invest £2,000 in trust with half of the interest to be paid to Thomas Mason and the other half to his older brother Nathaniel.[133] An identical allocation was given to their younger brothers Joseph and Langham, while their sisters Ann Harriet and Jane received separate though equally substantial investments. Moreover, Ann Harriet and Jane also each received one-third of the proceeds from the sale of Thomas Fletcher's real estate assets which were to be consolidated and then invested on their behalf.[134] Considering much of the Fletcher family's wealth passed down through Thomas Mason's grandmother Ann Hunt

---

[131] *Morning Post*, 19 January 1793.
[132] *Morning Post*, 19 January 1793; *St. James's Chronicle or the British Evening Post*, 2 March 1793; *Morning Herald*, 9 April 1793.
[133] England & Wales, Prerogative Court of Canterbury Wills, 1384-1858 for Thomas Fletcher.
[134] England & Wales, Prerogative Court of Canterbury Wills, 1384-1858 for Thomas Fletcher.

had been lost on bad investment choices up until this point, the money was well received by Thomas and his siblings.

Thomas Fletcher's will, however, would cause quite the commotion more than 60 years later, particularly considering it bequeathed the last remnants of generational wealth that iterations of the Fletcher, Hunt and Mason families could draw from. The resulting legal actions would likely have led to a very fractured family, though the extent to which it involved the Mason family is not known.

While all of this was well into the future, Thomas Mason and his wife Dorothea immediately benefitted from the contents of Thomas Fletcher's will, thus helping to support their ever-increasing family. By May 1794 the couple and their three daughters had moved to Little Park Street in Coventry where their first son, Thomas (Jr), was born on 30 July 1794.[135] He sadly died at the age of seven months and was buried on 1 March 1795 at the nearby St Michael's Church.[136] Another death occurred a few months later with the loss of Thomas Mason's youngest brother Langham. He had been living in Farnley, Yorkshire, since mid-1790, undertaking an apprenticeship with a cloth manufacturer.[137] Illness, however, likely brought Langham to Coventry where he died in August 1795 at the age of 22 and was buried at St Michael's Church.[138]

After administering Langham's effects, Thomas Mason and his four remaining siblings, Nathaniel, Ann Harriet, Jane and Joseph, resolved to sell the bulk of the closes that had been placed in trust for them since their uncle Thomas Hunt's death in 1785, i.e., Upper Broomfield Close, Middle Broomfield Close, Lower Broomfield Close, Great Meadow, Little Meadow, Crabtree Fields and Bull Fields. The properties were sold to James Troughton of Coventry for £2,100.[139]

Balancing these deaths with births, three more children were born to Thomas and Dorothea Mason in Coventry during the late 1790s. They were a daughter named Sophia born on 21 December 1795, a son named Nathaniel born on 1 March 1798 and another

---
[135] *Coventry Standard*, 12 May 1794; England & Wales, Non-Conformist and Non-Parochial Registers, 1567-1936 for Thomas Mason.
[136] National Burial Index For England & Wales for Thomas Mason.
[137] UK, Register of Duties Paid for Apprentices' Indentures, 1710-1811 for Langham Mason.
[138] National Burial Index For England & Wales for Langham Mason.
[139] National Archives UK, PA 184/5/10-11.

son named Thomas born on 12 August 1799.[140] All three children were baptised at the Great Meeting House in Smithford Street.

While Thomas and Dorothea and their growing family lived in relative comfort in the sheltered city of Coventry, there was much going on throughout the world that would impact various members of the Mason family and its appendages in different degrees in the decades to come. First, the British began colonising Australia with the First Fleet, a contingent of soldiers, convicts, settlers and government personnel, sailing into Sydney Harbour in January 1788. Over the next 80 years more than 162,000 convicts would be forcibly transported to Australia, reducing the stress of over-crowding on Great Britain's prison system and in the process establishing English colonies in the southern hemisphere. Second, and closer to home, the French Revolution, which began in 1789, had exacerbated into an international conflict with Britain officially declaring war on France in early 1793 following the beheading of Louis XVI on 21 January of that year. The two countries would fight one another for the next 23 years on both the land and the sea, initially as the French Revolutionary Wars (1792-1802) and then the Napoleonic Wars (1803-1815). With national interests directed towards the conflict, Britain mobilised its resources to expand its naval and military assets, in the process becoming a global industrial, economic and political powerhouse. The Industrial Revolution, in particular, placed Britain on a global pedestal, with technological innovations associated with manufacturing, iron production, transportation, equipment and tool-making pioneering a new era, including those associated with railways, steamships, textile manufacturing, and communication. With these new technologies, Britain's businessmen also became leaders in international commerce, banking, trade and shipping.

Given the war with France was played out mostly on continental Europe and its waterways, there was little direct impact felt by the Mason family firmly entrenched in Coventry. Having more of an influence on their assets and landholdings, nonetheless, were power struggles, political changes and continued calls for the abolishment of slave labour in the West Indies.

---

[140] *Coventry Standard*, 12 May 1794;
England & Wales, Non-Conformist and Non-Parochial Registers, 1567-1936 for Sophia Mason, Nathaniel Mason and Thomas Mason.

France had taken control of the island of Tobago in June 1781, capitalising on the fact that Britain had placed most of its naval resources towards America's battle for independence such that the island was largely left unprotected. However, the settlement had remained predominantly English in terms of its constitution, laws, civil government and customs, with landholders able to retain their property. In April 1793 the French Revolutionary Wars saw Britain once more regain control of Tobago, though again it was a bureaucratic change that had little bearing on the existing landholders. Tobago thus remained relatively peaceful, despite these changes in sovereignty. While Thomas Mason's older brother Nathaniel had been appointed administrator of their late father's plantations in Tobago, Jamaica and Grenada following his death in 1782, Nathaniel had remained in London, managing them from his home in the Inner Temple area where he was employed as a barrister.[141] The plantations, supervised on-site by an English colonist via a power of attorney, appear to have generated some income by way of mortgage repayments, at the very least, with little direct attention required.

On 27 March 1802, however, Britain, France, Spain and the Netherlands signed the Treaty of Amiens. The pact, amongst other changes of sovereignty of islands and regions, gave Tobago back to the French. Likely owing to this change in circumstance, as well as an increasingly resistant slave population, Nathaniel Mason saw the need to travel to Tobago in the early 1800s where he signed his last will and testament. Sadly, he died on 2 September 1802 at Demerary, a Dutch colony situated on the north coast of South America some 400 nautical miles south-east of Tobago that is now part of the country of Guyana, '*after an illness of four days*'.[142] Nathaniel was 41 years of age and unmarried. It is distinctly possible that he died of yellow fever, a mosquito-born virus that causes jaundice and fever, amongst other symptoms. The disease was extremely prevalent in the region at the time, causing hundreds and hundreds of mortalities.[143]

With his brother's death, Thomas Mason became the patriarch of the family. He also benefitted from Nathaniel's will. Specifically, Thomas received the bulk of the estate, apart from a share in

---
[141] www.coventrycollections.org/search/details/archive/110099410.
[142] *Sun*, 8 January 1802.
[143] *Saint James's Chronicle*, 10 August 1802.

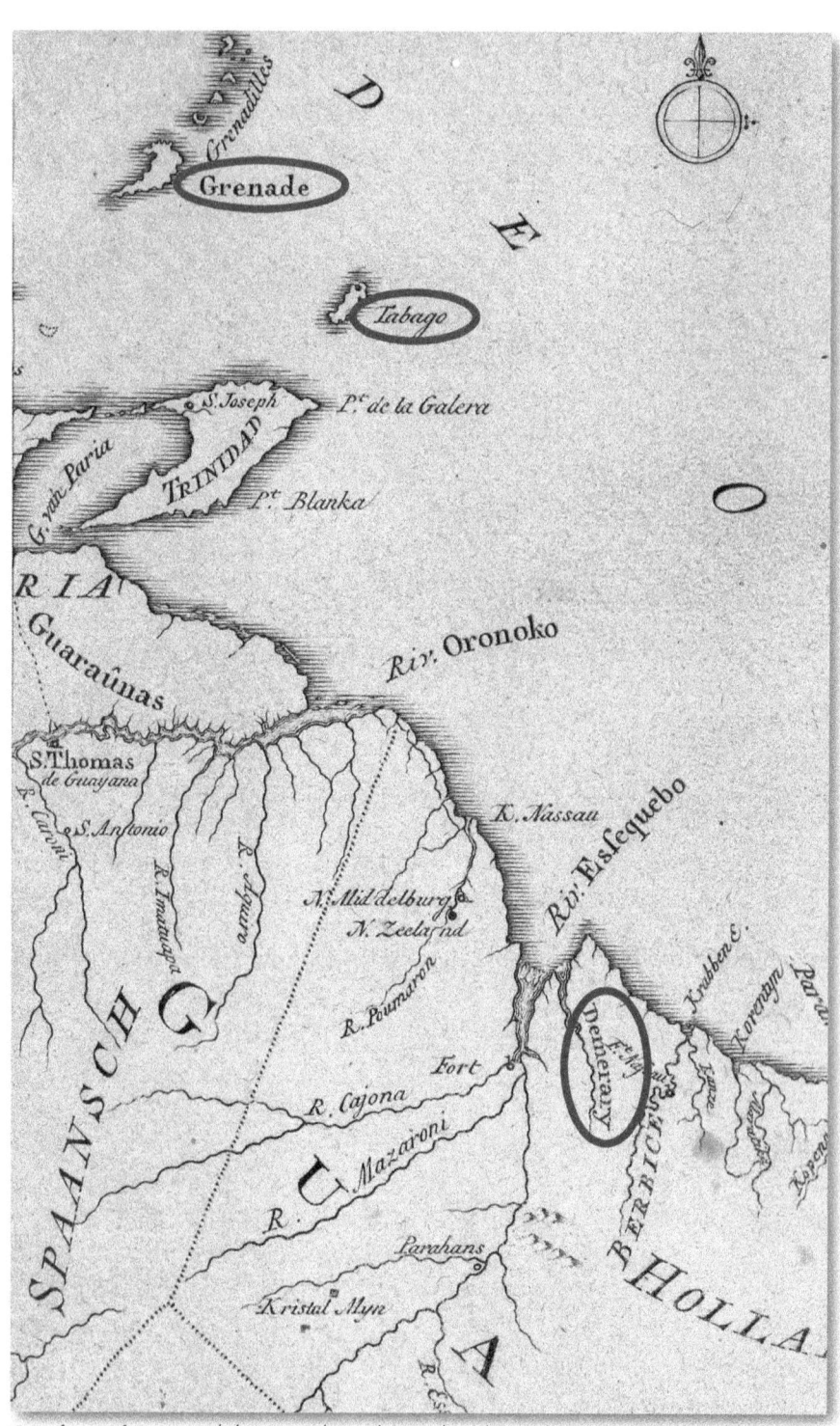

Partial map of Guyana and the West Indies with Grenada, Tobago and Demerary circled (1760s).
Library of Congress (hdl.loc.gov/loc.wdl/wdl.11339).

property in Southampton that had previously belonged to his father.[144]

By 1803 Thomas Mason and his family had moved to a larger residence in Bishop Street, Coventry, where he continued to work as an attorney.[145] His wife Dorothea gave birth to their final child, a daughter named Frances, on 15 April of that year. All told, she had given birth to eight children between 1790 and 1803, including five daughters and three sons, with all but one of their sons surviving infancy.

As their children grew, education, social and other opportunities became important. With a family history strong in education, Dorothea would have made certain that all of her children were well educated, including her daughters. She was also an advocate for women in her local community, including providing funds for the lying-in hospital charity.[146] Additionally, and indicating a sense of equity and equality for mistreated women, Dorothea is mentioned in a law suit whereby she persuaded Mary Milltis, '*a young woman extremely well connected, and the daughter of a respectable ribbon manufacturer in Coventry*', to sue Benjamin Flower, a widower, for breach of promise.[147] Though delicate details of the case were embarrassingly played out in the press, Miss Milltis won the suit and was awarded £500 for being deprived of marriage.

By this point in time, however, the Mason family's interest in Coventry was waning. The Oxford Canal was superseded by the opening of the Grand Union Canal in March 1805 which intentionally bypassed the city to significantly shorten the journey between the Midlands and London. Lack of trade slowed the Coventry economy. Established industries also remained stoic. With a population of under 25,000 people, most men were employed in the ribbon weaving industry, clock and watch making, as well as a growing interest in bicycle manufacturing. However, in general, increasing industrialisation was resulting in a de-skilling of the workforce. The influence of the weavers, considering their large numbers, gave them considerable leverage in local economic, social and political issues. As a member of the City Council's oligarchy based on intergenerational nepotism, Thomas Mason

---

[144] England & Wales, Prerogative Court of Canterbury Wills, 1384–1858 for Nathaniel Mason.
[145] *Coventry Standard*, 10 January 1803.
[146] *Coventry Standard*, 11 March 1805, 15 September 1806, 13 March 1809.
[147] *Coventry Standard*, 10 March 1810.

found himself out of favour. He and his wife Dorothea sought better opportunities for themselves and their children elsewhere. They resolved to return to London.

In September 1806 Thomas Mason began selling off the remainder of his real estate assets in and around Coventry.[148] In November of that year the family's house in Bishop Street was advertised for sale.[149] Most of their furniture and effects were advertised for sale in January 1807. The Mason family moved to London a few weeks later.

> **TO be SOLD by AUCTION,**
> **By RICHARD BOOTH,**
> On Wednesday the 14th Day of January Inst. and two following Days, on the Premises, in Bishop-Street, Coventry:—Part of the elegant and modern HOUSEHOLD FURNITURE, Brewing Vessels, Dairy Utensils, &c. &c. the Property of Mr. MASON, who is removing to London:—
> Comprising a general Assortment of Kitchen Requisites, Ovens, and Boilers, upon the best Constructions, a large Quantity of Iron-bound Vessels and Brewing Tubs, Large Cooler and Copper Furnaces, a Variety of Mahogany and other Chairs, Tables, Chests of Drawers, Swing and Pier Glasses, handsome Mahogany Wardrobes, Tent and other Bedsteads and Hangings, Feather Beds, blankets and Counterpanes, Mahogany Night Tables, Bason and Dressing Stands; an elegant and compleat Set of Furniture for a Drawing Room, consisting of 12 Black and Gilt Elbow Chairs and Sofa, with Cane Bottoms, Cushions, and Rich printed Furniture, with Window Curtains to match, Large Chimney Glass with three Plates, Diamond Cut, an elegant Mirror, Satin Wood Tea and Card Tables, Fire Screens, beautiful Brussels and other Carpets, a compleat Set of Dining Tables, with two Circular Ends, four Feet six Inches, by nine Feet three Inches, a fine toned Harpsichord, Mahogany Side Board, four Large handsome Library Bookcases, with Glass Doors, Circular Library Table with Drawers, Alphabetically arranged, a Large Library Ladder with Drawers, and other Writing Desks, Variety of Dairy Utensils, several Saddles, Bridles, Harness, &c. &c. a six-inch Cast, large Garden Frames and Glasses, &c.
> N. B. Several Alderney and other Cows, and valuable Merino or Spanish Sheep, in Lots, to be sold precisely at One o'Clock, on Thursday the second Day of Sale.
> Catalogues will be printed in due Time, and may be had seven Days previous to the Sale, at the Warwick Arms Inn, Warwick, and of the Auctioneer, Coventry.
> ☞ Sale to begin each Day precisely at Ten o'Clock.

Coventry Standard, 5 January 1807.

---

[148] *Coventry Standard*, 15 September 1806.
[149] *Coventry Standard*, 17 November 1806.

London and Napoleon

Anne Mason was 13 years of age when she moved with her family to London in early 1807. The Mason household quickly established themselves in the Cornhill area of London, close to Cheapside, taking up residence in the Rectory House located just behind St Michael's Church.[150] The vibrant and busy streets would have been a rather abrupt change for Anne, with new routines, sights, smells and sounds to become accustomed to. There was some familiarity, however, with Anne's grandmother Arabella living a few miles away in Brunswick Square.[151] As her only surviving grandparent, it would likely have been a welcome event to be reunited with such a spirited and talented woman and musician who was by now in her late 60s.

While Anne and her sisters were tutored at home, as was custom, her two younger brothers, Nathaniel and Thomas, were enrolled in the Merchant Taylor's School in Suffolk Lane in the parish of St Lawrence Pountney, located less than a mile from their new home.[152] Continuing his professional pursuits as an attorney, Thomas Mason retained clients in Coventry and generated new business in London, primarily dealing with bankruptcy cases and real estate transactions.[153]

Globally, there was still a lot going on. The Napoleonic Wars continued to be waged with Napoleon invading several countries in continental Europe, including Austria, Prussia, Spain and

---

[150] *Coventry Standard*, 10 January 1803.
[151] National Archives UK, Insured: Arabella Mitz 7 Kenton Street Brunswick Square widow.
[152] C. J. Robinson (1883). *A Register of the Scholars Admitted Into Merchant Taylors' School: From A. D. 1562-1874*.
[153] *Coventry Standard*, 9 July 1810; *The Day*, 15 May 1809; *Champion*, 6 November 1814.

Rectory House located just behind St Michael's Church, Cornhill, London (2024).
www.gryphonpropertypartners.com.

Portugal, with the goal of building a hegemony to weaken the British, as well as isolate it from countries that were once considered allies. The stakes were, however, immeasurable. All told, hundreds of thousands of men were wounded or died on both sides, with civilian casualties numbering in the millions. It was a dark period of history, with the Battle for Waterloo still eight years away.

Although the conflict was fought far from London, its effects would have been evident. Naval and military personnel and resources would have been noticeable in the city, including those returning from Europe sick or wounded. There was also the constant threat that Napoleon and his troops would make their way across the English Channel to invade Britain. Local volunteer movements were formed across the country to help thwart any attacks that may occur, with their presence apparent in major cities and towns. It is estimated that as many as one in four Britons took part in military service during this period.[154] Women of the English upper classes also supported the cause by fundraising and holding benefits and events to raise money to help equip and clothe soldiers, as well as support prisoners of war.

Economically, the war had a generally positive impact on the British economy. Any loss of trade with Europe and other French-aligned regions was supplemented by the diversion of resources to military causes. In addition to continued improvements associated with industrialised manufacturing, transportation and communication technologies, England further solidified its dominance in global sectors associated with commerce, banking, trade and shipping. As such, national wealth generally grew.

At the political level, changes were also occurring. In February 1807 the House of Commons passed the Slave Trade Act by an overwhelming majority. The legislation had a near-immediate effect of prohibiting the slave trade, though it did not automatically emancipate those enslaved at the time. The island of Tobago, for example, continued to be largely dependent on an enslaved workforce to run its plantations. However, it is not known if the Mason family still retained their landholdings in the West Indies by this point in time, though they remained the mortgagee of several properties.

For Anne Mason, now in her teenage years, albeit many years from her debut into formal society, her daily life was likely sheltered from the depth and extent of these global events. Instead, at the local level there was much for her to learn and experience. In addition to her continuing education, fashion would have become more important to her and her sisters after their move to London and as they grew in age. The ongoing Napoleonic Wars had coincided with new trends in clothing and, in its early years, due to trade embargoes, a divergence between what was considered vogue in France compared to what was fashionable in England.

---

[154] www.thenapoleonicwars.net/british-invasion-scares-overview.

While English women had initially adopted dresses with lower waistlines, once Parisian fashion again made its way across the Channel they quickly adopted the French look of higher waistlines. The silhouette also began changing from a vertical one established during the previous decade to one more angular. Less fabric was becoming prevalent with hemlines shortening to just above the ground. Military-style adornments also became popular, as an acknowledgment of the conflict.

There were also books, music, art and other entertainments to keep Anne and her sisters occupied. Jane Austen anonymously published her first book, *Sense and Sensibility,* in 1811. It was followed two years later by *Pride and Prejudice*. Other books released during this period were Mary Shelley's *Frankenstein* and the Grimm Brothers' book of fairy tales. These titles were likely supplemented with more classical ones such as Shakespeare.

What is not known, however, is if Anne's father Thomas was able to afford all of these items and opportunities for his seven children, including five daughters. What we do know is that more money came to the family by way of Joseph Paice's will. The 82-year-old charitable bachelor died in September 1810 leaving Thomas Mason £450 in trust.[155] Thomas' surviving siblings, Ann Harriet, Jane and Joseph, all received similar amounts.

Indicative of an upward trajectory, some time around this period Anne Mason and her family moved to a more fashionable residence at 13 John Street, Bedford Row, while her father established his professional offices in Foster Lane, Cheapside, and then at 27 Bread Street, i.e., the property that his father had received a half-share in many decades prior via the Paice family.[156] With the Mason children entering adulthood, there were several life-changing events that took place. First, Anne's second eldest sister Harriet Helen, then aged 21 years, married. On 7 September 1813 at St Andrew's Church in Holborn, London, a 15-minute walk from the Mason family's home in John Street, she married George Walker Marsh, a factor of Croydon, Surrey.[157] Witnesses to the event were Anne Mason, her father Thomas and her younger sister Sophia, along with George's sister Catherine. The couple

---

[155] England & Wales, Prerogative Court of Canterbury Wills, 1384–1858 for Joseph Paice.
[156] *The Day*, 25 November 1809; *Morning Chronicle*, 18 September 1810; *Coventry Standard*, 7 January 1811; *National Register*, 15 November 1812; *Morning Post*, 26 May 1813; *Leeds Intelligencer*, 16 January 1816.
[157] London, England, Church of England Marriages and Banns, 1754–1938 for Harriet Helen Mason.

settled in nearby Bloomsbury, London, where their first child George (Jr) was born in June of the following year.[158] Several more children would be born to the couple in the years that followed. Second, in May 1814, Anne's younger brother Nathaniel began a five-year clerkship with their father to become an attorney.[159] And finally, from an international standpoint, after years and years of conflict, on 15 July 1815 Napoleon surrendered to the British at Rochefort. The Treaty of Paris was signed a few months later, on 20 November 1815, formally ending the war. Napoleon was permanently exiled to the remote island of Saint Helena in the South Atlantic Ocean. Though casualties had been high, Britain emerged from the conflict as a global powerhouse, largely thanks to the sustained industrial and technological advances it had made over the previous decades. Its naval and military resources were also considered unsurmountable. Though Britain had obviously lost the War of 1812 with America, which actually spanned three years, its plight not helped by national resources being deployed to multiple regions throughout Europe as part of the Napoleonic Wars, overall it was a time to rebuild, regroup and recover.

The end of the Napoleonic Wars and the implementation of peace agreements between most of Europe, America and Great Britain heralded a period of relative international accord. Instead of directing resources to its defence, industrial and financial resources were directed towards domestic improvements throughout Britain, including the development of railways, ports, bridges and other modes of transport, as well as long distance communication systems. Improvements to manufacturing and farming practices were also significant during this period. However, the British economy initially suffered a marked downturn due to bad agricultural yields and declines in production associated with its textile industries. It took some time for the economy to recover and the nation to restore itself after decades of conflict.

In terms of Anne Mason's home life during this period, there was much going on, though sources of information confirming what transpired over the next few years are unfortunately lacking. What is known is that Anne's father Thomas Mason is noted as working as an attorney out of his Bread Street office up until at least May

---

[158] London, England, Church of England Births and Baptisms, 1813-1923 for George Henry Marsh.
[159] *Coventry Standard*, 7 January 1811.

1817.[160] Indicative of a change in professional circumstances and suggesting that he was no longer a practising attorney, however, her brother Nathaniel's clerkship had been transferred to one of Thomas' employees, Charles Becket of Compton Street, a month prior.[161] The clerkship would again be transferred two months later, in June 1817, this time to James Brooks of John Street, Bedford Row.[162]

By this period in time Anne's youngest brother Thomas was approaching 17 years of age. With an inclination for academic pursuits, it is reported that he wanted to go to Oxford to further his education. However, given the family's status, Thomas would have been required to enter the institution as a full fee-paying student but a lack of funds hindered his dream.[163] Instead, he found a position with the London-based mercantile firm of Heath, Son & Furze, of the Old Jewry, working as a clerk.[164]

Significantly, lack of means also meant that a *'capital family house'* located at 13 John Street, Bedford Row, was advertised for lease in February 1817 with immediate possession.[165] Containing six bedrooms, a large nursery and two drawing rooms, etc., the residence was advertised for lease by Charles Becket, solicitor of Compton Street. This is unquestionably the house that the Mason family occupied.

> To Professional Gentlemen, Merchants, and Families.—Excellent Residence, with Coach-house, and Stabling. John-street, Bedford-row.—By Mr. BOWLEY, at Garraway's, on THURSDAY, the 27th inst. at Twelve,
>
> THE LEASE of a capital FAMILY HOUSE, in complete, substantial, and ornamental repair, with immediate possession; containing six good bed chambers and dressing rooms, a large nursery and numerous closets, two lofty well-proportioned drawing rooms, 24 feet by 21, and 24 by 16, elegantly fitted up; a dining room, 24 feet by 21, breakfast parlour, a spacious entrance hall, kitchen, butler's pantry, and domestic offices; also a detached coach-house, stabling for six horses, with apartments over; the whole held for eleven years and a half, at a rent of only 120*l.* per annum; the coach-house and stable at present let off at 30*l.* per annum, to a tenant at will.
>
> May be viewed by tickets only, which, with particulars, may be had of Mr. Becket, 18, Compton-street, Brunswick-square; and of Mr. Bowley, 26, Brydges-street, Covent-garden; particulars also at Garraway's.

Morning Post, 20 February 1817.

---

[160] *Stamford Mercury*, 5 July 1816; *The London Gazette*, 13 January, 10 May 1817.
[161] UK, Articles of Clerkship, 1756-1874 for Nathaniel Mason.
[162] UK, Articles of Clerkship, 1756-1874 for Nathaniel Mason.
[163] adb.anu.edu.au/biography/mason-thomas-2436.
[164] adb.anu.edu.au/biography/mason-thomas-2436.
[165] *Morning Post*, 26 May 1813, 20 February 1817.

The reason for this drastic change in circumstances is undoubtedly because Thomas Mason was suffering financially. His professional status as a credible attorney was additionally being questioned. He was also being sued. The plaintiff: his mother-in-law Arabella Mitz, likely to recoup thousands of pounds loaned and then lost in wayward and speculative financial transactions.[166]

Just where the Mason family moved to after vacating their John Street home is not currently known. It is plausible that Dorothea and her children remained in London, living with her mother Arabella. Meanwhile Thomas may have relocated back to Coventry where in early June 1817 he was instructed to appear at the Shakespeare Inn in nearby Stratford-upon-Avon to provide a statement of the conduct and dealings associated with a decades-old bankruptcy proceeding involving the late Charles Henry Hunt.[167] Remaining in the region for several more years, a 'Thomas Mason, Esq.' is known to have donated £1 to the Warwick County Asylum at Streeton in 1819.[168] The same person donated £20 to the institution the following year.[169]

There is also the possibility that Thomas Mason moved overseas in an attempt to escape the mountain of debt he had accumulated, as well as his diminished reputation. A biography written about his son, Thomas (Jr), states that his father *'went to London in 1807 and in 1817 was appointed attorney-general at Tobago where he died'*.[170] Again, no evidence has yet been found supporting this claim.

What is known, however, is that Thomas Mason did die some time in 1820. This is confirmed by the transfer of the administration of his brother Nathaniel's 1802 will, including management of his properties in the West Indies, to Thomas' eldest son and heir, Nathaniel, who by now was a qualified solicitor based in London.[171] This transfer took place on 15 February 1821.[172] It is also confirmed by a law suit amongst various members of the Mason family that took place several decades later that specifically states that Thomas Mason died in 1820.[173] However, the exact date and

---
[166] The National Archives, UK (reference C 13/1694/34; Mitz v Mason); England & Wales, Prerogative Court of Canterbury Wills, 1384-1858 for Anne Harriet Mason.
[167] *Law Chronicle, Commercial and Bankruptcy Register*, 15 May 1817.
[168] *Birmingham Chronicle*, 20 January 1820.
[169] *Birmingham Chronicle*, 18 January 1821.
[170] adb.anu.edu.au/biography/mason-thomas-2436.
[171] England & Wales, Prerogative Court of Canterbury Wills, 1384-1858 for Nathaniel Mason.
[172] England & Wales, Prerogative Court of Canterbury Wills, 1384-1858 for Nathaniel Mason.
[173] Reports of Cases in Chancery, Argued and Determined in the Rolls Court During the Time of Lord Langdale, Master of the Rolls. [1838-1866], Volume 19.

location of Thomas' death is unknown. To date, no will has been located which, given his occupation as an attorney specialising in wills and estates, seems rather peculiar. Moreover, no death notice published in any British newspaper has yet been found.

With regards to Thomas Mason's financial assets, there was nothing left to endow. The legacy money and resources bequeathed to him from generations past, as well as via uncles and other family associates was gone. While Thomas' wife Dorothea would have been supported by her mother Arabella, moving in to her residence at 7 Kenton Street in Brunswick Square, London, where Arabella operated a circulating library and entertained her social set, there was likely not enough funds to maintain all of Dorothea's children that still remained at home. It also plausible that they felt the awkwardness of the new situation too.

To lessen the burden and gain some form of independence, Anne Mason and her older sister Arabella, both by now entering their mid-to-late 20s, sought employment in positions that their social standing would deem respectable: companions and governesses. It was far from ideal, but given the reality of their family's situation, it was a choice without an alternative. They had both refused to marry for anything but love, and they had detested the idea of slowly slipping into a barren and thrifty life of spinsterhood, particularly in London.

Arabella was the first to leave, gaining a position with a family in Ireland, looking after two boys following the death of their mother.[174] Anne advertised her availability in July 1819. By this point in time she also declared herself open to the prospect of becoming an upper maid.

> WANTED, by a Person of respectability, a CONFIDENTIAL SITUATION in either of the undermentioned capacities: as Companion, and to Attend on an elderly Lady (or Invalid), as Juvenile Governess, or Upper Maid; salary not so much an object as a comfortable situation. Address letters, post paid, M. M. to be left at the Circulating Library, No. 7, Kenton-street, Brunswick-square.

Morning Post, 9 July 1819.

---

[174] H. Lawrence (1901). *The Journal of Mrs. Fenton: A Narrative of Her Life in India, the Isle of France (Mauritius), and Tasmania during the years 1826-1830.*

Part Two

Clergy and Cholera

It is impossible to write a love story about two people when there is so little information with regards to how they met and what their first interactions were like. While we do have confirmation that George Frankland and Anne Mason married for love, seemingly effecting them to a lifetime of financial *'prudence'* since neither of them came armed with resources, unfortunately any *Bridgerton*-type biography will have to remain on the fiction shelves. What we do know, however, is that Anne Mason was 29 years of age when she married 22-year-old George Frankland in Bombay on 18 July 1822.[175] Just how she came to be living in India is worthy of a few explanatory pages.

A response to Anne Mason's advertisement for a *'confidential situation'* appears to have come from Mary Josepha Davies, the wife of Rev Henry Davies. Married at Bath in 1809, with their first child, a daughter named Sophia born two years later, the couple had spent the years 1814-1818 in India as part of Davies' role as Chaplain for the East India Company in Bombay, during this period also expanding their family.[176] For the benefit of their health, however, the couple and their children had returned to England in mid-1818 with Rev Davies spending much of the time travelling the country giving sermons.[177] With the Davies family's collective health restored, by early 1820 they were preparing to sail

---

[175] *Morning Chronicle*, 7 January 1823; H. Lawrence (1901). *The Journal of Mrs. Fenton: A Narrative of Her Life in India, the Isle of France (Mauritius), and Tasmania during the years 1826-1830.*
[176] Somerset, England, Marriage Registers, Bonds and Allegations, 1754-1914 for Henry Davis; Somerset, England, Church of England Baptisms, Marriages, and Burials, 1531-1812 for Sophia Browning Davies; University of Birmingham, Cadbury Research Library: CMS/B/OMS/C I E/63.
[177] The Missionary Register for MDCCCXX (1820).

back to India where Rev Davies would begin another stint for the East India Company based at St Thomas' Cathedral in Bombay.[178] However, with their oldest daughter Sophia now approaching 10 years of age, she was in need of a governess to provide a well-rounded and thoroughly British upper-class education as opposed to leaving Sophia at a boarding school in England. Befitting of her future status as a lady, her instruction would need to focus on European languages, literature, drawing, art, needlework and music. It was Anne Mason who gained the trust of Rev Davies and his wife Mary to travel with the family to India to undertake this role.

With her position secured, Anne needed to gain approval from the East India Company for her intended trip and to secure a bond of £200, guaranteed by two sureties, though no money would pass hands unless Anne was proven guilty of bad behaviour or a crime while in India. Generally obtained from London-based merchants and traders, she would have been thankful and very relieved that her brother Thomas' employer, John Benjamin Heath, who had previously been to India, agreed to act as one surety for her passage while George Tatlock acted as the other.[179] Anne's bond was authorised on 11 February 1820, several weeks before her scheduled trip.[180]

On 12 March 1820 Anne boarded the ship *Phoenix* at Gravesend, 20 miles south-east of London, after likely staying one last night with her grandmother Arabella and mother Dorothea in Brunswick Square.[181] As one can imagine, it was conceivably a period fraught with worry; about herself, about her family, and about money. Anne had to leave, nonetheless. There were no options for her in London. There was also no turning back.

Anne probably avoided the looks of concern and guilt in her family's eyes as she walked from their doorstep possibly for the last time to an awaiting carriage. She would have carried a retinue, placing it firmly in her lap and waved one last goodbye. It is highly plausible that she was accompanied by one of her brothers, most likely Thomas, on the ride, grateful to have someone familiar yet stoically unemotional by her side. The pair would have arrived at

---

[178] The Missionary Register for MDCCCXX (1820).
[179] search.fibis.org/bin/aps_detail.php?id=247186.
[180] search.fibis.org/bin/aps_detail.php?id=247186.
[181] search.fibis.org/bin/aps_detail.php?id=469745; *Public Ledger and Daily Advertiser*, 14 March 1820.

the Gravesend docks and quickly found the *Phoenix*. Rev Davies and his family were likely already on board. After a reserved goodbye, Thomas then undoubtedly placed in her hand some money, a collection gathered from various members of the Mason family, before Anne made her way up the gangplank.

With Anne's trunk delivered on board the *Phoenix* several days earlier, she likely went in search of her new charge Sophia and their accommodation. Finding both, the pair undoubtedly explored the cramped vessel some more before proceeding back up on the deck. With the vessel cleared to leave Gravesend, Anne would have been present to witness the ropes being thrown back from the dock, releasing the ship from its temporary home. Soon the masts would have been a hub of activity, the crew unfurling the sails and sending them into a flutter. The London breeze would have then come to assistance, with the *Phoenix* slowly but surely working its way down the river.[182]

Anne had likely never seen London from the water before, at least this far down the Thames, and would have wondered at its familiar sights and landmarks seen from a different viewpoint. Finally entering the welcoming months of spring after the harshness of winter, the city would have looked far from its best, the wanton waves of smoke from coal fires being absorbed into the gray sky. Anne would have remembered this day as one of her saddest, yet also one in which her curious mind and itch for adventure was likely fortified.

The *Phoenix* arrived off Deal, Kent, two days after traversing the Thames and turning southward into the English Channel.[183] After a fine passage along the English coast, with Anne taking in the various scenes pointed out to her by those that had made the voyage previously, the vessel entered the North Atlantic Ocean. Despite the heavier seas and at times belting winds, Anne no doubt made good use of the time giving lessons to Sophia and entertaining the other children on board. Her evenings would have been spent dining with other passengers, including Rev Davies and his wife Mary, members of the garrison and their family, as well as several traders and merchants who were also on board.

---

[182] *Public Ledger and Daily Advertiser*, 14 March 1820.
[183] *Statesman*, 15 March 1820.

The ship's passage to India was not direct, however. There were stops to make along the way to take on additional freshwater and food. Six weeks after leaving England, the *Phoenix* moored off the volcanic island of Madeira, a towering mountain rising out of the sea, with the busy town of Funchal situated at its base.[184] Here the vessel spent nine days at anchor taking on various supplies with Anne perhaps making several excursions to the island in the company of Rev Davies and Sophia.[185]

After leaving Maderia the *Phoenix* then made an unexceptional passage down the coast of Africa, rounding the Cape of Good Hope on 16 May 1820, and arriving off Bombay on 18 June; a passage of only 83 days at sea and several weeks shorter than most of the passengers had anticipated.[186] Thankful to have reached their destination, Anne would have immediately been overcome by the stifling humidity, heat and the monsoonal rains. She had heard that it would be the rainy season, which generally lasted between June and September, yet she likely could not believe the actual amount of rain that fell. Buckets and buckets of it. And the relentless humidity that was only temporarily relieved by the downpours. It would take some time to get used to the climate.

Surrounded by water on three sides, Bombay was a rapidly growing city at the time of Anne's arrival, helped by an increasingly prominent cotton industry. With a population of over 180,000 people and under British rule by way of a Royal Charter to the East India Company for two centuries, its architecture was an eclectic mix of Gothic, Neo-Classical and Indian styles. Anne would have stared at the city, its skyline dominated by red roofs, its structures mostly white in colour, its vivid vegetation and trees, and of course its people as the ship moved closer to the port. With so much of her attention focused on this part of the city, she possibly neglected to take in the lighthouse, rock formations and small islands that they also passed, including the celebrated island of the Elephanta, which she would have had heard so much about on the voyage. There would be time to view these landmarks later, nonetheless.

It would have taken some time for the *Phoenix* to come to rest and the formalities of its arrival to be dealt with. It was probably

---

[184] *Star*, 27 April 1820.
[185] *Star*, 27 April 1820.
[186] *Bombay Gazette*, 21 June 1820.

many hours before Anne and the Davies family were rowed ashore, the group then making their way to the parsonage, thankfully only a few blocks from the port. Anne was likely glad to walk the short distance, her legs wobbly from the ship's motion, thus taking some time to get accustomed to the firm ground.

Consecrated in 1718, St Thomas' Cathedral was the first Anglican church in Bombay, with its location strategically placed within the fortified walls of the British settlement. The parsonage was located near to the church, likely a spacious residence representative of those constructed for personnel serving with the East India Company, i.e., a few storeys high, surrounded by verandahs and lush gardens with low internal ceilings though fitted with many windows and doors to improve ventilation.

While Rev Davies soon commenced work overseeing St Thomas' Cathedral and catching up on all that he had missed in the two years since his family's departure back to England, Anne would have continued to tutor the Davies' daughter Sophia. She would also have become acclimated to the style of living, whereby

View of Bombay, from Mazagon Hill, 1831, hand-colored lithograph.
Yale Center for British Art, Paul Mellon Collection.

St Thomas' Cathedral, Bombay, 1831, hand-colored lithograph.
Yale Center for British Art, Paul Mellon Collection.

servants attended every facet of the household's needs, though the weather would have remained an obstacle to her settling in to this new environment. She no doubt could not become accustomed to the unrelenting heat and humidity nor the rain. Whereas in England Anne would have been outdoors during some part of the day, walking London's numerous parks and streets, and running errands, Bombay's weather would have been a barricade to this pastime. Exploring the streets and taking in the rich scenery, new flowers and trees would have to wait until the rainy season was over.

    There were other deterrents that limited options for outside activities and entertainment in general: boundaries and illness. At the time of Anne's arrival in Bombay, the city and the surrounding region was enjoying a period of relative peace with the British East India Company defeating the last of an indigenous-lead confederacy several years prior. The garrison still remained, however, with its administration and construction activities helping Bombay to emerge as a significant trading hub. It was also being re-imagined into a metropolis through large-scale civil engineering works aimed to amalgamate several of the local islands.

Given Bombay's British settlement was largely made up of those connected with the East India Company who lived and worked within its fortified walls, there would have been ample opportunities for dinners, dances, concerts and other social events with those that lived within the bastion. However, at the time of Anne's arrival the newspaper reported on the rate of mortality affecting the local British population due to a cholera epidemic. The statistics provided below are astonishingly only for the period 13 to 19 June 1820 and are in fact a reduction from previously published data.

Since our last, the Rain has fell in torrents and as we had conjectured, a diminution of the Cholera has certainly taken place, as will be noticed in the annexed statement.

Died of Cholera Morbus from 13th June to the 19th June 1820, inclusive.

	Males	Females	Children	Total
13 June	22	29	9	60
14	24	14	4	42
15	17	21	7	45
16	18	24	8	50
17	24	13	6	43
18	17	13	3	33
19	13	15	4	32
	135	129	41	305

Bombay Gazette, 21 June 1820.

The result of ingesting water or food contaminated with the bacterium *Vibrio cholerae*, symptoms of cholera include severe diarrhoea, vomiting and dehydration. The infection was so acute and life-threatening at the time, however, that patients often died within hours of the first symptoms appearing, including those previously considered of good health. Unfortunately the bacterium thrived in unsanitary environments and with Bombay's incessant rains, humidity and limited capabilities to treat its drinking water supply and manage sewage, it was common for outbreaks to occur and be widespread, particularly during the rainy seasons.

It was into this environment that Anne Mason initially adapted, though thankfully the threat of cholera began to wane.[187] There were other health threats, however, including 'bilious fever', most commonly caused by malaria, which appeared to effect sometimes fatal consequences in a matter of days. Sadly, the local *Bombay Gazette* was filled with death notices for young and active East India Company personnel and members of their families who died within hours or days of contracting an illness.

Did Anne Mason regret her decision to relocate to India? The answer to this question is not known, but it would have been uncharacteristic for any new arrival in a foreign land to not feel a sense of homesickness or doubt. It was definitely a new and harsh reality that Anne now faced, though she was likely sheltered by the environment of the parsonage and her position as a governess.

Slowly but surely Anne would have settled into a new routine, though it would have remained quintessentially 'British' in how she taught her charge Sophia, spent her spare time, and who she interacted with. Still, Anne Mason would have begun to experience new foods and flavours, including fruits such as mangoes and watermelons, as well as curries and different types of seafood. Moreover, she would have been exposed to some of the local culture and traditions and experienced first-hand the social hierarchy of Bombay, including the caste system.

There was also society to join with the British contingent and garrison staunchly tight with their interactions predominantly only associating with one another. It was a large society, in the realms of thousands of British subjects living in Bombay during this period, though it was predominantly male-orientated. Very few single women had made their way to India from Britain during this period such that the community was largely made up of wives, daughters and sisters of those working for the East India Company, those acting as members of the British government and their administrators, or those men involved in trade. Given its military dominance, it was also a fluid community with arrivals and departures of personnel and their families a regular occurrence due to promotions, resignations and leave approvals.

---
[187] *Bombay Gazette*, 28 June 1820.

There was also the persistent threat of death, whereby cholera and other diseases could render a relatively healthy person dead in a matter of hours.

While she would have been deemed past the age of marriage in England, with so few English women present in India at the time Anne Mason was considered an eligible spinster in the British community of Bombay, even though she was by now in her late 20s. Promulgating her opportunity to find love would have been the numerous events that military personnel attended with single women present, far more in number and opportunity than back in England, including informal dinners and dances.

It was at one of these functions that Anne Mason and George Frankland first met. Seven years her junior, George was notably the son of Rev Roger Frankland, Canon of Wells Cathedral in Wells, Somerset, and the grandson of Admiral Sir Thomas Frankland, 5th Baronet, a British naval officer with a legacy of daring piracy, a member of parliament for the borough of Thirsk, Yorkshire, and a slave trader.[188] Sir Thomas was also the father of an astonishing 19 children born to his wife Sarah, daughter of William Rhett, Chief Justice and Governor of South Carolina, whom he had met while stationed in the region.[189] Described as a highly gifted woman, a descendant later suggested that from Sarah *'were derived those powers of understanding which distinguished the next generation of Franklands'*.[190]

Regardless of provenance, the surviving children of Sir Thomas and Sarah Frankland proved quite impressive with similar diplomatic and military service to Britain, including being stationed on the Isle of Man, in Paris, Italy, India and Portugal, as well as taking expeditionary and defensive cruises to Africa and Asia Minor.[191] There is also an anecdote of a meeting with Napoleon that proved more in depth than expected owing to a misidentification.[192]

Growing up George Frankland would have been told tales of these global escapades and adventures, particularly those concerning his grandfather Sir Thomas Frankland. Born in India

---

[188] en.wikipedia.org/wiki/Sir_Thomas_Frankland,_5th_Baronet; *The Scots Magazine*, 1 April 1782; J. Waylen (1897). *The House of Cromwell: A Genealogical History of the Family and Descendants of the Protector.*
[189] J. Waylen (1897). *The House of Cromwell: A Genealogical History of the Family and Descendants of the Protector.*
[190] J. Waylen (1897). *The House of Cromwell: A Genealogical History of the Family and Descendants of the Protector.*
[191] J. Waylen (1897). *The House of Cromwell: A Genealogical History of the Family and Descendants of the Protector.*
[192] J. Waylen (1897). *The House of Cromwell: A Genealogical History of the Family and Descendants of the Protector.*

Portrait of George Frankland's grandfather, Sir Thomas Frankland, 5th Baronet, by Henry Walton. Wikimedia Commons.

around 1718, unfortunately Sir Thomas died in 1784 in Bath, Somerset, i.e., 16 years prior to George's birth.[193]

Meanwhile George Frankland's mother was the Hon Catharine Colville, youngest daughter of John, the 8th Lord Colville of Culross, Scotland, and his wife Amelia (nee Webber).[194] Her

---

[193] en.wikipedia.org/wiki/Sir_Thomas_Frankland,_5th_Baronet.
[194] J. Debrett (1808). *Debrett's Peerage England, Scotland, and Ireland*.

father had retired from the British Army in the early 1760s after a distinguished career spanning 24 years of service, including being stationed in the West Indies and Gibraltar, afterwards taking up a position as Inspector General to the Outposts in Scotland where Catharine spent most of her childhood.[195]

As suggested there is a lot more to George Frankland's history than these short statements imply, including a connection to Oliver Cromwell.[196] George Frankland and his ancestors are in fact worthy of having their own books written about them, delving deeper into these generational legacies of diplomatic, military and religious service, along with the customary marriage contracts, law suits, worldwide travel, complicated wills and premature deaths. They were also honorary members of the British peerage, with some corresponding with Sir Joseph Banks due to a shared interest in botany and a possible family connection.[197]

To be somewhat brief, with relevance primarily to George Frankland, he was born in the fashionable town of Bath, Somerset, England, on 31 January 1800 to Rev Roger Frankland and his wife, the Hon Catharine.[198] Unfortunately for George, in a period where male lineage and birth order were important, he was the sixth of twelve children born to the couple and the fourth of six sons.[199] This position thus propelled him into a future without the benefit of financial nepotism, being three derivatives from the heir, though the influence of maternal and paternal relations would be apparent in the career opportunities that came George's way. So too would the inherent privilege of his upper-class upbringing.

Though born and baptised in Bath, George Frankland was raised in the rural village of Yarlington, some 30 miles to the south, where his father was Rector since 1797. A year before George's birth, Rev Roger Frankland had additionally been appointed Vicar of Dulverton, another small village located 70 miles to the north-west of Yarlington.[200] He likely split his time between the two locations, the extra income proving necessary to help support the ever-expanding Frankland family.

---

[195] W. Anderson (1864). *The Scottish Nation; or the Surnames, Families, Literature, Honours, and Biographical History of the People of Scotland.*
[196] J. Waylen (1897). *The House of Cromwell: A Genealogical History of the Family and Descendants of the Protector.*
[197] *Stamford Mercury*, 4 August 1820.
[198] Somerset, England, Church of England Baptisms, Marriages, and Burials, 1531-1812 for George Frankland.
[199] Frankland Family Tree compiled by author on Ancestry.com.
[200] J. Nichols (1826). *The Gentleman's Magazine and Historical Chronicle from January to June, 1826.*

Yarlington offered an idyllic playground for George Frankland and his many brothers and sisters. The small village, with a population of around 300 people, was situated amongst rolling hills and valleys intersected by numerous streams feeding into the rivers Cam and Cale.[201] The local economy was primarily supported by agriculture with crops such as wheat, barley, oats and potatoes grown.[202] The parsonage house, where the Frankland family lived, was stated to be a *'very good dwelling in a pretty, romantic situation'*, though they appear to have moved to Holebrooke House near Wincanton, three miles from Yarlington, by 1808.[203]

Given the small population, there were no schools in Yarlington nor Wincanton. Instead, George and his brothers would have initially been educated by their father or a tutor before being sent to a boarding school, possibly located in one of the other larger towns within the county of Somerset.

Holebrooke House now Holebrook Manner, near Wincanton, Somerset (2024).
theholbrookmanor.com.

---

[201] A. P. Baggs & M. C. Siraut (1999). *A History of the County of Somerset: Volume 7, Bruton, Horethorn and Norton Ferris Hundreds.*

[202] A. P. Baggs & M. C. Siraut (1999). *A History of the County of Somerset: Volume 7, Bruton, Horethorn and Norton Ferris Hundreds.*

[203] *British Press,* 9 January 1808; *Salisbury and Winchester Journal,* 1 May 1809, 20 January 1812, 7 February 1814.

While his oldest brother Frederick left home to attend the Royal Military College at Woolwich in early 1809, and his two older brothers, Edward and Charles, had both entered the Royal Navy in 1807 and 1810, respectively, initially serving as midshipmen, George was more inclined to pursue academic-based interests, with a love of art and science.[204] Unfortunately his desire for a more philosophical and genteel lifestyle may have been thwarted by a lack of family resources. The death of his maternal grandfather, Lord Colville at Bath in March 1811, however, proved beneficial for George Frankland and his family.[205] While £5,000 was settled on his mother, George and his older brother Frederick received £200 each to be put in trust with the sum due at the age of 21. George was 11 years of age at this time so it is assumed that the interest generated via the trust would have gone to his education.

It was shortly thereafter, in January 1812, that Rev Roger Frankland was promoted to the position of Canon of Wells Cathedral, a prominent appointment considering the size of the parish, in the realm of thousands of people, and the cathedral itself being the seat of the Church of England Diocese of Bath and Wells.[206] Wells was also located 20 miles to the south-west of Bath and 16 miles north-west of Yarlington, putting the Frankland family closer to this prestigious and sought-after town. However, it appears that they did not immediately move to Wells, remaining at Holebrooke House for at least several more years. Rev Frankland also remained Rector of Yarlington until at least 1817.[207]

With his older brothers away from home, it was likely that their return during vacations and holidays were joyous ones for the entire Frankland family. In his memoirs published in 1874, George's oldest brother Frederick remarks on his sisters being pleased that he was learning to play the flute in military college such that he was able to accompany their pianoforte playing. Frederick also notes that his uncle, Major General the Hon Sir Charles Colville, often stayed with them, including in mid-1812 following his return to England from Spain after being wounded

---

[204] F. W. Frankland (1874). *A Memoir of the Early Military Life of Sir Frederick William Frankland, VIII. Baronet of Thirkleby*; J. Marshall (2010). *Royal Naval Biography, or Memoirs of the Services of all the Flag-Officers, Superannuated Rear-Admirals, Retired Captains, Post Captains and Commanders.* Vol. IV. Part II; H. Colburn (1876). *Colburn's United Service Magazine and Naval Military Journal, Volume 141*.
[205] England & Wales, Prerogative Court of Canterbury Wills, 1384–1858 for Lord John Coville.
[206] *Bristol Mirror*, 26 July 1817.
[207] *Pilot*, 3 January 1812.

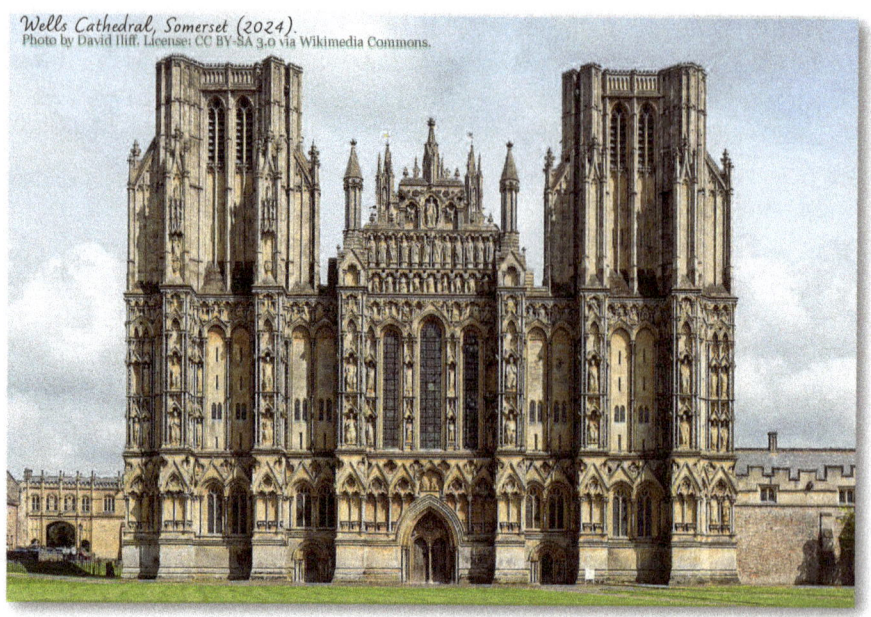

Wells Cathedral, Somerset (2024).
Photo by David Iliff. License: CC BY-SA 3.0 via Wikimedia Commons.

at Badajos.[208] Soon thereafter, Frederick received a summons from Sir Charles Colville to join him as part of Lord Wellington's army based in Lisbon, Portugal. It was the start of a prestigious military career for Frederick. In fact he and his brothers Edward and Charles would all be commended for their exceptional service, in the process seeing large areas of the world and being involved in some of Britain's more historical conflicts, including Waterloo.[209]

While his three older brothers had found professional callings in their early teens, it took some time for George Frankland to settle on a career path. He appears to have travelled to Europe, specifically France and Switzerland with his brother Edward around 1816 to 1818, and on his return may have attempted to follow in his father's footsteps at Oxford.[210] However, there is no evidence to date that George formally completed a university degree such that it was via family connections that he was able to join the British Army, initially as a Cadet, i.e., the lowest rank of any member of service. However, it was a position without purchase indicating he lacked financial resources at the time.

[208] F. W. Frankland (1874). *A Memoir of the Early Military Life of Sir Frederick William Frankland, VIII. Baronet of Thirkleby.*
[209] F. W. Frankland (1874). *A Memoir of the Early Military Life of Sir Frederick William Frankland, VIII. Baronet of Thirkleby.*
[210] J. Marshall (1835). *Royal Naval Biography or Memoirs of the Services ...*; Jane Franklin (21 June 1838). Letter to her sister Mary Simpkinson, University of Tasmania Library Special and Rare Materials Collection.

George Frankland was assigned to the 24th Regiment of Foot, a battalion which his brother-in-law William Robison was a member.[211] At the time, the regiment was stationed in India with George first arriving in Calcutta per the ship *Princess of Charlotte of Wales* in October 1819.[212] Under the command of Captain C. B. Gribble, the vessel had departed Gravesend on 18 May 1819, arriving in Calcutta on 6 September. Also on board was Lieutenant Colonel William Robison and several other officers of various regiments.[213] It is likely that Robison's wife Matilda, who was George Frankland's older sister, was scheduled to join them at some stage, though she had sadly died a week prior to the ship's departure and only a few days after giving birth to the couple's first child.[214]

The 24th Regiment had been stationed in India for several years, being involved in multiple conflicts. At the time of George Frankland's arrival, it was based at Ghazepoor, on the Ganges River, nearly 500 miles north-west of Calcutta.[215] Thus George, William Robison and other personnel from the regiment that had been on board the *Princess of Charlotte of Wales* would have been transported up the Hoogly River via barge, then travelled overland for several days to connect with the Ganges River system. The trip likely took several weeks to complete. George, however, arrived in the region in October 1819 when the climate was more forgiving, with daily temperatures moderate compared to those experienced in April through August.[216] Though situated inland and rather remote, Ghazepoor was considered an important outpost for the British who had only taken it over in 1818, primarily due to its importance in opium production and trade.[217] At the time of George Frankland's arrival, the British had commenced construction of an opium factory.

Upon arrival in Ghazepoor, Lieutenant Colonel Robison assumed command of the 24th Regiment. Settling in to the local British community, it would have been at this location that George Frankland and other members of the 24th Regiment received

---

[211] *Salisbury and Winchester Journal*, 24 May 1819.
[212] search.fibis.org/bin/aps_detail.php?id=962367; *Bombay Gazette*, 6 October 1819.
[213] search.fibis.org/bin/aps_detail.php?id=962367; *Bombay Gazette*, 6 October 1819.
[214] Frankland Family Tree compiled by author on Ancestry.com.
[215] G. Paton, F. Glennie & W. Penn Symons (1892). *Historical Records of the 24th Regiment, from its Formation*.
[216] en.wikipedia.org/wiki/Ghazipur.
[217] en.wikipedia.org/wiki/Ghazipur.

news of the death of King George III who had died on 29 January 1820 and the subsequent accession of King George IV. There was personal news for George Frankland too, having been promoted to the position of Ensign in March 1820.[218]

The 24th Regiment remained around a year in Ghazepoor before making preparations to relocate to Cawnpore, leaving in mid-November 1820.[219] Considering the two locations were over 250 miles apart and the march performed at an average of eight miles per day, it would have been a long and arduous trek, taking over a month to complete. Before they left Ghazepoor, the local British community reflected that the *'utmost harmony has pervaded the Society of Ghazepoor ever since this Regiment came to the station. Its officers appear as one Family, and the orderly good conduct of the Soldiers make their departure regretted no less than that of their officers'*.[220]

It is likely that George Frankland did not travel to Cawnpore with the 24th Regiment. On 12 January 1821 he was officially appointed an Aide de Camp with the 65th Regiment of Foot, though had likely received the news a few months prior.[221] At the time, the 65th Regiment was assembling in Bombay with some companies due to be transferred to the Persian Gulf to campaign against an Omani tribe known as Bani Bu Ali.[222] However, given that this particular expedition had left Bombay on 11 January 1821, George would have missed their departure.[223] Directly making his way from Ghazepoor to Bombay would have taken over a month or more considering the distance to be covered was around 1,000 miles. It would also have involved multiple modes of transport, including horse, elephant, carriage, barge and foot.

Upon his arrival in Bombay, George Frankland would have been pleased to rejoin several members of his family. Notably, his uncle Lieutenant General Sir Charles Colville had been appointed Commander in Chief of Bombay in April 1819.[224] He had arrived in India with his wife Lady Jane Colville (nee Mure) and their infant son Charles (Jr), as well as George's sister Emma Frankland, from England per the ship *Barossa* in October 1819.[225] The Colvilles had

---
[218] *New Times*, 6 March 1820.
[219] *Government Gazette (India)*, 23 November 1820.
[220] *Government Gazette (India)*, 23 November 1820.
[221] www.abhilekh-patal.in/jspui (PR_000002479883).
[222] *Government Gazette (India)*, 11 January 1821.
[223] en.wikipedia.org/wiki/Bani_Bu_Ali_expedition.
[224] *Bombay Gazette*, 14 April 1819.
[225] *Bombay Gazette*, 13 October 1819; search.fibis.org/bin/aps_detail.php?id=246869.

Map of India (1818).
Library of Congress (www.loc.gov/resource/g7650.fi000237/).

also expanded their family, welcoming a daughter, born at Loujee Castle in December 1819.[226] In addition, Emma Frankland had married William Chaplin at St Thomas' Cathedral, Bombay, in October 1820.[227] Though George would have missed the birth and the wedding by a matter of months, he likely cheerfully welcomed the new members to his family.

Settling in to Bombay, George Frankland became Aide de Camp to his uncle. It was an extremely lucrative position though one probably given to him through influence rather than merit. Despite being far from the remote areas of India that he had previously been stationed at, George would have enjoyed the cosmopolitan city flavour of Bombay though still would have endured the risk of cholera, malaria, dysentery and other diseases then extremely prevalent. There were also more opportunities for entertainment than he had previously been associated with as part of his last regiment, as well as more opportunities to mix with single women deemed worthy of his hand. Sir Charles and Lady Colville frequently held and attended dinners, levées, dances and balls. Horse racing was another outlet for recreation with the attendance of Lady Colville given special mention in the press with regards to her beauty and fashion.[228]

Given George Frankland worked closely with his uncle, he undoubtedly resided at Loujee Castle, enjoying the comforts of a full house of servants and a lifestyle symbolic of the English upper class. His days would have largely been filled with administrative and political tasks, as well as attending ceremonial events. It would have been a far better situation for George, who seems to have had a penchant for desk work and socialising, as opposed to what he had been accustomed to as a Cadet then Ensign with the 24th Regiment. However, there may have also been some cavalry-related tasks, with Sir Charles Colville personally touring with some battalions of the British Army while in India.[229] In the absence of Bombay's then Governor, Sir Charles additionally acted in this role.[230]

Having arrived in Bombay from England in June 1820, Anne Mason would have been present in the city for at least eight

---

[226] *Bombay Gazette*, 8 December 1819.
[227] *Bombay Gazette*, 18 October 1820.
[228] *Bombay Gazette*, 7 February 1821.
[229] *Bombay Gazette*, 26 October, 1 November 1820.
[230] *Bombay Gazette*, 29 November 1820.

Portrait Miniature of George Frankland (c1823).
www.christies.com/en/lot/lot-2471869.

months before there was opportunity to meet her future husband George Frankland. It is not known if the couple had a long or short courtship or where they met. It is assumed they were first introduced by mutual associates at one of the many social events occurring in Bombay at the time.

Regardless of introduction, 29-year-old Anne Mason and 22-year-old George Frankland were married by licence on 18 July 1822, the ceremony taking place at St Thomas' Cathedral and performed by Rev Henry Davies.[231] There were numerous witnesses to the union, notably Sir Charles Colville, as well as Mountstuart Elphinstone then Lieutenant Governor of Bombay. Also listed is a 'William Mason', though to date a familial relationship between him and Anne Mason is yet to be confirmed. Other witnesses were no doubt friends of the bride and/or groom.

Upon receiving news of the couple's marriage back in England some five months later, the Mason family placed notices in the London-based press. Perhaps giving themselves more 'airs and graces' than reality, Anne Mason was described as the daughter of the *'late Thomas Mason, Esq. of John-street, Bedford-row'*.[232] The Mason family had not lived at this residence for at least five years.

> At Bombay, on the 18th July, by the Rev. Henry Davies, Lieut. George Frankland, of the 65th Regiment of Foot, son of the Rev. Roger Frankland, Canon of Wells, and grandson of Sir Thos. Frankland, Bart. to Ann, third daughter of the late Thomas Mason, Esq. of John-street, Bedford-row.

Morning Chronicle, 7 January 1823.

While they very likely married for love, neither Anne Mason nor George Frankland had any assets or resources such that no marriage contract was necessary. This fact would have immediately became apparent when they went to set up their marital home. George's salary would not have been enough for the couple to maintain an upper-class lifestyle in India where they were expected to not only acquire, furnish and equip a residence but also secure and pay for the services of numerous servants. Conceivably, and in an attempt to secure more pay and status for George Frankland, he had been promoted to the position of Vice Lieutenant, no doubt thanks to the patronage of his uncle.[233]

---
[231] UK, British Army and Navy Birth, Marriage and Death Records, 1730-1960 for George Frankland.
[232] *Bombay Gazette*, 29 November 1820.
[233] www.abhilekh-patal.in/jspui (PR_000002480592).

Vol 6
P. 150

Marriage record of George Frankland and Anne Mason (1822).
UK, British Army and Navy Birth, Marriage and Death Records, 1730-1960.

These are to Certify to all whom it doth or may concern that the Court of Directors of the East India Company did on the Twenty sixth day of April One thousand Eight hundred and Twenty five receive from their Government at Bombay by the Ship "Katherine Stewart Forbes" a paper entitled "Marriages Solemnized at the Presidency of Bombay in the East Indies in the year 1822" Certified by "Henry Davies Senior Minister of St Thomas's Church." and in which paper I find the following entry; viz:

"1822
"July 18th George Frankland of Bombay Esquire one of the Aid de
" Camps to His Excellency the Honble Sir Charles Colville,
" Bachelor, and Miss Anne Mason, of Bombay, Spinster,
" were married in this Church by Licence from the Honble
" the Court of the Recorder, this Eighteenth day of July in
" the Year of Our Lord, One thousand Eight hundred
" and Twenty two. " By me Henry Davies
" Senior Minister

"This marriage was solemnized ⎱ George Frankland
" between us ⎰ Anne Mason

" In the presence of us — Eliza Hunter Blair — Chs Colville
" Elizabeth Bruce D. Leighton
" Amelia Williams James Jackson
" Isabella G Leighton William Mason
" M. Elphinstone. F. N. B. Tucker."

In Witness whereof I have hereunto set my hand at the East India House in London this Twenty Eighth day of June in the year of our Lord One thousand eight hundred and thirty nine

For Anne Mason, now Frankland, who had been working in Bombay as a governess, her new status as a military wife would have taken some time to become accustomed to. Suddenly she also found herself interacting with George's family, including Sir Charles and Lady Jane Colville. More changes in circumstances came late in 1822 when Anne Frankland realised that she was expecting the couple's first child.

Given Bombay, and India more generally, suffered from high rates of infant mortality and a lack of educational facilities considered adequate for the children of British subjects, it was customary for children born in India to be sent back to England, usually at a very young age. These children were then placed with family members or sent to boarding school. When Anne Frankland found herself pregnant, the harsh reality of their situation became more apparent. While George had only recently been promoted, he resigned from his position as Aide de Camp for his uncle effective 1 January 1823.[234] This decision was likely predicated on a need for a higher-paying role rather than his work with Sir Charles Colville not being satisfactory.[235]

There were many changes taking place. Lady Colville and her children left Bombay, sailing back to Britain with the intention that Sir Charles would soon follow.[236] However, he remained in India for several more years.[237] So too did George Frankland and his new bride. In a risky move, in early 1823 George was appointed to an engineering department charged with developing the 1,300-mile Dawk Road from Nagpore to Bombay via Poona.[238]

Strikingly it was convention in India at the time, and for many decades following, for wives to accompany their husbands during any travel required as part of their vocations. Thus Anne joined George as the couple travelled through remote regions of western India. Setting up camp and becoming acquainted with the practicalities and arduousness of her new husband's work surveying for roads, bridges and boundaries was something that Anne would never have dreamed possible when she first sailed for India less than three years prior. She was also preparing to give birth for the first time. What verily extremes they faced.

[234] *Bombay Gazette*, 8 January 1823.
[235] *Bombay Gazette*, 30 January, 26 February 1823.
[236] *Bombay Gazette*, 30 January 1823, 30 November 1825.
[237] *Bombay Gazette*, 30 January 1823, 30 November 1825.
[238] *Bombay Gazette*, 24 March 1824; Historical Records of Australia, Series 3, vol. 5.

Babies and Voyages

Sophia Catharine Frankland was born at Nagpore in central India on 22 July 1823, coinciding with her parents' first wedding anniversary. Given the remoteness of the location, Anne and George Frankland waited many months for her to be baptised. This event finally took place upon the couple's return to Bombay in early 1824, by this time Sophia was six months of age. She was baptised by Rev Henry Davies on 24 January 1824 at St Thomas' Cathedral. It was likely a compelling period for the Frankland family with George notified that he had been promoted to Lieutenant a few weeks earlier.[239] The couple would have also been happy to be back in Bombay amongst friends. There was more news too. Anne Frankland was once again pregnant.

Baptism record of Sophia Catharine Frankland (1824).
UK, Officers' Birth Certificates, Wills and Personal Papers, 1755-1908.

---

[239] *Weekly Globe*, 11 January 1824.

For the benefit of their own health and that of their infant daughter and unborn child, Anne and George Frankland departed Bombay on 28 January 1824, four days after Sophia's baptism. They sailed as passengers on board the ship *Sarah* under the management of Captain Thomas Bowen.[240] The vessel was en route to London, though the Franklands only sailed as far as Cape Town, South Africa.[241] Anne, George and Sophia Frankland disembarked from the *Sarah* in early April 1824.[242]

A British colony since the Anglo-Dutch Treaty of 1814, Cape Town at the time of the arrival of the Franklands was a bustling port town with a population of over 100,000 people of whom around half were of European descent.[243] It was also a haven for English military personnel on leave from India as it allowed them to retain their position and full salary while enjoying a break in a gentler climate. For reasons unknown, however, Anne, George and Sophia did not stay in Cape Town long, instead making their way to Stellenbosch, a town located 30 miles directly inland. It was here that their second daughter Georgina Anne was born on 22 June 1824. She was baptised on 21 July, a day before Anne and George's second wedding anniversary with her sponsors, by proxy, being Frederick Frankland and Emma Chaplin (George's eldest brother and sister), and Arabella Jane Mason (Anne's eldest sister).

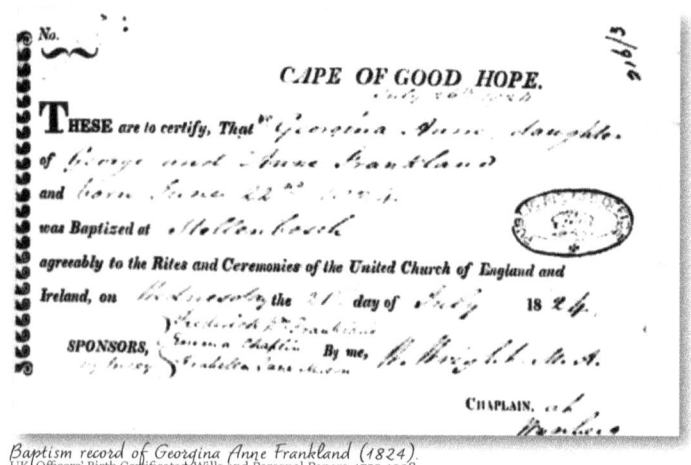

Baptism record of Georgina Anne Frankland (1824).
UK, Officers' Birth Certificates, Wills and Personal Papers, 1755-1908.

---

[240] *Bombay Gazette*, 4 February 1824; *Sun*, 15 June 1824.
[241] *Bombay Gazette*, 4 February 1824; *Sun*, 15 June 1824.
[242] *Nation*, 17 May 1824.
[243] A. Wilmot (1869). *History of the Colony of the Cape of Good Hope*.

While George Frankland had remained a Lieutenant, by now with the 67th Regiment of Foot, during his time in South Africa possibly undertaking some form of administrative or surveying work, he had also applied for a leave of absence. Official approval for 12 months of absence was given to him by Thomas McMahon, the Commander in Chief in India, on 23 November 1824.[244] The leave was to take effect from the date of his departure from Cape Town. Given this order was made in India, however, it would have taken some months before George was notified.

Now a family of four, the Franklands departed Cape Town for London as passengers on board the East India Company's ship *Berwickshire* on 31 January 1825.[245] After calling at Saint Helena, though only staying one day, the vessel arrived at Portsmouth on 11 April. After disembarking the Franklands would have travelled by coach to Bath or London, either way a distance of 80 miles. Upon arrival at one of these locations, Anne and George would have finally had the opportunity to meet their respective in-laws and associated family members for the first time. There had obviously been many significant events since they both sailed to India over five years prior. In addition to several marriages and births, Anne's grandmother Arabella Mitz had died in London in August 1823 at the age of 81.[246]

Anne and George Frankland and their two daughters Sophia and Georgina, now aged 21 months and 10 months respectively, returned to England to find George's parents and sisters part of 'The Ton' such that their movements were printed in local newspapers, including their interactions with the Royal Family and the fashions that they wore.[247] Unfortunately very few of these publications name George or Anne Frankland's presence specifically such that we are unable to grasp our couple's particular movements, though they no doubt would have spent some time with Rev Roger Frankland, his wife the Hon Catharine and their youngest daughters Catherine, Octavia and Sophia.

The 12 months of absence from his military service, however, would have gone by quickly for George Frankland, especially considering it began on 31 January 1825 when he departed South

---

[244] *Sun*, 14 April 1825; *British Press*, 14 April 1825.
[245] *Sun*, 14 April 1825; *British Press*, 14 April 1825.
[246] *Morning Post*, 4 September 1823.
[247] *London Courier and Evening Gazette*, 21 May 1824.

Africa. Very likely dreading a return to India, as convention would have meant that Anne and their two young daughters remained in England, he sought new opportunities, though by late January 1826 was still yet to return overseas. Entirely out of the question would have been for the Franklands to stay in England. Though descendants on both sides of their families had been, and in some cases still were, landed gentry, George and Anne had no land with which to tenant out and earn an income. They also had no home of their own and very little money. Any hospitality provided to them during their stay in England would have been bestowed by family 'gratis', though George was likely receiving half of his pay.

While George waited for news of a more agreeable appointment from the British Army, he and his wife Anne continued to enjoy being part of the Frankland family's social circle. For example, the press report for a *'Fancy Ball at Cheltenham'* held by Major and Mrs Hamerton at their residence in Montague Place in late January 1826 notes the presence of *'the Hon. Mrs Frankland, ... Miss Frankland,* [dressed as a] *Lady of the ancient Court; Miss _ Frankland, a Dutch peasant; ... Mr. George Frankland, an Arab ...'.*[248] The newspaper report further noted that *'Miss Blakeney and Mr. George Frankland personated a Gipsey Tinker and his wife, with infinite spirit and talent'.*[249]

However, in the days and weeks following this soirée, there was much melancholy for the entire Frankland family. First, George's eldest sister Emma Chaplin passed away at Ramsgate, Kent, on 1 February 1826 at the age of 30.[250] Less than two months later, on 25 March, George's father, Rev Roger Frankland, passed away at his home, 70 Poulteney Street, Bath, Somerset, aged 63.[251] He left the bulk of his estate to his wife, the Hon Catharine, though some provisions were placed in trusts for all of his surviving children, including George.[252]

In May 1826 George finally received a new appointment from Henry Bathurst, 3rd Earl Bathurst and Secretary of State for the Colonies: he was to be Assistant Surveyor of Van Diemen's Land at a salary of £250 per annum, with the proviso that George be promoted to a superior position, i.e., Surveyor General or

---

[248] *Morning Post*, 25 January 1826.
[249] *Morning Post*, 25 January 1826.
[250] *English Chronicle and Whitehall Evening Post*, 9 February 1826.
[251] *Sun*, 28 March 1826.
[252] England & Wales, Prerogative Court of Canterbury Wills, 1384-1858 for Roger Frankland.

Deputy Surveyor General, as soon as one became open given '*Mr. Frankland's qualifications render him eligible for higher employment*'.[253] Whether George requested this position or was awarded it based on merit or family influence is not known. However, it was certainly a big change compared to India, particularly in terms of climate, though one which George and his wife Anne welcomed, including in terms of raising their children. The only issue: Anne was once again pregnant.

Armed with a letter of introduction from Downing Street via R. W. Hay, Under Secretary, George, Anne and their two daughters took their leave from England. While their exact movements during the following months are unknown, it is likely they sailed to Cape Town where their son Augustus Charles Frankland was born on 21 September 1826, though no record of the exact location of his birth has yet to be found.

> UNDER SECRETARY HAY TO LIEUT.-GOVERNOR ARTHUR.
>
> Dear Sir, Downing Street, 20 May, '26.
>
> I am directed by Earl Bathurst to introduce to your notice the Bearer of this letter, Mr. George Frankland, whom Lord Bathurst, as you are aware, has appointed one of the Assistant Surveyors at Van Diemen's Land. Mr. Frankland, besides being a person of Education and Science, has had very considerable experience as a Trigonometrical Surveyor, having been employed in India for some years in that capacity; and, as he possesses much zeal and enterprize, his Lordship anticipates that he will prove himself eminently useful in conducting a general survey of the Colony, for which undertaking, from his acquaintance with the superior branches of his profession, he is peculiarly qualified. He may also at the same time be employed in collecting information in regard to Geology and the Natural History of the Country in which he is about to take up his residence. You will therefore be pleased to recommend him to the Surveyor General in such manner, as shall induce him to avail himself of Mr. Frankland's Services in the way best calculated to turn the Talents which he possesses to the advantage of the Public. I remain,
>
> R. W. HAY.

Letter of Introduction for George Frankland (1826).
Historical Records of Australia, Series 3, vol. 5.

[253] Historical Records of Australia, Series 3, vol. 5.

While Anne and George Frankland and their now three children were still making their way to Hobart Town, news of George's appointment as Assistant Surveyor reached Van Diemen's Land via letters carried per the ship *Woodford*. The 522-ton vessel had had left London in late July 1826, arriving in the River Derwent four months later, on 22 November, with 99 convicts on board as well as a detachment of the 99th Regiment.[254] It would be another eight months, however, before the Franklands themselves arrived in Hobart Town via the 300-ton ship *Harvey*.

Under the management of Captain Findley, the *Harvey* had navigated the southern coast of Van Diemen's Land in early July 1827, entering Storm Bay to drop anchor off Hobart Town's Old Wharf area on 10 July.[255] On board were Anne Frankland, by now 34 years of age, her husband George, aged 27, and their three children: Sophia, aged three; Georgina, aged two; and baby Augustus now nine months old. The vessel had sailed from England via Cape Town where it had landed troops and remained for six weeks before making its way to Van Diemen's Land.[256]

It is likely that the Frankland family boarded the *Harvey* during its stop-over in Cape Town. If so, they had undoubtedly missed a stressful first leg of the voyage whereby, after leaving London, the vessel had sprung a leak in the English Channel and was forced to undertake repairs at Plymouth over the course of several weeks.[257] Upon getting back underway, there had been unrest amongst some of the passengers such that several duels involving personnel from the 55th Regiment who were to disembark at Cape Town had taken place. Unfortunately, one of these conflicts had resulted in the death of a lieutenant when a bullet had struck his forehead and he was killed instantly.[258] The *Harvey*'s delay leaving Cape Town was likely the result of a criminal investigation which had been carried out upon its arrival in South Africa. It is not known what the passengers on board the vessel thought of these duels, though it is obvious that they would have been concerned for their own health and safety since the *Harvey* was only a 300-ton craft.

It was thus with a sense of relief for all on board that the *Harvey* finally sailed up the River Derwent in the midst of Hobart

---
[254] *The Hobart Town Gazette*, 25 November 1826.
[255] *Colonial Times and Tasmanian Advertiser*, 13 July 1827.
[256] *Colonial Times and Tasmanian Advertiser*, 13 July 1827.
[257] *The Hobart Town Gazette*, 14 July 1827.
[258] *The Hobart Town Gazette*, 14 July 1827.

Town's winter. In addition to cargo and livestock, the vessel had 30 passengers on board, mostly middle and upper-class immigrants, including barristers and merchants and their families, intending to make a new life in the developing colony.[259]

For many thousands of years the traditional owners and custodians of nipulana (Hobart Town), the Mouheneener band of the South East Nation of Aborigines had utilised the land and its associated waterways. All of this changed in February 1804 following the arrival of Lieutenant Governor David Collins and his contingent of British convicts, marines and free settlers. Named Hobart Town in honour of Lord Hobart who served as Secretary of State for War and the Colonies from 1801 to 1804, it was initially a rudimentary population, in its infant years being constantly on the verge of starvation.

By the late 1820s, concurrent with the arrival of the Franklands, the European settlement of Hobart Town (and Van Diemen's Land generally) had matured, with commerce and industry spurred by the increasing availability of convict labour. Free settlers began arriving to take advantage of vast expanses of land made accessible for farming and the cultivation of wheat and wool began. The era also saw the development of local and intercolonial trade, and the establishment of a whaling industry. This period additionally coincided with arrival of the colony's fourth Lieutenant Governor, George Arthur, who would oversee a more self-governing, organised and authoritative administration.

In 1824 the European population of Van Diemen's Land stood at around 12,000 people, over half of whom were convicts. With more and more free settlers arriving, it had become apparent that a comprehensive and systematic map of the island needed to be developed, particularly since parcels of land in varying sizes and locations were being more frequently awarded to free settlers and emancipated convicts alike. Better plans for the development and expansion of towns, as well as infrastructure in the form of roads, bridges and water courses were also much in need. The *ad hoc* nature of Hobart Town's establishment was also being aligned for corrective action, especially considering that some of the early land grants were believed to have been incorrectly measured, often to the benefit of the grantee, becoming somewhat of a political

---

[259] *The Hobart Town Gazette*, 14 July 1827.

Painting by George Frankland showing an immigrant family arriving at Hobart Town (1827).
Allport Library and Museum of Fine Arts, State Library of Tasmania (AUTAS001139593552).

issue.[260] It was in this situation that George Frankland found himself upon assuming the role of Van Diemen's Lands' Assistant Surveyor.

Likely introducing himself to Lieutenant Governor George Arthur near immediately upon his arrival in Hobart Town, in addition to determining a start date and place of office, another priority would have been finding accommodation for his family. With all of this going on, George found time to paint a scene.

Known for his '*exquisite caricature sketches*', George Frankland's painting from 1827 of an immigrant family arriving in Hobart Town remarkably still exists, part of the State Library of Tasmania's Allport Library and Museum of Fine Arts.[261] It is a unique mix of an extraordinarily detailed landscape painting with a comical scene assumed to show George with daughter Georgina in his arms and daughter Sophia by his side, as well as his wife Anne scrambling up the banks near the Old Wharf seemingly covered in mud. A larger vessel, possibly the *Harvey,* is moored out in the river.

What is apparent in the painting and is known to be factually correct: Anne Frankland was once again pregnant, expecting the couple's fourth child. Missing from the artwork is their baby son Augustus and the bulk of their luggage. Still, it is a fascinating depiction of Hobart Town and the context in which George and Anne Frankland and their family arrived.

---

[260] *Colonial Times and Tasmanian Advertiser*, 9 February 1827.
[261] Copies of letters from Jane, Lady Franklin, Van Diemen's Land, to her sister Mary Simpkinson 1838 - 1843. University of Tasmania Library Special and Rare Materials Collection, Australia;
Allport Library and Museum of Fine Arts, State Library of Tasmania (AUTAS001139593552).

Surveys and Society

Five months after the Franklands' arrival in Hobart Town, Anne gave birth to the couple's third daughter. Matilda Roberta Frankland was born on 20 December 1827.[262] During the interim the family had settled into a cottage at the upper end of Collins Street and George had started work. There were, however, some hiccups. The Franklands had departed England on the assumption that George's appointment as Assistant Surveyor would stand and that he would be promoted as soon as a position became open.

> Sir,   Downing Street, 17 May, '26.
>
> In conformity with the arrangement communicated to you in my dispatch of the 1st Instant, I have the honor of acquainting you that I have appointed Mr. George Frankland to be the first Assistant Surveyor at Van Diemen's Land, with a Salary of £250 pr. annum, the same rate of remuneration which, according to the Scale I have forwarded to you, I have assigned to Mr. Scott, whom it is my intention to appoint to the head of that Department, whenever the retirement of Mr. Evans shall take place. In the mean time its Establishment will consist of the following persons:—
>
> 1. Mr. Evans, Surveyor General.
> 2. Mr. Scott, Deputy Surveyor General.
> 3. Mr. Frankland, First Assistant.
> 4. Mr. Wedge, Second   do
> 5. Mr. Sharland, third   do
>
> As Mr. Frankland's qualifications render him eligible for higher employment, it is my wish that he may be appointed to the first Vacancy, which may occur in the Colony in any of the appointments of a superior description for which he may be fitted, and to which I may not have nominated a different person.
>
> I have, &c.,
>
> BATHURST.

Historical Records of Australia, Series 3, vol. 5.

---

[262] Tasmanian Archives (RGD32/1/1 no. 2554 and no. 2555).

George would therefore likely have been frustrated to find out that in the months following his initial appointment, George Evans had in fact retired from the position of Surveyor General but that Captain Edward Dumaresq had been appointed in his place, with Thomas Scott acting as Deputy.[263] Thus George Frankland was relegated to third in the Survey Department's hierarchy. This predicament was entirely the result of the fact that it took many months for letters to be sent between administrative officials in England and those in the Australian colonies, a distance by sea of 16,000 miles, with notices often crossing paths mid-ocean. There was also a perceived flexibility by those present on both sides to make decisions and then notify the other not realising that decisions had already been made at either end. For George's situation in particular, it did not help his cause that Edward Dumaresq was the brother-in-law of General Darling, i.e., then Governor of New South Wales, and had been appointed '*to that lucrative post*' without the approval of Downing Street.[264] Perhaps placating the situation was the fact that Edward Dumaresq was likely a well-known acquaintance of George Frankland as he had spent several years in India with the Bombay Native Infantry, including working with the Survey Department at the same time that George was there.[265]

The local press reported on the conundrum three days after the Frankland's arrival and offered a possible solution. '*Lieut. Frankland, H. P.* [assumed to infer half-pay] *has arrived per the ship Harvey, bearing the King's Commission as Deputy Surveyor-General. Mr. Scott, who also received his appointment from Home, as Surveyor-General, is now acting as Deputy, until answers are received from England, to dispatches forwarded by the local government respecting the appointment of Mr. Scott. As Captain Dumaresq acts as Surveyor-General, we can see no other mode of proceeding than, that Mr. Frankland will act as Deputy, according to his Commission, at Launceston, where the want of a branch of the Survey Department is most seriously felt; and that Mr. Scott, from his great knowledge of every part of the interior, will still continue in active service, at the head of the outdoor department. We believe that Mr. Frankland imagined that by virtue of his appointment he would be entitled to act as Surveyor-General, in the event of any thing happening to Mr. Scott; but in this respect he has found himself under the*

---
[263] *Colonial Times and Tasmanian Advertiser*, 9 March 1827.
[264] *Hobart Town Gazette*, 27 February 1827.
[265] adb.anu.edu.au/biography/dumaresq-edward-2002.

*disagreeable necessity of considering that he is a peg lower than he thought for ...'.*²⁶⁶ While this issue took some months to sort out, George Frankland was appointed Aide de Camp to Lieutenant Governor George Arthur much to the chagrin of the Editor of the *Colonial Times* newspaper. On 5 October 1827 he opined, *'Mr. Frankland, the new Deputy Surveyor General has been appointed Aide de Camp to His Excellency Lieutenant Governor Arthur, at a salary, we understand, of ten shillings per diem, to be paid, it is said, out of the Colonial Revenue. This we cannot however believe; for, in all our peregrinations, we never heard of a Military Officer being a Civilian, and paid out of the Civil Fund. Considering Mr. Frankland's arduous (if performed) duties, as Deputy Surveyor General, we are of the opinion that he must neglect the avocations of one office, to perform those of the other; and that one of the Officers of the 40th Regiment would have been better appointed -- We do not like the plurality of offices in one individual'.*

Finding himself in favour with the Lieutenant Governor, though not the press, George Frankland settled into his new role as Aide de Camp, as well as his work with the Survey Department. As stated, in the days before Christmas 1827, he and his wife Anne also welcomed their fourth child, Matilda. Becoming acquainted with Hobart Town, the couple would have relished the more favourable temperate climate Van Diemen's Land offered as opposed to the oppressive heat of India. The threat of diseases, particularly malaria and cholera, was also much reduced though there was still the ever present risk of scarlet fever, tuberculosis, influenza, measles and dysentery, more likely to affect infants and children.

In the early days of January 1828, while Anne stayed at home convalescing with their new baby, George took the opportunity to climb Mount Wellington, the behemoth of a landmark that dominates the Hobart Town skyline. With its summit 4,000 feet above sea level, the climb up the mountain would have taken George and his companion (Captain d'Urville) many hours to complete with the pair noted as collecting specimens of rare plants and minerals along the way.²⁶⁷ A further few hours would have been spent navigating their descent back to Hobart Town.

Two weeks later, on 16 January 1828, the Franklands attended St David's Church in Hobart Town where their two youngest

---

²⁶⁶ *Colonial Times and Tasmanian Advertiser*, 13 July 1827.
²⁶⁷ *The Hobart Town Courier*, 5 January 1828.

Baptism records of Augustus Charles and Matilda Roberta Frankland (1828).
Tasmanian Archives (RGD32/1/1 no. 2554 and no. 2555).

children, Augustus and Matilda, were baptised by Rev William Bedford.[268] It is interesting to note that Augustus was now 16 months of age, though why the couple had waited so long to get him baptised is not known. Still, the day would have been a happy occasion for George and Anne albeit one where the distance between themselves and their families was extremely apparent.

On a professional level George Frankland's expertise soon became apparent and he was commended for surveys of Sullivans Cove and Hobart Town's harbour generally which were then used to develop a plan for alterations and improvements by John Lee Archer, a civil engineer and architect in the government's employ.[269] It was proposed that a quay be erected and mercantile stores be built as part of the development of a 'New Wharf' area.[270] A few weeks later George was praised in the local press for surveys he had made of several streams located in the foothills of Mount Wellington with the intention of diverting them into the Hobart Town Rivulet thereby increasing the town's water supply.[271]

Obviously eager to see the interior of Van Diemen's Land, on 8 March 1828 George Frankland left Hobart Town in company with Lieutenant Governor George Arthur and others on an exploratory expedition to Launceston and associated regions.[272] It was during this trip that letters arrived from London confirming George's appointment within the colony's Survey Department. In particular, he was appointed Surveyor General with Captain Dumaresq alternatively appointed Collector of the Internal Revenue.[273] In officially publishing George's appointment in *The Hobart Town Gazette* on 22 March 1828 it was appeasingly stated that, '*In the promulgation of this Order, The Lieutenant Governor considers it due to Mr. Dumaresq, to point out, that during periods*

---

[268] Tasmanian Archives (RGD32/1/1 no. 2554 and no. 2555).
[269] *The Hobart Town Courier*, 19 January 1828.
[270] *Colonial Advocate, and Tasmanian Monthly Review and Register*, 1 March 1828.
[271] *The Hobart Town Courier*, 23 February 1828.
[272] *The Tasmanian*, 14 March 1828.
[273] *The Hobart Town Courier*, 8 March 1828; *Colonial Times*, 15 May 1829.

(exceeding Two Years), that he has been intrusted with the charge of the Survey Department, His Excellency has had the zeal, integrity and ability which he has manifested in conducting this very important Department'.

It was likely an awkward period for George as he assumed the higher position of Surveyor General from his associate. Given the two men and their wives belonged to the same social circle, which based on Hobart Town's size was at the time quite small, they undoubtedly shared some delicate moments. For example, both '*Mr. and Mrs. Frankland*' and '*Mr. and Mrs. Dumaresq*' were attendees of a ball that took place at 10 pm on the evening of Monday 17 March.[274] The Hobart Town Courier's reporting of the event is worth reprinting. '*This evening the spacious apartments recently erected in the Barrack-square, were thrown open by the Officers of the 40th Regiment, to a numerous and fashionable assemblage of their friends, for a splendid Ball and Supper, to which most of the principal inhabitants had received cards. The rooms filled soon after 10 o'clock; and quadrilles and Spanish dances were kept up during the whole night with great spirit. The Mess room was appropriated to dancing. It was brilliantly illuminated, and the floor was well and very tastily painted. ... In all, we believe there were nearly 120 persons present, forming an assemblage of fashion, beauty, and elegance, worthy of Almacks itself ...*'.[275]

Another social occasion was the Sunday morning church service held at St David's Church. Hobart Town's social hierarchy was no more apparent than in the placement of the congregation amongst the pews. It was also a crowded event, with the ladies noted to be '*most fashionably dressed*'.[276] Quickly becoming accepted members of this upper-class society, George Frankland was not only elected to the committee of the Society for Promoting Christian Knowledge for Van Diemen's Land but also its Honorary Secretary and Treasurer.[277] He remained in this role for many years.

As life often throws curve balls, despite these career and social successes there was much grief within the Frankland family when Anne and George's youngest child Matilda died in late April 1828, aged just four months. Cause of death is not known. She was buried on 28 April at the Burial Ground near St David's Church.[278] Matilda was the last child born to the couple.

[274] *The Hobart Town Courier*, 22 March 1828.
[275] *The Hobart Town Courier*, 22 March 1828.
[276] *The Hobart Town Courier*, 22 March 1828.
[277] *The Hobart Town Courier*, 26 April 1828.
[278] Tamanian Archives (RGD34/1/1 no. 1683).

While the Frankland family mourned the death of their youngest child, George continued to receive praise for his survey work, as well as his efforts to overhaul regulations stipulating the granting, renting and selling of land, including by a more efficient tender process. Further exploratory trips were also undertaken with George and his deputy, Thomas Scott, exploring the Wellington Range in May 1828 with the goal of making preparatory steps for the potential development of a road between Hobart Town and Port Davey on Van Diemen's Lands' south-west coast.[279] Another purpose of the trip was to survey the country west and south of Mount Wellington and report on the availability of suitable land, as well as minerals, animals, timber and other resources.[280] Intending to travel to the region via New Norfolk, this was densely forested, remote and rugged bushland, often steep with which the two men had to negotiate with the trip likely taking several weeks to complete. However, given the time of year the trip was curtailed. The pair returned to Hobart Town having been forced back due to snow and heavy rains.[281] Still, they managed to navigate the River Derwent to a waterfall of about 30 feet in height, with some worthwhile tracts of land discovered such that they vowed to return to the region when weather conditions were more favourable.[282] George Frankland also created a map from the survey.

Back in Hobart Town, Anne and George Frankland sought a new home for themselves and their three children. In July 1828, exactly one year after their arrival in Van Diemen's Land, they gave up the lease on their six-room cottage situated at the upper end of Collins Street at the Ellinthorpe Mill.[283] Both Anne and George Frankland also continued to be very active members of the Society for Promoting Christian Knowledge.[284]

On 1 September 1828 George Frankland was appointed a Justice of the Peace.[285] More employees had also been allocated to his Survey Department such that he sought to delegate one surveyor to each district thereby further increasing the efficiency

---

[279] *The Hobart Town Courier*, 24 May 1828.
[280] *The Tasmanian*, 30 May 1828.
[281] *The Tasmanian*, 6 June 1828.
[282] *The Hobart Town Courier*, 7 June 1828.
[283] *The Hobart Town Gazette*, 5 July 1828.
[284] *The Hobart Town Courier*, 23 August 1828.
[285] *Colonial Advocate, and Tasmanian Monthly Review and Register*, 1 September 1828.

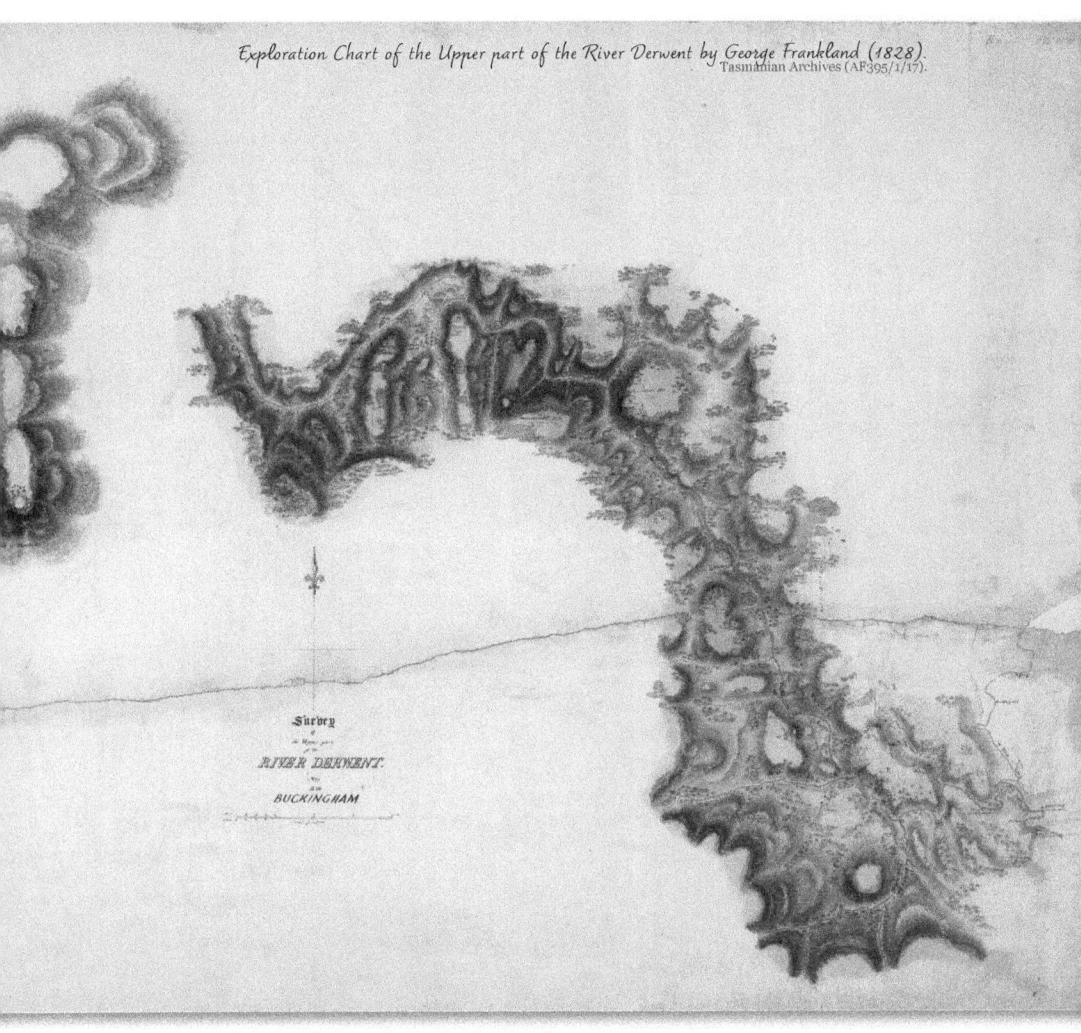

Exploration Chart of the Upper part of the River Derwent by George Frankland (1828).
Tasmanian Archives (AF395/1/17).

of the department, including with regards to the management of boundary and planning disputes. With the volume of land being awarded increasingly commensurate with the arrival of more and more industrious immigrants and the emancipation of convicts, Van Diemen's Land was slowly being turned into an antipodean England, with those more resourced immigrants higher up on the social scale also more likely to receive larger land grants. Under George Frankland's directives, enterprising settlers who had increased the value of their existing properties were also generously awarded further grants. Convict labour still formed the backbone of the economy throughout the colony, however, with settlers benefitting from an ever-increasing influx of incarcerated men and women from Great Britain, many from the agricultural and labouring classes. All of these changes completely neglected to consider the traditional owners and custodians of the land, with altercations and incidents occurring more frequently as contact between the Palawa people and European settlers increased. Local tribes of Aboriginals were also disproportionately affected by the introduction of diseases and viruses they had little to no immunity to.[286] This issue would soon come to a precipice under the direction of Lieutenant Governor George Arthur, resulting in the systematic removal and subsequent annihilation of the island's indigenous population.

For Anne Frankland and her three children more specifically they remained largely within the boundaries of Hobart Town interacting predominantly within its upper-class society, sheltered from the sensitive situations going on throughout Van Diemen's Land. Anne would have also commenced giving the children their lessons, with their oldest child Sophia now five years of age. Ever the explorer George, however, continued his expeditions. In November 1828 he accompanied Lieutenant Governor Arthur and Captain Montagu to Maria Island and Great Oyster Bay, on Van Diemen's Lands' east coast, with the group intending to travel back to Hobart Town via Ross.[287] In early January 1829 Lieutenant Governor Arthur, Captain Montagu, George Frankland and several others left Hobart Town on another tour, intending to visit the north-west coast as far as the Van Diemen's Land Company's establishment at Circular Head.[288] They returned several weeks later after a successful venture, also visiting Westbury, Quamby Bluff, the Meander River and Western Creek.[289] In March and May 1829 George, in the company of several associates, took multiple excursions to the Huon River region.[290]

While George Frankland was continuing to prosper in Hobart Town in terms of his professional commitments, his wife Anne was taking care of their children and household, as well as making new friends. Though it is not known if Anne maintained a diary during this period, we are fortunate that one of her peers did.

[286] H. L. Roth (1899). *The Aborigines of Tasmania*.
[287] *The Hobart Town Courier*, 8 November 1828.
[288] *The Hobart Town Courier*, 3 January 1829; *Colonial Times*, 9 January 1829.
[289] *The Hobart Town Courier*, 31 January, 7 February 1829.
[290] *The Hobart Town Courier*, 21 March, 2 May 1829.

The Journal of Mrs. Fenton: A Narrative of Her Life in India, the Isle of France (Mauritius) and Tasmania During the Years 1826-1830 details Elizabeth Fenton's time in India, Mauritius and, finally, Van Diemen's Land.[291] The wife of a major in the British Army, the couple had met in India and then made their way to Mauritius, awaiting the arrival of their first child. Notably Sir Charles Colville, i.e., George Frankland's uncle, was Governor of Mauritius at the time Elizabeth Fenton and her husband Michael arrived there in early 1829. While Michael Fenton almost immediately then sailed to Hobart Town, Elizabeth remained in Mauritius preparing to give birth. She stayed with Sir Charles Colville and his wife Lady Jane for part of this period.

There are some fascinating, honest and obviously confidential parcels of information in Elizabeth Fenton's diary, particularly regarding a feminine perspective of colonial Van Diemen's Land in the late 1820s, as well as its residents, including George and Anne Frankland. It is fortunate to historians that the diary survived and was first published in 1901.

For example, in February 1829 Elizabeth Fenton wrote, '*Lady Colville speaks highly of the talents of an elder brother* [should be nephew] *in the Survey Department in Van Diemen's Land, who it seems was with them in India, and made there a marriage with more love than prudence. Such being the case, his uncle procured for him a situation in Van Diemen's Land from pure necessity. Mrs. F. she describes as being very gentle and unpretending -- rather than pretty or animated -- but she says she feels certain I must like her.*'[292]

This passage of course refers to George Frankland and his wife Anne with the '*more love than prudence*' statement confirming that the pair had married for love rather than money. The statement also confirms that Sir Charles Colville had a hand in securing George Frankland's appointment to the Survey Department in Van Diemen's Land.

Elizabeth Fenton's diary continues. '*Lady C. is a right pleasant person herself and as gay as need be -- indeed her spirits often quite bring me to a stand from the mere effect of contrast.*[293]

---

[291] H. Lawrence (1901). *The Journal of Mrs Fenton: A Narrative of Her Life in India, the Isle of France (Mauritius) and Tasmania During the Years 1826-1830.*

[292] H. Lawrence (1901). *The Journal of Mrs Fenton: A Narrative of Her Life in India, the Isle of France (Mauritius) and Tasmania During the Years 1826-1830.*

[293] H. Lawrence (1901). *The Journal of Mrs Fenton: A Narrative of Her Life in India, the Isle of France (Mauritius) and Tasmania During the Years 1826-1830.*

In mid-August 1829, upon sailing up the River Derwent with her newborn baby Flora, Elizabeth Fenton wrote that if her husband 'Fenton' was in the interior of Van Diemen's Land and away from Hobart Town, '*Lady Colville desired me to send for Mr. Frankland, to whom she had written to be ready to assist me.*'[294] However, it was soon determined that Fenton had only a few days prior sailed for Mauritius per the *Orelia* in search of his wife. Upon reaching anchor Elizabeth thus wrote, '*How fortunate it appears, how providential, that the Colvilles should have written to Frankland to assist me in case of Fenton's absence. My purpose is this: I will send by the port officer my letter to Mr. F. and write to know if he can give me any information as to Fenton's movements.*'[295]

Several days later her diary replays the scene. '*I am impatient to go on with my story. Well, my letter to Mr. Frankland was hardly written, before the port officer was introduced to me by Mr. Betts, as Lieutenant Hill, a very mild and gentlemanly person. On the first mention of my name, he expressed the kindest interest, and begged an immediate introduction, as he said he was intimate with Fenton, whose movements he was fully aware of, also his intentions in leaving the Colony. ... I then told Mr. Hill I had just been engaged in enclosing letters for Mr. Frankland, and writing to ask his advice. This he said was the very best thing I could have done, as Fenton and the Franklands were always together ...*

A consultation was held between the gentlemen, as to the possibility of a whale-boat overtaking the Orelia, in which Fenton sailed, as the pilot affirmed that the fresh breeze, which brought us in during the night, must have retarded them; it was impossible they could round a certain cape, and might be still beating about "Storm Bay." So the result was that Mr. Hill, after leaving my letters with Mr. Frankland, would proceed to Colonel Arthur, to request assistance on my behalf. ... How very greatly it lightened my disquiet, to find so much ready kindness displayed where I had expected none. But on the possibility of Fenton's return I would not suffer my mind to dwell. It was too vague.

By eleven the next day we saw a boatful of gentlemen push off from the beach, and in a few minutes after Mr. Frankland's name was announced. I had sent Mrs. Hughes to put up our things within, and had seated myself near the window with Flora asleep on my knee. One glance at Mr.

---

[294] H. Lawrence (1901). *The Journal of Mrs Fenton: A Narrative of Her Life in India, the Isle of France (Mauritius) and Tasmania During the Years 1826-1830.*
[295] H. Lawrence (1901). *The Journal of Mrs Fenton: A Narrative of Her Life in India, the Isle of France (Mauritius) and Tasmania During the Years 1826-1830.*

Frankland assured me he was above the common style of men, and a few minutes' conversation convinced me he was equally high-bred and kindly obliging. He had a gaiety of voice and manner more French than English, but still there was that which bespoke the high-caste English gentleman, and we became well acquainted in half an hour, as if we had lived together ten years.

He presented a letter left with him, by Fenton, in the event of my coming during his absence. This I only glanced over, and gathered enough for my guidance -- that Fenton had advised me to consult with Frankland. After many questions about his uncle's family, and his brother Arthur, a little nursing and much admiration of Flora, and every kind intention that could be expressed in words, he rose to depart, previously arranging that I should be ready by twelve next day, to go on shore to his house. He much regretted they had no spare apartment, but that should not prevent our being together all the day, and he would engage commodious rooms for me at the Macquarie Hotel, near his house.'[296]

The next day George Frankland made his way on board the vessel with a party of others, his wife Anne being included; the first time the two ladies had been introduced. After formalities, the group soon began to walk up Macquarie Street. Elizabeth Fenton later wrote. '*About half-way up I could not resist the temptation of stopping to lean upon a fence almost breathless, this being the longest walk I had taken for some years; and further being equipped in black satin shoes, they were penetrated by wet and fringed with mud. Mrs. Frankland's recollections of the habits of India soon explained my distress, and the party kindly accommodated themselves to my feebleness and unequal strength, until we reached the hotel, when, after inspecting the rooms ordered, Mr. Frankland, with equal kindness and tact, proposed they should all leave me to rest for an hour, when he would return and take me to his house, which proposal I readily agreed to.*

Well, suppose the hour past. I am on my way, attended by the nurse and Flora, and enter a very pretty cottage within a little compound of shrubs and flowers, in all the lavish fragrance of Australian spring. The cottage itself, as well as its inmates, the very beau ideal of taste and good order. Small indeed was the cheerful drawing-room, by how much did it contain bearing evidence of the high tone of its occupiers' education and tastes!'[297]

---
[296] H. Lawrence (1901). *The Journal of Mrs Fenton: A Narrative of Her Life in India, the Isle of France (Mauritius) and Tasmania During the Years 1826-1830.*
[297] H. Lawrence (1901). *The Journal of Mrs Fenton: A Narrative of Her Life in India, the Isle of France (Mauritius)*

And it is from Elizabeth Fenton's diary that next comes an honest and pure description of our subject, Anne Frankland. '*Mrs. Frankland was then dressed for dinner. Lady Colville had told me I should think her cold, but not so. She was exceedingly kind, though calm and still in manner, which her aspect of fragility and paleness led you to attribute to physical causes. Her lady-like, quiet demeanour prepossessed me, and there was in her a most living resemblance of some one I had known before, though who I could not tell -- or where.*

While I was making my toilet in her room, I felt so exhausted by the length and weight of my hair, I expressed my desire to cut it off; she declared her horror at such a sacrifice, saying for many years she had seen nothing like it, and that there was some peculiarity in this climate very injurious to its growth. ...

With much pleasant conversation the evening passed, for ... to find listeners to all I had to relate of the most estimable family I had quitted was an enjoyment.

I could fill some pages with trifling matters, which all created interest, but it would not be worth your attention; one remark only -- I was almost childishly pleased by the evening aspect of an English drawing-room, the windows covered with graceful blue merino drapery, the "carpet," even the polished steel fender and fire-irons brought back so many dormant remembrances.'[298]

Several more days passed and Elizabeth Fenton was thankfully reunited with her husband who had returned to Hobart Town via the whaleboat dispatched to retrace his nautical whereabouts. Elizabeth relayed the scene from her hotel room. '*And while I wrote I heard some bustle below, soon followed by steps on the stairs; a moment after -- Fenton flew in. Was not this a crisis! After being four days out at sea, the wind continuing contrary, they had brought to in some bay, and there spied the distant speck on the water, whose errand was so momentous to us both. Fenton was playing chess with some one called Gelebrand, when there was a cry of a boat following the ship. He started up, exclaiming that it was coming for him. A very brief space elapsed before himself and his baggage were in it, and on their way again to the Derwent.*

After Fenton had been a few minutes in the house, Frankland entered with the greatest delight. He said he had heard the news from twenty people as he ran down the street. After a little unconnected and very joyful

---

and Tasmania During the Years 1826-1830.
[298] H. Lawrence (1901). *The Journal of Mrs Fenton: A Narrative of Her Life in India, the Isle of France (Mauritius) and Tasmania During the Years 1826-1830.*

conversation, -- for still we all felt as in a dream, -- Frankland pleaded my engagement, would not remit it, so we agreed to dine with them, and that Fenton should take me there in due time. He then left us.'[299]

The Fentons soon established themselves in a home further up Macquarie Street yet in close proximity to the Franklands; the foursome becoming fast friends and confidantes. Elizabeth Fenton also detailed her household, consisting of '*a nurse, cook, laundress, housemaid, a man who cuts wood and is groom, and a boy she brought from India ... with the idea of training him for an inside servant*'. It is assumed that the Frankland family had a similar staff, if not more, considering they had three children by this stage in their lives. In describing her social life in her diary, Elizabeth Fenton also acknowledged, '*You will perceive that altogether the tone of society here is very superior to what I had expected to find -- indeed, I was fully prepared to be without any that I could mingle in.*'[300]

A few months later, Elizabeth relayed more detail on Anne Frankland. '*I was saying to him* [her husband Fenton] *one evening that Mrs. Frankland's likeness to someone I had known before was so striking, it haunted me, and that I wished to hear her name. "Oh," he replied, "Lady Colville told me it was Mason." "I have it all now," I said, "she must be sister to a lady who was governess to a family connected with ours in Ireland -- and I well remember her telling me of her sister 'Anne' going to India. How strange that I should thus meet the two sisters at such intervals of time! I am sure I must have spoken to you of Arabella Mason, for we were great allies. Her situation was rather peculiar. She had taken the charge of two boys whose mother was dead. Their father, a man of immense fortune, was anything but the kind of person whom it was pleasant for a young woman to be domesticated with ... My sister lived immediately beside them, and when she found how uncomfortable poor Miss M. was, she invited her to spend the evenings with us, which she did, and we all liked her. She had been very well educated, and was indisputably a 'lady.' Her society was a great advantage to me, for I was too much the mistress of my own actions, and she commenced reading French and Italian with me, which I had too much neglected. She often told me my "Saying and Doings" were a perfect curiosity to her, accustomed to the conventional regularities of London life which I can now well understand.*

---

[299] H. Lawrence (1901). *The Journal of Mrs Fenton: A Narrative of Her Life in India, the Isle of France (Mauritius) and Tasmania During the Years 1826-1830.*
[300] H. Lawrence (1901). *The Journal of Mrs Fenton: A Narrative of Her Life in India, the Isle of France (Mauritius) and Tasmania During the Years 1826-1830.*

She invariably wound up all her exhortations by deploring that I had been allowed "to run wild." Nevertheless, many and many a pleasant excursion had we over those beautiful glens and mountains, aided by a quiet pony we rode alternatively, and escorted by Richard Webb, regarding whom many a sage admonition she bestowed on me -- pity they were thrown away -- and where is he, I wonder?

I lost no time in communicating my discovery to Mrs. Frankland, and at first it appeared to embarrass her, which made me repent having referred to it, but whatever the first impulse was that operated in her, it passed off, and we spoke of her sister and other members of her family I knew by name. And she after that told me something of the story of her life, and she had many trials.'[301]

Elizabeth Fenton's diary ended in December 1830. By this time she had moved with her husband and baby daughter to a property north of New Norfolk such that there is nothing more reported on the Frankland family, though they would have kept in contact by letter and visited together when the Fentons travelled to Hobart Town.

---

[301] H. Lawrence (1901). *The Journal of Mrs Fenton: A Narrative of Her Life in India, the Isle of France (Mauritius) and Tasmania During the Years 1826-1830.*

Secheron and Security

Having lived in Hobart Town for two years, Anne and George Frankland took steps to become homeowners for the first time. On 6 August 1829 the couple purchased three acres of land at Battery Point from William Kermode. Located south of the Mulgrave Battery, the property was situated on the edge of the River Derwent overlooking a small bay. It was purchased at a cost of £124, payable in two instalments over a 12-month period.[302] The Franklands named the property Secheron, a nod to the locale of the same name near Geneva, Switzerland, where George had apparently been a boarder during his teenage years.[303]

While plans were developed for their home the Franklands remained living in Macquarie Street in a house containing six rooms on the ground floor, four rooms on the second floor and two large rooms on the third floor, with servant apartments and offices detached.[304] The family also began visiting Secheron, often inviting friends to join them. On 23 December 1829 Elizabeth Fenton noted, *'We had a very delightful party at Secherone - Mr. Frankland's location at the Battery point - a picnic in a tent. I was solicited by all parties to produce a curry as my part of the feast, which gave general satisfaction; Mrs. Stephen declared it to be the nicest dish she had ever tasted.'*[305] The 'Mrs. Stephen' referred to was Virginia Stephen, the wife of Alfred Stephen, the colony's Attorney General.

---

[302] www.thelist.tas.gov.au (Historical Deed 01/0223).

[303] Jane Franklin (21 June 1838). Letter to her sister Mary Simpkinson, University of Tasmania Library Special and Rare Materials Collection.

[304] *The Hobart Town Courier*, 4 April 1829.

[305] H. Lawrence (1901). *The Journal of Mrs Fenton: A Narrative of Her Life in India, the Isle of France (Mauritius) and Tasmania During the Years 1826-1830.*

George Frankland was also prospering professionally, tasked with leading a trigonometrical survey of the entire island of Van Diemen's Land, quite a substantial and complicated undertaking.[306] He had additionally received a raise, with his annual salary increased to £700 per annum plus allowances for housing and travel.[307] With more appointments from England arriving in Hobart Town, the Survey Department was stated to be *'pretty well supplied with assistants'*.[308] George was also appointed by Lieutenant Governor George Arthur to the colonial government's Land Board in January 1830 with the *Colonial Times* commending this decision stating that no person of *'higher character'* could have been selected.[309]

It was during this period that the Van Diemen's Land Society was also established *'For the Publication of Local, Scientific Information and the Establishment of a Museum and Botanic Garden'*.[310] With the organisation's patron Lieutenant Governor Arthur, George Frankland also volunteered his services and was duly elected Vice-President, as well as to a committee tasked with establishing a museum and library.[311] It was notably one of the earliest scientific bodies established in the colony. George was eager to be involved. At the organisation's first meeting he gave a speech, indicative of his exuberance and optimism, noting, '*I cannot refrain from congratulating the present company, and the country in general, on the formation of a Society so well calculated to elicit its capabilities and to promote its welfare*'. He continued. '*Many persons there are who consider scientific research merely as the appropriate occupation of a particular class of men who are supposed to devote their time and minds solely to theoretical speculations, unconnected with practical advantages; but upon better consideration they would perceive that not only the principal changes in the relations of the world, but also most of our ordinary pursuits, and most of our comforts are the result of scientific discoveries, and that reflection should induce every resident in a new country, where the field for discovery is of course great, to turn his attention to such subjects as he may have the opportunity of investing.*'[312]

---

[306] *The Hobart Town Courier*, 9 May 1829.
[307] *Colonial Times*, 14 August 1829.
[308] *Colonial Times*, 6 November 1829.
[309] *The Hobart Town Courier*, 16 January 1830; *Colonial Times*, 22 January 1830.
[310] *Colonial Times*, 18 December 1829.
[311] *Colonial Times*, 18 December 1829.
[312] *The Hobart Town Courier*, 23 January 1830.

The next few paragraphs of George Frankland's speech offer an interesting window into his mindset, particularly with regards to science and innovation, but moreover his praise of European colonisation of distant countries due to its superior scientific and industrial innovation, as well as its religion, coming at the expense of indigenous populations. It is an intriguing and rather ironic dichotomy. This compassion and circumspection was likely in opposition to those seated in the room and definitely from those within the colonial government given the policies towards Van Diemen's Lands' Aborigines that were on the cusp of being introduced under Lieutenant Governor Arthur.

'Our very residence in this island may be termed the offspring of science, for it was the progress of astronomy and navigation which led to its occupation. Without that progress the navigators of Europe would still be creeping timourously along the western shores of Africa, dreading every gust of wind that might drive them out of sight of the known land marks. That ideal barrier, the torrid zone, would still be deemed an insurmountable obstacle, and the fables of ignorance would still paralyze every effort towards geographical discovery. But the progress of science induced far more glorious results: it rendered the most ungovernable elements the very instruments of the will of man. Bold spirits, armed with those powers with which science supplied them, launched forth, and discovered New Worlds! The great promontory of southern Africa was passed, and the vast regions of the east were at once opened to the flow of European adventure, and European history.

The amelioration in the state of those nations of India, which have become subject to England, is perhaps the most beautiful illustration of the practical effects of science that can be cited. These great counties which from time immemorial had been a prey to every species of intestine rapine confusion are now, by the introduction of our institutions, resting in peace and security under the magic shield of their influence, and may, I think, be considered as gradually though slowly approaching the great era when they will embrace Christianity.

These, among many others, may be classed with the advantage which, as regards India, have sprung from the culture of science. Would that it were possible to trace her steps with equal satisfaction to this naturally favoured little island!

Science led to its discovery, but its discoveries instead of bringing blessings in their train have heaped ruin and destruction upon those

Painting of Battery Point by Mrs A. Prinsep (1829). The Secheron land is behind the large vessel on this page.
Dixson Galleries, State Library of New South Wales.

children of misfortune, the Aboriginal owners of the soil - a people naturally amiable and intelligent, who with better treatment on the part of those who have come in contact with them, might have been rendered valuable friends, and have continued a happy nation! However, I should hope that there is yet time to restore that harmony which, but for the brutal inhumanity of white men, had never been broken; and surely no more glorious object could this Society propose to itself than that of acquiring to more intimate acquaintance with this much wronged people, with a view of ameliorating their condition, and of saving them from being extirpated from the face of that earth on which the Almighty had placed them!'[313]

After several speeches encompassing chemistry, botany, nomenclature and expeditions given by other members of the society, all holding prominent positions within Hobart Town's government and civil offices, the group sat down to a meal and the toasts began. George Frankland offered up his own. '*We all remember*', he began, '*that melancholy day, when standing upon the poop of the good ship, that danced beneath our feet, we strained our eyes to catch a last glimpse of our native land; and not less so the many succeeding hours, which were occupied in looking over the bulwarks, and recollecting the many joys, from which we were quickly sailing away. Our hearts filled with these recollections, we then thought it impossible, that we could ever feel a permanent interest in any land but that of our early love. But these fears were changed to hope, when we came and saw the richness and beauty of the country for which we had left our home, we found the soil productive of abundant harvests, the climate most congenial to our constitutions, the scenery magnificent and new, and the land altogether full of the most interesting curiosities. Who will deny, that his sensations, in making these discoveries, were joyous, and at the same time preparatory to those of permanent interest in the place of his new residence? Such, I believe, are the feelings of all who hear me, and I propose to them a toast, which they will joyfully pledge, "Prosperity to the land we live in".*'[314]

The speeches and toasts were printed in the local press, with the meeting said to be positive for the Van Diemen's Land Society and its future success. Unfortunately not all of Hobart Town's inhabitants were impressed with this reporting, offering up their own opinions as to the political nature of the organisation and the behind-the-scenes criticism and gossip that had taken place in the days immediately following the Society's inaugural meeting. The

---

[313] *The Hobart Town Courier*, 23 January 1830.
[314] *The Hobart Town Courier*, 23 January 1830.

Editor of *The Tasmanian* newspaper was downright combative of the organisation, in intense language stating that the patronage of Lieutenant Governor Arthur would lead to its demise.[315] Further, there was much criticism of the process for electing new members which was deemed '*prejudicial*'.[316] In particular, an '*unpleasant circumstance*' had apparently occurred and caused a '*sensation*' in Hobart Town whereby an old colonist had been excluded from the Society's membership.[317] The resulting editorial thus piqued '*old established colonists*' against '*late arrivals and almost strangers in the colony*'.[318] With such a controversial start, unfortunately the Van Diemen's Land Society met its death within a few years, unable to break free from embedded preconceptions and punctured egos from some within the hierarchy of Hobart Town, even though the colony had only been established less than 30 years prior. At a follow-up meeting George Frankland rose to move an amendment to correct the error and issue an honourable apology to those that had been denied membership.[319] However, it was not approved.[320]

All told the Van Diemen's Land Society appears to have been incompatible with the establishment. Within this milieu, however, there was one newspaper that picked up George Frankland's speech with regard to Van Diemen's Lands' Aborigines, its editor agreeing with '*every word of this eloquent appeal to the feelings of the present*'.[321] The same editorial also lamented that since the ongoing future of the organisation was not viable, it was to be much regretted '*when we bear in mind how much good it might have done*'.[322]

While George Frankland's participation in the Van Diemen's Land Society was short-lived, it is evident that he and his wife Anne were personally taking a permanent interest in Van Diemen's Land with plans for the development of their new home at Battery Point coming into fruition. Both Anne and George had lived in multiple homes across multiple countries: in England, India and South Africa. Just what type of home would they build based on their past experiences, their tastes and their family's needs? Secheron began to take shape.

---

[315] *The Tasmanian*, 29 January 1830.
[316] *The Tasmanian*, 29 January 1830.
[317] *The Tasmanian*, 29 January 1830.
[318] *The Tasmanian*, 29 January 1830.
[319] *The Tasmanian*, 12 February 1830.
[320] *The Tasmanian*, 12 February 1830.
[321] *Colonial Times*, 29 January 1830.
[322] *Colonial Times*, 29 January 1830.

Drawing of Sullivans Cove and Battery Point, including part of Secheron, by George Frankland (1832).

Scale of Chains

HOBART TOWN
By Mr Frankland

Government Gardens

In addition to the time and effort spent on designing and creating their new family home, on the domestic front there was much going on, the bulk of which would have been managed by Anne Frankland. For example, in March 1830 the Frankland's groom and footman, William Smith, an indentured convict, absconded from their service.[323] A reward was offered for his return. A few months later Anne advertised for the services of a nursery maid, specifically *'a Woman who came free to the Colony'*.[324] Continuing their patronage of the local christian community, the couple donated money to the building of a new Hobart Town church in September 1830.[325] More exploratory excursions also took place, with George often in the company of Lieutenant Governor Arthur, including to the White Hills district.[326] Meanwhile a map of Van Diemen's Land delineating the police districts was released by the Survey Department.[327] It also included new townships.

With Van Diemen's Lands' outer-lying settlements growing proportionately with the arrival of new immigrants, the emancipation of convicts who had completed their sentences, and the increasing availability of new lands made available by the Survey Department, the conflict between the European population and the island's Aborigines increased. Though there had been deaths on both sides, by the early 1830s there were believed to be only a few hundred indigenous peoples remaining; their population decimated in a matter of only three decades. Obviously protective of their land and culture, they remained resolute.

Lieutenant Governor Arthur had introduced several policy-related solutions to alleviate the conflict over the previous years though none of them had much impact in lessening the dissension. In late 1830 he implemented a highly ambitious strategy now referred to as the 'Black Line'. Specifically, approximately 3,000 men, made up of soldiers, convicts, volunteers and a handful of Aborigines formed 12 corps and were spread out along a 180-mile line with the intention of coalescing the indigenous peoples to the Tasman Peninsula via its isthmus at Eaglehawk Neck, which would thereafter act as an Aboriginal reserve.[328] While he undoubtedly

---

[323] *The Hobart Town Gazette*, 6 March 1830.
[324] *The Hobart Town Courier*, 19 June 1830.
[325] *Colonial Times*, 24 September 1830.
[326] *The Hobart Town Courier*, 18 October 1830.
[327] *The Hobart Town Courier*, 23 October 1830.
[328] *The Tasmanian*, 5 November 1830, en.wikipedia.org/wiki/Black_War.

thought of himself as an ally of the Aborigines, helping foster them to a safe place, George Frankland appears to not only have been heavily involved in the campaign but also with its publicity.

On 5 November 1830 *The Tasmanian* published a report based on a field memorandum issued by the Lieutenant Governor in which it stated that a *'field sketch of the ground was annexed to this memorandum, executed, we apprehend, by Mr. Frankland, the Surveyor General'*.[329] With regards to the sketch specifically, the press report further detailed that, *'It is plain, simple, and comprehensive, and exhibits at one view the different positions which the line is to occupy on the 4 days during which this important operation is to be brought to a close'*.[330] A copy of this diagram is provided on the following pages.

Plagued by rugged and remote country, including rivers, deep gullies and steep mountainous ranges, as well as bad weather, the campaign failed. The targeted Aborigines were also fearful of the Black Line, successfully managing to avoid it. Still, Lieutenant Governor Arthur commended the actions of those involved stating, *'upon the merits of the Individuals composing the Force, the Lieut. Governor nor feels it difficult to attach the need of praise which they have deserved, and when ALL have shewn so much alacrity, zeal, patience and determination to overcome every difficulty ... although it is quite impossible to avoid noticing the extraordinary exertions which have been so cheerfully afforded by the Surveyor General and every officer of his department'*.[331] On reflection, it is obviously a poignant moment in Australian history and for George Frankland personally, particularly since he considered himself a friend to the traditional owners of Van Diemen's Land, a populace that only 10 months prior he had called *'children of misfortune ... a people naturally amiable and intelligent, who with better treatment on the part of those who have come in contact with them, might have been rendered valuable friends, and have continued a happy nation!'*.[332]

An avid communicator and painter, it was at this juncture in time that George Frankland sought to convey a message to the Palawa people by way of images as opposed to text or proclamation. He presented a *'little sketch, executed with much spirit, of the consequences of the Aborigines adopting a peaceable demeanor, or of continuing in*

---
[329] *The Tasmanian*, 5 November 1830.
[330] *The Tasmanian*, 5 November 1830.
[331] *The Tasmanian*, 26 November 1830.
[332] *The Hobart Town Courier*, 23 January 1830.

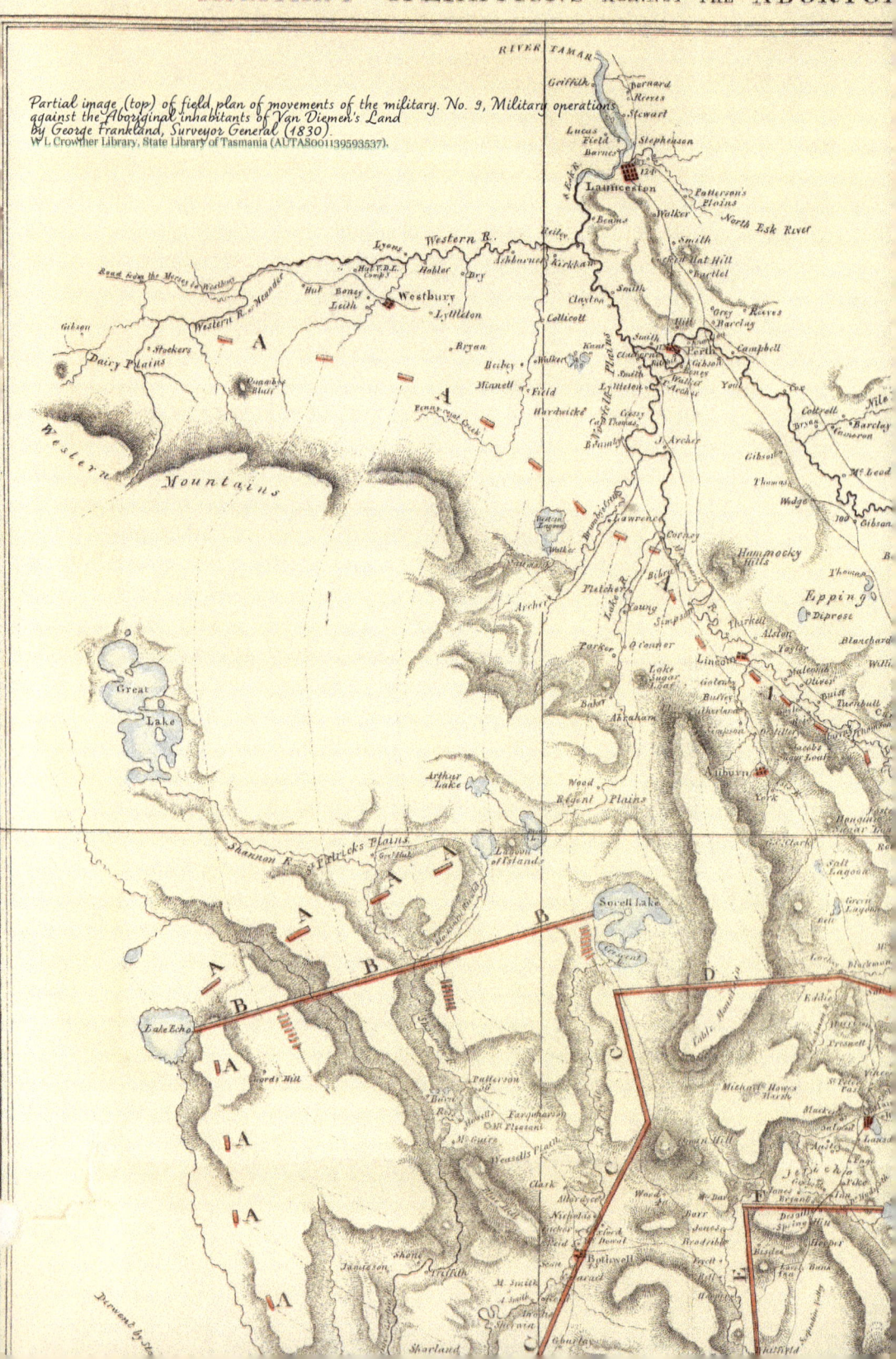

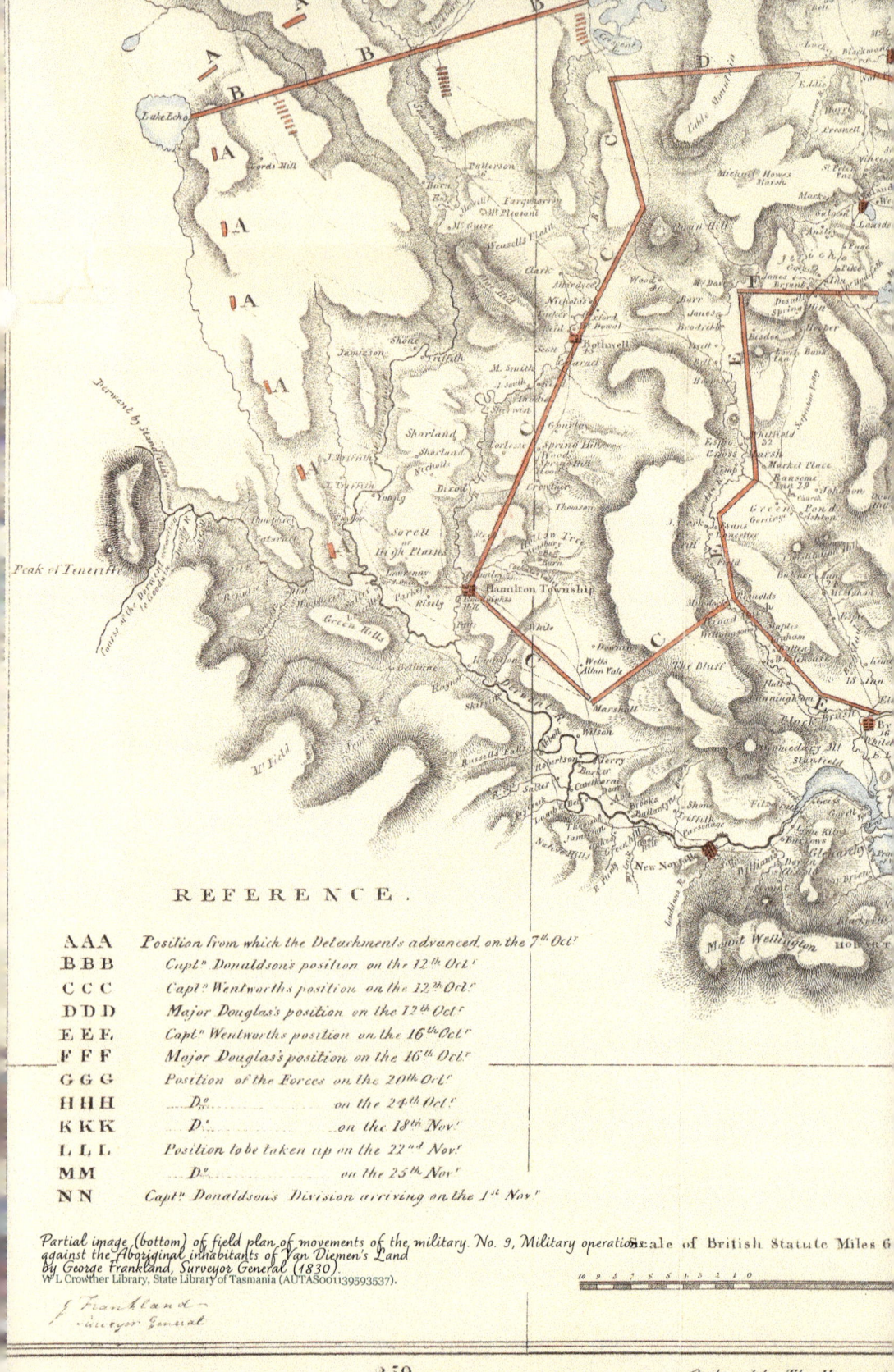

REFERENCE.

A A A	Position from which the Detachments advanced on the 7th Oct.r
B B B	Capt.n Donaldson's position on the 12th Oct.r
C C C	Capt.n Wentworth's position on the 12th Oct.r
D D D	Major Douglas's position on the 12th Oct.r
E E E	Capt.n Wentworth's position on the 16th Oct.r
F F F	Major Douglas's position on the 16th Oct.r
G G G	Position of the Forces on the 20th Oct.r
H H H	D.o on the 24th Oct.r
K K K	D.o on the 18th Nov.r
L L L	Position to be taken up on the 22nd Nov.r
M M	D.o on the 25th Nov.r
N N	Capt.n Donaldson's Division arriving on the 1st Nov.r

Partial image (bottom) of field plan of movements of the military. No. 9, Military operations against the Aboriginal inhabitants of Van Diemen's Land by George Frankland, Surveyor General (1830)
W L Crowther Library, State Library of Tasmania (AUTAS001139593537)

Scale of British Statute Miles 6

J. Frankland
Surveyor General

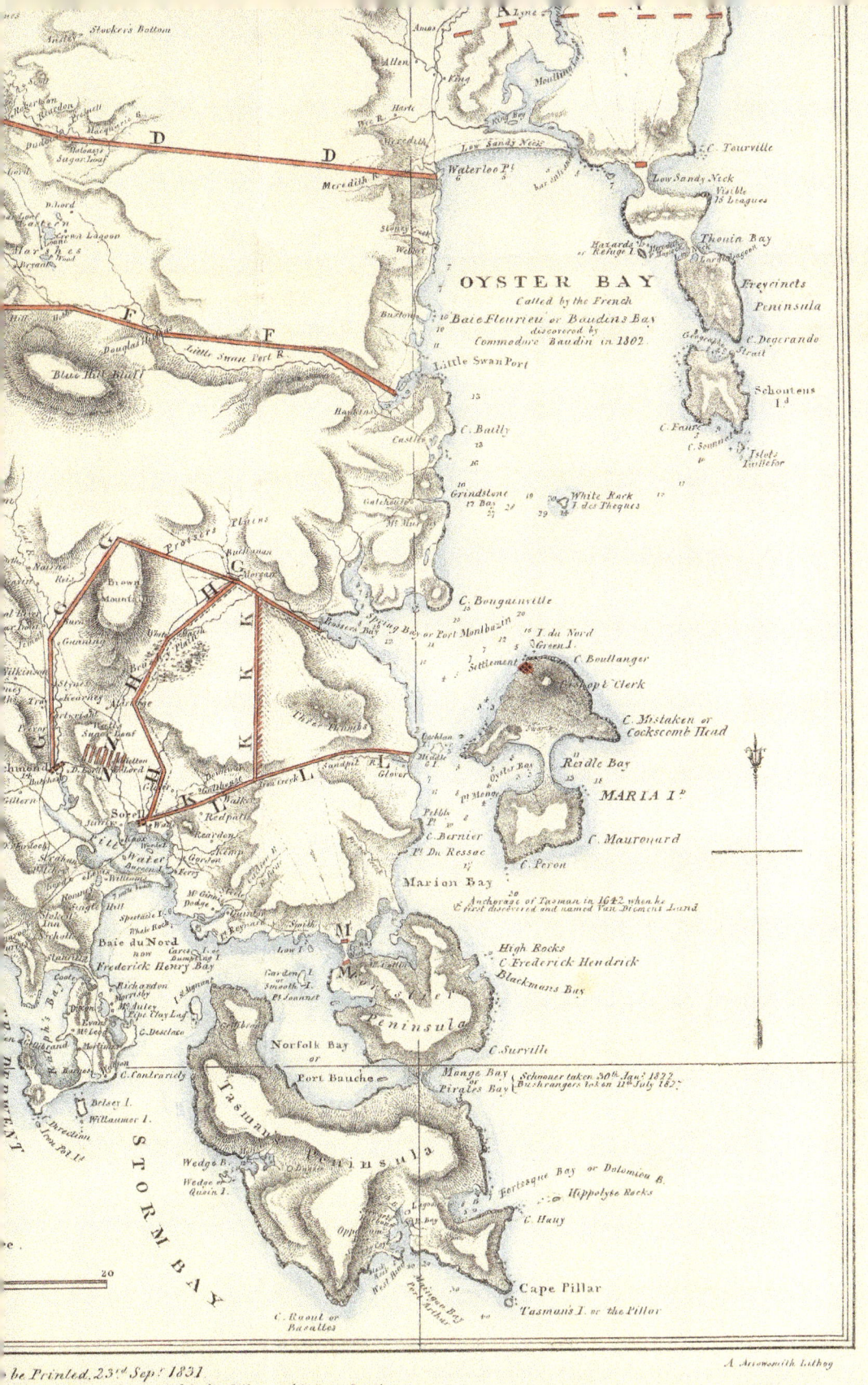

their present murderous and predatory habits' to one of the Aborigines who had assisted with the Black Line.³³³ A press report described its detail. '*In one part of the sketch, the soldiery were represented firing upon a tribe of the Blacks, who were falling from the effects of the attack. On the other part were seen, another tribe, decently clad, receiving food for themselves and families.*'³³⁴ This may have been the second 'picture board' that George painted, as there is an earlier artwork attributed to him that conveys Lieutenant Governor Arthur's Proclamation to the Aborigines, illustrating equality under the law, that was issued in April 1828. The picture board is now part of the collection of the Mitchell Library, State Library of New South Wales.³³⁵

While Lieutenant Governor Arthur persevered with his directives targeting the remainder of Van Diemen's Lands' Aboriginal bands and removing them from their traditional lands, it is not known to what degree George Frankland remained involved, though it could have been substantial since his department would have continued to provide the necessary surveys, plans and maps. However, George is noted in Hobart Town in December 1830 attending a ceremony marking the Proclamation of King William IV.³³⁶ On 18 January 1831 he attended the quarterly meeting of the District Committee for Promoting Christian Knowledge.³³⁷

Meanwhile, the Frankland family continued to expand their Secheron estate, purchasing an additional three acres, two roods and seven perches from William Kermode on 16 May 1831.³³⁸ The property was directly south of their existing parcel of land, with the two allotments separated by a boundary of 367 links. The purchase price was £148.³³⁹ George and Anne's plans for their new home were also surely coming together. So too was their family. On 11 May 1830 Anne's brother Thomas Mason arrived in Hobart Town per the ship *Arab* from London.³⁴⁰ Thomas was 30 years of age and single. He moved in with the Frankland family in their house in Macquarie Street and sought help from his brother-in-law George with finding a job. Eight months later it was reported that Thomas had been appointed Under Sheriff for Buckinghamshire,

---

³³³ *The Tasmanian*, 26 November 1830.
³³⁴ *The Tasmanian*, 26 November 1830.
³³⁵ collection.sl.nsw.gov.au/record/YK5Qpgjn/NROKZPVZloeD0.
³³⁶ *The Tasmanian*, 10 December 1830.
³³⁷ *The Hobart Town Courier*, 15 January 1831.
³³⁸ www.thelist.tas.gov.au (Historical Deed 01/1001).
³³⁹ www.thelist.tas.gov.au (Historical Deed 01/1001).
³⁴⁰ Tasmanian Archives (CU30/1/1 p11); *The Tasmanian*, 14 May 1830.

Lieutenant Governor Arthur's Proclamation to the Aborigines by George Frankland (circa 1828-1830).
Mitchell Library, State Library of New South Wales.

though not all were pleased with this decision, the *Colonial Times* stating, '*It is generally reported, that the situation of Under-Sheriff for Buckinghamshire is either filled or about to be, by a Mr. Mason, a person, we understand, of high pretensions, both as regards his abilities and family connections*'.[341] While this appointment turned out to be a rumour, in March 1831 Lieutenant Governor Arthur officially announced that Thomas Mason was appointed to the position of Assistant Police Magistrate and Muster Master, as well as a Justice of the Peace for Van Diemen's Land.[342] This decision resulted in more derision in the local press, particularly considering Thomas' lack of local knowledge. In particular, questions were asked about how he had become '*head of a department, without having passed the grades necessary to acquire a knowledge of local affairs*'.[343] The editorial continued, '*That Mr. Mason may be a very worthy, clever young man, we do not pretend to deny; but when such a sudden start is taken, to bring him high in rank, we say it will naturally instigate inquiry as to what qualifications rendered him deserving of becoming the "head of a department"*'.[344] George Frankland likely scorned over the implications of this and several other similarly worded press reports, all calling out his influence within the ranks of government and his intentional act of nepotism towards his brother-in-law. The *Colonial Times,* for example, went as far as to state that Thomas Mason would be more at home '*in the ball or drawing-room, than in mustering such "tag-rag and bob-tail" as our prison ships bring*'.[345]

Soon, however, the dust settled and Thomas Mason began his role within the colony's Police Department where he would remain employed for many decades in ever-increasing roles. For Anne Frankland, all of the criticism the couple faced from the press was likely worth having her brother with them after not seeing him for so many years.

A few months later, the Franklands would have been overjoyed by the arrival of another sibling. George's youngest brother Arthur, by now 22 years of age, arrived in Hobart Town per the ship *Drummore* on 18 August 1831.[346] He had sailed from Port Louis, Mauritius, where his uncle Sir Charles Colville had been serving

---

[341] *Colonial Times*, 7 January 1831.
[342] *The Hobart Town Gazette*, 12 March 1831.
[343] *The Independent*, 28 March 1831.
[344] *The Independent*, 28 March 1831.
[345] *Colonial Times*, 19 April 1831.
[346] *The Hobart Town Courier*, 20 August 1831.

as Governor since 1828. Like George previously in India, Arthur had spent three years acting as Sir Charles' Aide de Camp.[347]

Having now been in Van Diemen's Land for four years, George Frankland was once again being praised by certain arms of the press for the worthy role he had undertaken as head of the Survey Department. Specifically, his efforts had led to the laying out of numerous townships in the interior of the colony, as well as roads, schools and churches; discoveries of resources in the west and north-west; and surveys of the Van Diemen's Land Company's immense grant, as well as of King Island, various parts of the north and east coasts, and towards Port Davey. Further, he had shepherded the development of Sullivans Cove, the measurement of suburban allotments, including Lansdowne Crescent which he named after the famous location in Bath, England, and settlements just outside of Hobart Town, as well as the division of the island into police districts.[348] Moreover, the Survey Department was continuing its trigonometrical survey of the whole island.

There had been a lot of progress in a short period of time yet the Survey Department and George Frankland regularly came under criticism in the press for an apparent lack of efficiency and high payroll. Their work, however, was not helped by the continual need to settle claims from landholders regarding boundary issues that were an artefact of historical land grants being incorrectly measured and surveyed.[349] More criticism, this time seemingly warranted, was directed at George when it became known that he had sold an immense parcel of land that he had been granted by the colonial government owing to his position as an officer of the British Army. Furthermore, he had apparently used his influence within the Survey Department to alter the boundaries of it several times. The property was sold to Richard Dry in May 1832 for the substantial sum of £1,600.[350]

Comprising over 2,560 acres, the parcel was located near Westbury in Van Diemen's Lands' north. The proceeds of the sale undoubtedly went towards the building of the Frankland family's new home at Battery Point. In June 1832 George also purchased another acre of land at Battery Point from William Kermode

---

[347] *The Hobart Town Courier*, 3 September 1831.
[348] *Launceston Advertiser*, 6 June 1831; *The Hobart Town Courier*, 1 October 1831.
[349] *The Independent*, 8 October 1831.
[350] *The Tasmanian*, 26 May 1832; www.thelist.tas.gov.au (Historical Deed 01/1564).

Survey Office 21 June 1828

Sir

His Majesty having been pleased to appoint me to a situation which is likely to detain me many years in this Colony, I am very desirous of obtaining a Grant of Land, and I have therefore the honor to request that you will do me the favor of submitting to the Lieut. Governor this my application, in the hope that His Excellency will be pleased to give it a favorable reception.

I have the honor to be
Sir
Your obedt Servant
G. Frankland

The Honble
The Colonial Secretary.

George Frankland's application to the Government of Van Diemen's Land for a land grant (1828).
Tasmanian Archives (CSO1-1-296 File Number 7188, page 198).

and Daniel Callaghan for the total sum of £200.[351] All told, the Secheron property now comprised over seven acres of land.

By this point in time, Anne and George Frankland were considered part of Hobart Town's upper echelon of society. The couple's presence at concerts, balls and other entertainments where the *'whole of the first-rate fashionables were present'* was regularly noted.[352] The Franklands and their three children kept up to date in fashion by shipping cases of apparel direct from London.[353] They also continued to employ servants, preferring those that came 'free' to the colony as opposed to serving or emancipated convicts.[354] Meanwhile, Anne Frankland joined committees concerned with various charitable quests.[355]

Obviously in Lieutenant Governor Arthur's favoured circle of allies, in July 1832 George Frankland was appointed a Commissioner of the Caveat Board, established to correct early survey errors, making him one of the highest paid government employees in Van Diemen's Land.[356] The *Colonial Times* again lambasted the decision arguing that *'putting into his pocket this additional money wrung from the public, in order that he may neglect the duties of Surveyor General, and which are most important'* was wrong.[357] The article went even further, accusing the Survey Department of failing to satisfactorily undertake its duties. Moreover, the editorial questioned George Frankland's work ethic stating, *'It is not enough that Mr. Frankland should be in his office for a few hours daily, where, contrary to the usual practice of open doors, he shuts himself up in the most impenetrable manner; in some instances, perhaps, deigning to allow a very importunate personage to enter his presence, but who is soon bowed out again with the pleasing remark usual on all these state occasions, "write to us"'*.[358]

A few weeks later a letter to the editor of another publication suggested that a petition be developed calling for the resignation of George from the office of the Survey Department based on his *'utter incapacity to fulfil the duties of the situation'*.[359] George

---

[351] www.thelist.tas.gov.au (Historical Deed 01/1640).
[352] *The Tasmanian*, 9 July 1831.
[353] *Colonial Times*, 19 June 1829, 18 May 1831.
[354] *The Hobart Town Courier*, 26 May 1831.
[355] *The Tasmanian*, 31 August 1831.
[356] *Colonial Times*, 24 July 1832.
[357] *Colonial Times*, 24 July 1832.
[358] *Colonial Times*, 24 July 1832.
[359] *The Colonist and Van Diemen's Land Commercial and Agricultural Advertiser*, 10 August 1832.

made several attempts to defend his department and his own professional reputation, though the jeering and mockery would only grow louder and louder in the years to come.

During the interim, the Franklands continued to plan their estate at Battery Point. George's brother Arthur also remained living with the family. In September 1832 he posted an advertisement in *The Hobart Town Courier* asking for help with finding his small female pet monkey named Adelaide that he had no doubt brought with him from Mauritius or India.[360] The animal had escaped from the Frankland family's then home, Stephenville in Macquarie Street. The property at the time was owned by Alfred Stephen, but since he and his family were in England he had leased it to the Franklands from 1 January 1832.[361] Still in existence, Stephenville is on the present-day site of St Michael's Collegiate School, though has undergone substantial and multiple renovations and additions in its history.

While George Frankland's sole source of income came from his employment, apparently his younger brother had independent means. Somewhat of a rogue, Arthur instead spent his time undertaking recreational pursuits. For example, he was noted as competing in a race for six-oared galleys at the 1832 Hobart Town Regatta.[362] He was also noted as spending time fishing, often in company with his brother George.[363]

In late 1832 the Frankland family, including Arthur, finally moved from Macquarie Street into their new home, Secheron.[364] However, not all were congratulatory of the relocation. The press reported that George had enlisted men employed within the Survey Department to assist with transporting furniture and other items.[365] It was another faux pas for him which seemed to be frequently accumulating.

Given the size of the property, George Frankland also began requesting loans of convict labour from the colonial government.[366] These would have been for tradesmen and outdoor labourers as any servants employed inside the house were stipulated by the

---

[360] *The Hobart Town Courier*, 21 September 1832.
[361] *The Hobart Town Courier*, 12 November 1831, 21 January 1832; *The Hobart Town Gazette*, 16 November 1832.
[362] *Colonial Times*, 11 January 1832; *The Tasmanian*, 25 February 1832.
[363] *Colonial Times*, 16 October 1832.
[364] *The Hobart Town Courier*, 3 March, 21 April 1832; *Colonial Times*, 34 July 1832.
[365] *The Colonist and Van Diemen's Land Commercial and Agricultural Advertiser*, 7 December 1832.
[366] *The Hobart Town Courier*, 14 December 1832; *Launceston Advertiser*, 5 September 1833.

Franklands as having arrived free to the colony. The loaning of convict labour, however, would also see George Frankland under scrutiny, particularly over his abuse of the system to his own financial benefit.

With regards to Secheron, the house itself was built into the hill of the estate angled towards the Mulgrave Battery and Sullivans Cove. A two-storey sandstone residence, it was a merging of Gothic and Georgian inspired lines, and encompassed a reception hall, dining room, drawing room, parlour, five bedrooms, with a detached kitchen, pantry, storeroom and coach house as well as detached rooms for servants.[367] There were also two large rooms on the lower floor that opened out onto the sloping allotment.[368] A pump supplied water to the house.[369] A verandah was later erected on two sides.

Anne Frankland would have been heavily involved in the layout of the home, for the first time having input into how her family intended to live and entertain. Secheron, for Anne's purposes, would have been a merging of practical application, specifically with regards to kitchen and laundry facilities, and ostentatious and exuberant furnishings and styling, befitting of their standing within the upper-class of Hobart Town's society.

Pencil sketch of Secheron House by Thomas Chapman (1846).
University of Tasmania, Charles Darwin in Hobart Town - February 1836.
www.utas.edu.au/library/exhibitions/darwin/hobart.html.

[367] *The Mercury*, 20 September 1870.
[368] *The Mercury*, 8 February 1879.
[369] *The Mercury*, 20 September 1870.

Photo of Secheron House (circa 1930s).
Tasmanian Archives (NS3302/1/65).

Distress and Death

Settling in to Secheron was a period of new beginnings for Anne and George Frankland and their three children: Sophia, aged 9, Georgina, aged 8, and Augustus, aged 6. Their estate at Battery Point had a commanding view of the River Derwent, the Mulgrave Battery and the Port of Hobart Town, as well as the settlement's eastern shore. The residence that Anne and George created was designed for their family's needs and significantly marked the first time that either of them had lived in a home that they could truly call their own. The nearly eight acres of property that surrounded the house was prime for ornamental and kitchen gardens, as well as pastures. It was their utopia.

It did not last long. Criticism in the press continued to escalate about George Frankland's management of the Survey Department, as well as his influence over government affairs. There were other matters too that suggested ineptness. In April 1833 George's decision making was questioned concerning an expedition which he had taken with Lieutenant Governor George Arthur into Van Diemen's Lands' interior with the goal of reaching Macquarie Harbour. Only previously travelling as far as O'Briens Bridge himself, the group had travelled without anyone familiar with the type of country they would endure.[370] This reckless risk taking had become apparent when at one point during the trip the Lieutenant Governor had to be extracted from a gully in which he had been stuck for several hours.[371] The group also faced bad weather.

---
[370] *Colonial Times*, 16 April 1833.
[371] *Colonial Times*, 16 April 1833.

More aspersions came the way of the Franklands when the net worth of those associated with the colonial government was published in the local press in May 1833. George Frankland's fortune was estimated at £7,000.[372] The report also rather truthfully insinuated that this wealth had all been accumulated from his time in Van Diemen's Land. Others called out for their personal profiteering at the apparent expense of the struggling free settler were Lieutenant Governor Arthur, worth £30,000; Alfred Stephen, worth £15,000; and Rev William Bedford, worth £15,000.[373] The daily grind of the common man and their approval of the government was not being helped by the poor state of the colony's economy at the time. The article writer opined, *'thus from Minister to Minister are we cursed, without the chance of a change, by being taxed without our consent, to pay a host of needy adventurers, enormous salaries, for doing nothing, or perhaps what is worse than doing nothing - and to create a surplus revenue for His Excellency to boast about in his despatches to the Colonial Office'*.[374] A groundswell movement for change in leadership was slowly but surely generating momentum. Though it was initiated by a small agitated faction of the press, in the intervening years more and more frustrations were publicly vocalised, espousing Lieutenant Governor Arthur's government and his band of merry men, which included George Frankland.

Audits of the government's finances also revealed other expenses and exuberances associated with the Survey Department. In particular, questions were raised about George Frankland's *'forage allowance'* and his need for three horses and whether they were solely used for official work.[375] It did not help the situation that George soon disposed of one of the horses and gave it to his brother-in-law Thomas Mason at the government's expense.[376]

This period of the Franklands' lives also coincided with more development of Battery Point and Hobart Town's New Wharf area, incorporating Salamanca. Construction of a pier forming the New Wharf, extending from Sullivans Cove to the Mulgrave Battery had started in July 1830.[377] This ambitious project further enhanced Battery Point's appeal to merchants and shipowners. The

---

[372] *The Colonist and Van Diemen's Land Commercial and Agricultural Advertiser*, 7 May 1833.
[373] *The Colonist and Van Diemen's Land Commercial and Agricultural Advertiser*, 7 May 1833.
[374] *The Colonist and Van Diemen's Land Commercial and Agricultural Advertiser*, 7 May 1833.
[375] *The Austral-Asiatic Review*, 20 August 1833.
[376] *Colonial Times*, 27 August 1833.
[377] *The Hobart Town Courier*, 3 July 1831.

wharf was first noted to be in use in April 1831.[378] The Franklands' neighbours were additionally taking the opportunity to make improvements to their properties. Thomas Smith, who owned land between Secheron and the Mulgrave Battery, constructed a wharf on his four-acre site, optimising its use for shipbuilding and repair work.[379]

Subdivision of large land plots at Battery Point also occurred, resulting in new streets being developed and homes constructed; George Frankland naming Colville Street after his mother's family. The area's new residents coalesced to improve their neighbourhood too, noted in April 1834 as forming a subscription for the erection of a church.[380]

Not all were impressed by the rapidity in which improvements were being made, however. *The Colonist and Van Diemen's Land Commercial and Agricultural Advertiser* in May 1834 criticised the use of 200 convicts as part of a chain gang at the time '*employed in making a road near the Battery; along the whole extent of which there is not one single house, or one single inhabitant. The only reason which can be assigned for thus uselessly employing this large body of men at this spot, while the principal streets of the town, thickly studded with houses, and densely populated, are left impassable, from the immense traffic of the inhabitants cutting the surface into mud, knee deep, to the great injury of the tax-paying people, is, that the ****** and other Crown Officers of the Colony, have speculated largely in the purchase of the included land, which the cutting of these roads will force into immediate value!!!*'[381] This reproval was obviously directed at George Frankland. Specifically, a similar article reported that '*a large portion of the men belonging to the chain gang are most actively engaged in cutting a road to Mr. Frankland's gothic cross house, which road, after meandering, as the auctioneers would have it, in serpentine elegance along the brow of the battery-hill*'.[382]

With regards to their home life, Arthur Frankland visited Sydney during this period, participating in a boat race on the harbour.[383] He returned to Hobart Town in early December 1833,

---

[378] *The Hobart Town Courier*, 9 April 1831.
[379] *The Hobart Town Courier*, 11 September 1835.
[380] *The Hobart Town Courier*, 11, 18 April 1834.
[381] *The Colonist and Van Diemen's Land Commercial and Agricultural Advertiser*, 27 May 1834.
[382] *Colonial Times*, 27 May 1834.
[383] *The Hobart Town Courier*, 6 December 1833.

staying with the Franklands at Secheron.[384] A few months later he participated in the Hobart Town Regatta where he was heavily favoured.[385] Enjoying musical entertainments, Arthur Frankland took part in a concert held at the Hobart Town Court House in October 1834, playing an instrument called a seraphine, a new type of organ, that the Franklands had imported from England.[386]

By now the Franklands, along with the Arthur, Pedder, Stephen, Sorell and Kemp families, formed the upper class of Hobart Town's society, with their social interactions preferenced amongst those considered wealthy, well-born and/or powerful. Collectively referred to as the colony's '*haut ton*', the families wielded great political power.[387] With regards to the management of Secheron, however, retaining employees to assist with household duties appears to have been an issue for Anne and George as they regularly advertised for housemaids and cooks that '*have come to the colony free*', as well as footmen.[388]

In April 1834 Anne's brother Thomas Mason was promoted to Assistant Police Magistrate.[389] Upon receiving the news, the press once again chastised the preferential treatment that was endemic amongst higher-ranking government officials. The chorus calling for Lieutenant Governor Arthur's recall only grew louder, with other issues, including lack of trial by jury and a legislature not voted by the public, adding much impetus to the disenfranchised.[390] Still continuing the trigonometrical survey of Van Diemen's Land, George Frankland avoided the publicity by embarking on an expedition to find the source of the Derwent and Huon rivers in the colony's south-west region in early 1835.[391] The exploration proved successful with the source of the Derwent traced as far as Lake St Clair which George named, as well as Mount Ida, Mount Olympus and the Peak of Tenerife.

After several months away George Frankland returned to Hobart Town to face more criticism, this time regarding the diverting of town water to his Secheron estate, as well as the

---
[384] *The Hobart Town Courier*, 6 December 1833.
[385] *The Tasmanian*, 21 February 1834.
[386] *The Hobart Town Courier*, 31 October 1834.
[387] *The Tasmanian*, 30 January 1834.
[388] *The Hobart Town Courier*, 24 January 1834; *Morning Star and Commercial Advertiser*, 31 March 1835.
[389] *Colonial Times*, 3 June 1834.
[390] *The True Colonist Van Diemen's Land Political Despatch, and Agricultureal and Commercial*, 7 January 1835.
[391] *The True Colonist Van Diemen's Land Political Despatch, and Agricultureal and Commercial*, 7 January 1835; *The Tasmanian*, 20 February 1835.

houses of his associates, including Captains Forster and Montagu, at the public's expense.³⁹² The committee representing the Catholic Church in Van Diemen's Land also called out George's lack of progress towards them obtaining land settlements stating that he had acted *'in a manner highly injurious to a large and respectable body of the King's subjects; and thereby in direct opposition to the duties of his office'*.³⁹³

It must have been frustrating for Anne and George Frankland to find their names constantly in the press and most often in negative contexts. They had now been living in Hobart Town for eight years and likely considered themselves key and good standing members of the local community. The Franklands persevered, defending themselves and their reputation when the opportunity arose.

While Anne Frankland is rarely mentioned in Van Diemen's Lands' newspapers or statutory records, her charity and benevolence are apparent when she offered to take in a child from the ill-fated wreck of the convict ship *George III*.³⁹⁴ En route from England to Hobart Town under the command of Captain William Hall-Moxey, the ship carried a total of 308 persons, including 220 male convicts, plus guards, their families and crew.³⁹⁵ On the evening of 12 March 1835, the *George III* hit a rock off the southern end of the D'Entrecasteaux Channel and broke up in a heavy swell over a period of several hours. Shockingly, the convicts were locked below deck while the women and children were safely evacuated by the ship's boats. A total of 133 people died in the wreck, of whom 128 were convicts, mostly drowned.³⁹⁶ Upon hearing of the plight of the survivors in Hobart Town, Anne Frankland offered to take care of a child of one of the officers on board, Major Ryan, whose six-year-old son had broken his thigh while being loaded into one of the boats.³⁹⁷ At Secheron, under the Franklands' care, the child's health improved.

While the subsequent aftermath of the wreck of the *George III* was distressing for the Van Diemen's Land community as a whole, and investigations revealed the ill-treatment of the convicts below deck, as well as the plight of the survivors, the period marked the

---

[392] *The True Colonist Van Diemen's Land Political Despatch, and Agricultureal and Commercial*, 23 January 1835.
[393] *The Tasmanian*, 6 February 1835.
[394] *The Tasmanian*, 24 April 1835.
[395] en.wikipedia.org/wiki/George_III_(ship).
[396] en.wikipedia.org/wiki/George_III_(ship).
[397] *The Tasmanian*, 24 April 1835.

start of a series of anguishing events for the Frankland family more specifically. In May 1835 George Frankland was fortunate to escape serious injury when a pistol he was holding was accidentally discharged.[398] He received a severe wound to his hand though was able to recover. Next, a court case 15 months in the making, its delay likely coming at George Frankland's interference, was heard in Hobart Town.[399] A contractor named Henry Graham sued George Frankland for money lost when, through George's insistence, he was coerced into hiring a convict on loan to the Franklands over a three-month period to help plaster Secheron. The work only took two months, however, and instead of finding additional work for the convict, George Frankland demanded that Henry Graham take him on and cover expenses for the remaining month though it was obviously not his responsibility since the man was loaned to the Franklands.[400] It was one of many abuses regarding the loaning of convict labour at the time. George Frankland lost the case and, in another admonishment of his professionalism, had the government pay the costs.[401]

While Secheron and its gardens were being developed into the vast estate befitting of its upper-class residents, sourcing proficient help continued to be a menace for the Franklands. In September 1835 the couple advertised for the services of both a lady's maid and housemaid.[402] However, their household complement was reduced by one when Arthur Frankland left the colony to return to England two months later.[403] He appears to have left under dubious circumstances as a few weeks after his departure Arthur's name was embroiled in a court case for libel wherein several young men of the haut ton, including Alfred Stephen's brother George and Charles Arthur, nephew of the Lieutenant Governor, had accused one another of cheating during a game of cards.[404] The episode marked the start of a divide between the Lieutenant Governor and members of Hobart Town's high society.

The Frankland family were also looking to return to England, with the goal of seeing to their children's tuition and education.[405]

---

[398] *The Tasmanian*, 8 May 1835.
[399] *The True Colonist Van Diemen's Land Political Despatch, and Agricultural and Commercial*, 10 June 1835.
[400] *The True Colonist Van Diemen's Land Political Despatch, and Agricultural and Commercial*, 10 June 1835.
[401] *The True Colonist Van Diemen's Land Political Despatch, and Agricultural and Commercial*, 10 June 1835.
[402] *The Hobart Town Courier*, 25 September 1835.
[403] *Colonial Times*, 20 October; *The Hobart Town Courier*, 20 November 1835.
[404] *Colonial Times*, 12 January 1836.
[405] *Colonial Times*, 22 December 1835.

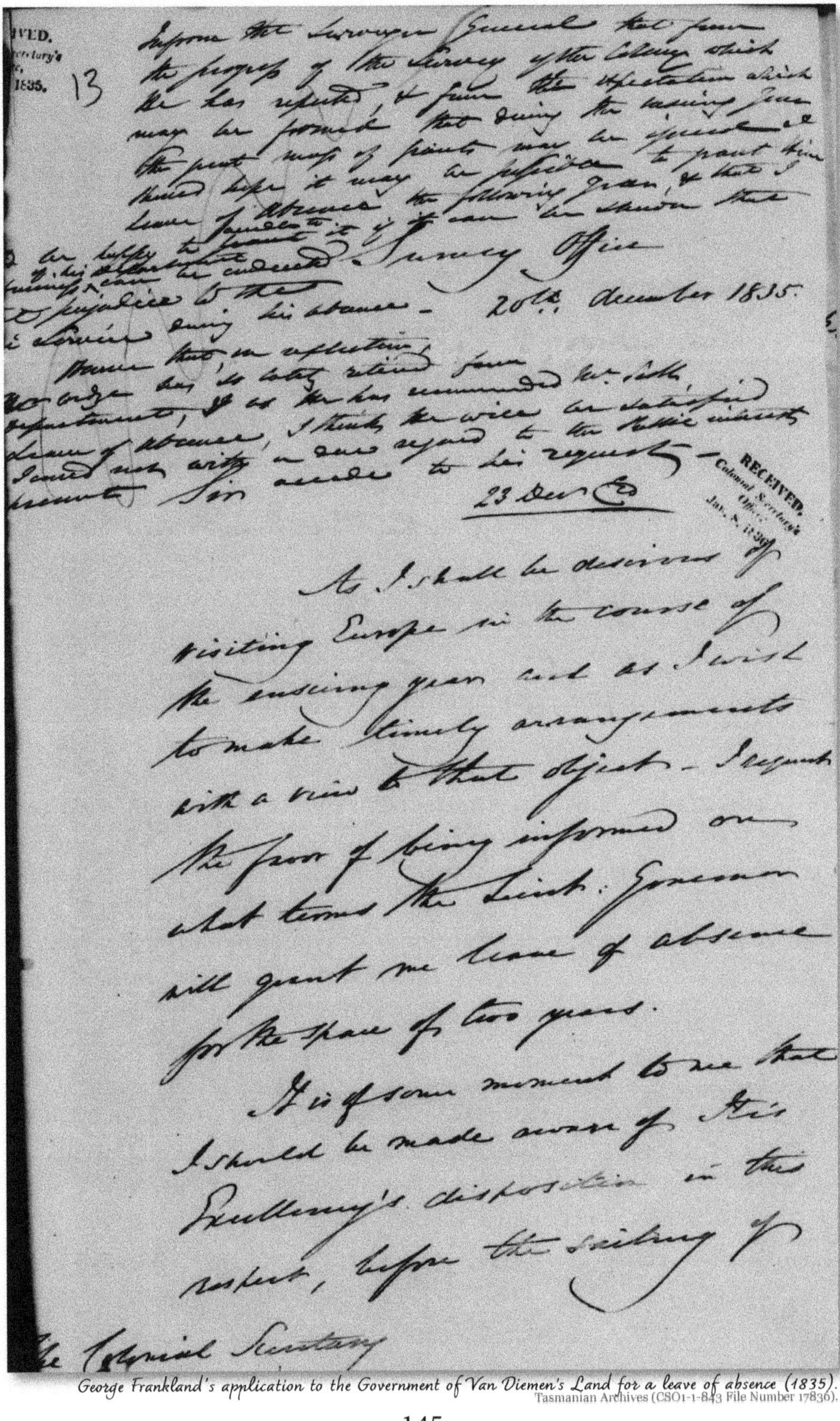

before the Surveyor General that from
the progress of the survey of the Colony which
he has reported, & from the expectation which
may be formed that during the ensuing year
the great mass of points now be reduced it
would seem it may be possible to grant him
leave of absence the following year, & that I
am [?] to [?] it if it can be shown that
[?] prejudice to the
[?] service during his absence –
Survey Office
20th December 1835.

[margin notes illegible]

23 Dec [?]

As I shall be desirous of
visiting Europe in the course of
the ensuing year and as I wish
to make timely arrangements
with a view to that object — I request
the favor of being informed on
what terms the Lieut. Governor
will grant me leave of absence
for the space of two years.

It is of some moment to me that
I should be made aware of His
Excellency's disposition in this
respect, before the sailing of

The Colonial Secretary

On 20 December 1835 George Frankland sent a letter to the colonial government requesting two years' leave of absence from his position with the Survey Department. While it appears that approval was initially given for the leave, with a start date of 1 January 1837, it was soon rescinded, owing to his position as head of the Survey Department being of high importance. The Attorney General, Alfred Stephen, also requested leave and was similarly dismissed.[406] George Frankland then spent many months corresponding with the colonial government arguing his case.[407]

Coinciding with his leave application, George Frankland became a trustee of the newly-created Hobart Town Grammar School, a co-educational school established with the goal of *'enabling the inhabitants of Hobart Town, at a trifling expense, to give their children a sound religious education on the principles of the Established Church'*.[408] Anne and George Frankland obviously wanted to return to England for the benefit of their children's education, though needed to find an alternative option while their application was under consideration. The Hobart Town Grammar School offered a possible solution. By now 10 years of age, their son Augustus would have been their highest priority since both daughters Sophia and Georgina could be educated at home by a governess or by the couple themselves. With regards to boys, the Grammar School was to provide instruction in reading, writing, grammar, arithmetic, measurement, the principles of navigation, as well as geography and history. In comparison the girls would be given the same subjects, substituting measurement and navigation for plain and fancy needlework.[409] All students were to receive religious instruction with their attendance at Divine Service each Sunday compulsory. Students would attend school between 9 am and noon and 2 pm and 5 pm during the warmer months and 9 am and noon and 2 pm and 4 pm during winter.[410] The cost of tuition was £5 per student. The school first operated out of premises at 60 Murray Street, contiguous to St David's Church.[411]

While George Frankland became heavily involved in the establishment of this educational institution suitable for his

---

[406] *Colonial Times*, 12 January 1836.
[407] Tasmanian Archives (CSO1-1-843 File Number 17836).
[408] *The Tasmanian*, 22 January 1836.
[409] *The Tasmanian*, 22 January 1836.
[410] *The Tasmanian*, 22 January 1836.
[411] *The Tasmanian*, 22 January 1836.

children, he and his wife Anne continued to socialise as part of Hobart Town's haut ton. There may have been some personal animosity between the Franklands and the Arthurs, however, regarding the leave request. In late January 1836, for example, Lieutenant Governor Arthur hosted a ball and supper to a '*select party of friends*'. Amongst the distinguished guests were George and Anne Frankland and Alfred Stephen and his wife Virginia, though the press report of the evening may have intended to create scandal, stating that all present enjoyed themselves quite merrily with the exception of '*Mr. Stephen and Mr. Frankland, who are, with the people, suffering from the "system"*'.[412] Given the assumed friendship between all of the ladies in the room, included amongst them Anne Frankland, it may have been an awkward situation for their small social circle to endure.

The following month the Franklands entertained the celebrated naturalist Charles Darwin who had arrived in Hobart Town on board the *Beagle* on 5 February. From his diary we learn of 27-year-old Charles Darwin's interactions with the Franklands and their peers. '*The Beagle stayed here ten days, and in this time I made several pleasant little excursions, chiefly with the object of examining the geological structure of the immediate neighbourhood ... I had been introduced to Mr. Frankland, the Surveyor-General and during these days I was much in his society. He took me on two very pleasant rides and I passed at his house "Secheron" Battery Point, the most agreeable evening since leaving England. There appears to be a good deal of Society here: I heard of a Fancy Dress Ball at which 113 were present in costumes! I suspect also the Society is much pleasanter than that of Sydney. They enjoy the advantage in there being no wealthy convicts. The Colony moreover is well governed; in this convict population, there certainly is not more, if not less, crime than in England.*'[413] The following day, on 13 February 1836, Charles Darwin spent the evening with Alfred Stephen and his family at Stephenville. He wrote, '*The house large, beautifully furnished, dinner most elegant. An excellent concert of rare Italian music. Stephenville had been the site of that mighty fancy-dress ball, while 96 guests had recently danced at 'Secheron'. Is not this astonishing in so remote a part of the world?*'.[414]

---

[412] *The True Colonist Van Diemen's Land Political Despatch, and Agricultural and Commercial*, 29 January 1836.
[413] www.thedomainhobart.com/charles-darwin.html; www.literature.org/authors/darwin-charles/the-voyage-of-the-beagle/chapter-19.html.
[414] www.thedomainhobart.com/charles-darwin.html.

At this juncture, however, George Frankland, Alfred Stephen and Lieutenant Governor Arthur all had other issues to deal with. By 1836 the population of Van Diemen's Land was estimated to be over 37,000 people, including 16,000 convicts; a tripling in ten years.[415] In the eight years since the Franklands' arrival in Hobart Town, demands on the Survey Department had been great and its inefficiencies a burden to those wanting to not only obtain land but also develop it with commercial and residential buildings, as well as for farming. Applications took far more time than anticipated and since accurate surveys were needed to determine boundaries for allotments in relation to streets, roads, public facilities, churches, waterways and fencing, etc., there was much criticism regarding the delays. It was one of several blights on the legacy of the government, as was the holdup with the trigonometrical survey of the entire colony. The stranglehold of Lieutenant Governor Arthur over his administration was also continually being called into question. As was he.

On 25 May 1836 it was publicly announced that Lieutenant Governor George Arthur had been recalled back to England.[416] Apparently conveyed in the '*most courteous and commendatory terms*', the message had arrived in Hobart Town per the convict ship *Elphinstone*.[417] A successor was not appointed.

While much of the population of Van Diemen's Land viewed the news as positive, Anne and George Frankland would have been apprehensive about their future, particularly since George had been a key component of Lieutenant Governor Arthur's administration. The recall also put the Franklands' plans to travel back to England in jeopardy. It was a period fraught with indecision and concern for their future, especially considering there was no way of knowing who would be appointed to the role. The Franklands waited for further news, though it would be months before anything was confirmed.

In late August it was finally revealed that Sir John Franklin had been appointed Van Diemen's Lands' new Lieutenant Governor.[418] While the colony waited for his arrival, factions of the unrelenting Hobart Town press, having claimed the scalp of George Arthur,

---

[415] *The Tasmanian*, 19 June 1835.
[416] *Colonial Times*, 31 May 1836.
[417] *The True Colonist Van Diemen's Land Political Despatch, and Agricultural and Commercial*, 27 May 1836; *The Hobart Town Courier*, 27 May 1836.
[418] *The Cornwall Chronicle*, 27 August 1836.

SUPPLEMENT.

GOVERNOR GEO. ARTHUR

Is Ordered HOME!

LORD GLENELG closes his Despatch as follows :—" I have felt it my duty, to advise his Majesty, that you should be IMMEDIATELY RECALLED; and I have to convey to you, his Majesty's commands, that, on receipt of this Despatch, you will, with as little delay as possible, repair to this Office. ("Signed) GLENELG."

TO-MORROW OUGHT TO BE A DAY OF GENERAL THANKSGIVING!

For the deliverance from the iron-hand of GOVERNOR ARTHUR. We have now a prospect of breathing. The accursed gang of bloodsuckers will be destroyed. Boys will be seen no more upon Police Benches, to insult Respectable Men. Perjury will cease to be countenanced, and a gang of Felons will be no longer permitted to violate the

LAWS OF CIVILIZED SOCIETY.

COLONISTS,

The dismissal of Arthur from the Governorship of unhappy TASMANIA, is a BLESSING, that will be felt by the worthy, and be duly appreciated. The Impounding Law, which was made to benefit the great Members of Council, will be abolished. The Turkey and Persian Act will meet with the same fate; and the Act of abomination practised by the hirelings, and secret emissaries of the Government, upon the People, will no longer be countenanced.

◆ REJOICE! ◆
FOR THE DAY OF
Retribution HAS ARRIVED.

Announcement of Lieutenant Governor George Arthur's recall in The Cornwall Chronicle (28 May 1836).
Tasmanian Archives (NS1013/1/625).

moved their hostilities to his allies. George Frankland endured much embarrassment from their comments with the public criticism so great that he and Anne were unable to attend a play at the Theatre Royal with their children for fear of retribution.[419] The press persisted, in particular the *Colonial Times* on 20 September 1836 published the following commentary on George Frankland's work ethic, or lack thereof. *'As the Surveyor General has not intimated to the public the change made for some time past in the routine of the duties of his office, we consider it imperatively necessary to do so, in order that the "unfortunates" who may be subjected to undergo the ordeal of passing the Survey Department and all its intricacies may not lose more time than they already do, in walking to no purpose to the top of Macquarie-street. Be it known, therefore, that George Frankland, Esq., is to be consulted at the house of that eminent artist, Mr. Bock, in Campbell-street, at any hour between ten and three o'clock daily, where he is at present busily engaged in having a full length likeness taken of his exquisite person. From three to five, the indefatigable Surveyor General will be found indulging in aquatic amusements, and learning to steer clear before the arrival of Sir John Franklin. From five to half-past six o'clock the over-worked and ill-paid Gentleman is to be found taking a turn around the beauteous walks of Secheron, or making his toilette for the night. From half-past six to eight, dinner, and all its pleasures, occupy his time, and from eight until eleven, coffee -- conversatione -- music -- singing, &c., fill up the space, until repose after the fatigues of a well spent day is required. In the morning a constitutional walk -- playing with the children -- breakfast, a ride on the long tailed Arabian to the residence of Mr. Bock's at ten o'clock, concludes the daily journal of the amusements of the Van Diemen's Land Surveyor General. The remainder of the twenty four hours is spent by the great man in attending to his vast duties in the Survey Office.'*

It was in this context that, after nearly 12 years of service governing Van Diemen's Land, Lieutenant Governor Arthur and his family departed Hobart Town for England on board the *Elphinstone* on 30 October 1836.[420] In the months and weeks prior many farewell dinners, addresses and other events had been held, with Anne and George Frankland part of the loyal well wishers. Given Sir John Franklin was still yet to arrive in the colony at the time of Lieutenant Governor Arthur's departure, Colonel Kenneth Snodgras, then in New South Wales, was temporarily appointed to

---
[419] *The True Colonist Van Diemen's Land Political Despatch, and Agricultural and Commercial,* 8 July 1836.
[420] *Colonial Times,* 1 November 1836.

the role.[421] Perhaps in an effort to dispose of assets in anticipation of his own family's intended departure back to England, in early November 1836 George Frankland advertised several building allotments situated within the grounds of Secheron for sale.[422] The parcels failed to sell.

On 6 January 1837 Sir John Franklin, his family and entourage arrived in Hobart Town per the ship *Fairlie*.[423] He was officially sworn in as the colony's fifth Lieutenant Governor the following day. With a vested interest, the population of Van Diemen's Land anxiously awaited to see whether he would shepherd in a more liberal administration, free of corruption and tyranny. Feeling the need to make himself known and approach the change in leadership with a positive influence, George Frankland met Sir John Franklin and his wife Lady Jane Franklin on board the *Fairlie*, presenting a bouquet of flowers to the latter. In a letter to her father, John Griffin, Lady Jane wrote that George '*was the first person on the morning of our disembarkation of Hobarton to pay his respects to us on board the Fairlie, bringing me a bouquet of beautiful flowers, the most characteristic and acceptable compliment which my new country could furnish*'.[424]

After this initial introduction George Frankland likely spent the first few weeks of the new administration hoping that Lieutenant Governor Franklin did not read the accumulating criticisms levelled at him and his Survey Department, including shouts of negligence, dereliction of duty and incompetence. Instead, George sought to placate and consolidate their association, inviting Sir John Franklin to personally tour the Survey Department. It was during the course of this meeting, which took place on 13 January 1837, that George exhibited a lithographed plan of Hobart Town and its suburbs.[425] Presented on the following page, it is not known if George Frankland produced the plan or if it was created by one or more of his employees. Regardless of provenance, George soon found himself in favour with the new Lieutenant Governor, by the end of January also receiving invitations to dine with the Franklins at Government House.[426]

---

[421] *Bent's News and Tasmanian Three-Penny Register*, 5 November 1836.
[422] *The Tasmania*, 4 November 1836.
[423] *The Tasmania*, 6 January 1837.
[424] Jane Franklin (4 January 1839). Letter to her father John Griffin, University of Tasmania Library Special and Rare Materials Collection.
[425] *The Tasmania*, 20 January 1837.
[426] Jane Franklin. Dinner Engagement book, Tasmania, 1837-1843, University of Tasmania Library Special

Map of Hobart Town and surrounding Suburbs produced by the Survey Department (c1837).
Allport Library and Museum of Fine Arts, State Library of Tasmania (AUTAS001131821480).

Sadly this period coincided with the death of Virgina Stephen, Anne Frankland's friend and confidante. She died during childbirth on 23 January 1837 and was buried three days later at St David's Burial Ground, Hobart Town, aged 33.[427] Her newborn daughter Emily also died the same day and was buried with her.[428] Alfred Stephen was left with two daughters and five sons in his care, all 10 years of age and under.[429] The Franklands, particularly Anne, no doubt stepped in to help the grief-stricken family, a day after the burial declining an invitation to dine at Government House with the Franklins.[430]

A month later Anne Frankland left a rosewood work box inlaid with mother of pearl sprigs on the evening coach while returning to Hobart Town from New Norfolk. She had no doubt been in the region visiting her brother Thomas, his wife Abigail and their infant daughter Emily.[431] Anne offered a £1 reward for the box's return.[432] Its misplacement would have been disheartening to her as it was likely a practical family heirloom containing her sewing supplies that she would have used daily.

Doubling down on his work George Frankland and his entire Survey Department spent the next few months employed in finishing his comprehensive map of Van Diemen's Land. The map was published in April 1837 with copies sent to England where it would be reproduced and printed. A copy is provided on the following pages.

Perhaps indicative of the continued negative targeting of George Frankland and his Survey Department, Sir John Franklin requested more oversight, including being given copies of field notes.[433] As part of this exercise it was revealed that the department had surveyed over 1,185,000 acres between 1832 and 1836.[434] The new Lieutenant Governor's directive, however, may have been two-fold. Ever the explorer, he was likely after information regarding the island's interior and coastlines with the view to undertaking expeditionary trips. Sir John Franklin also took an interest in

and Rare Materials Collection, Australia.
[427] Tasmanian Archives (RGD34/1/1 no 4794).
[428] Australia Cemetery Index, 1808-2007 for Emily and Virginia Stephen.
[429] adb.anu.edu.au/biography/stephen-sir-alfred-1291.
[430] Jane Franklin. Dinner Engagement book, Tasmania, 1837-1843, University of Tasmania Library Special and Rare Materials Collection, Australia.
[431] Tasmanian Archives (RGD32/1/2 no 6802).
[432] *The Hobart Town Courier*, 10 March 1837.
[433] *The Tasmanian*, 10 March 1837.
[434] *The Hobart Town Courier*, 10 March 1837.

Hobart Town's water courses, touring the local rivulet with the goal of removing obstruction and improving supply in April 1837 in the company of George Frankland.[435] The press tried in vain to convince Sir John Franklin to conduct further investigations into the incompetencies of the Survey Department in the weeks and months ahead, by now going so far as to issue personal attacks and rather brutal denigrations, but it was not forthcoming. George Frankland had been accepted into the Franklins' fold. He had also finally received two years' leave to travel back to England.[436]

Perhaps in an effort to secure funds for the family's return to Britain, on 7 June 1837 George Frankland took out a mortgage for £1,600 with the Derwent Bank on the Secheron property.[437] The rate of interest was a substantial 10 per cent per annum. A few months later the estate was advertised for lease.

> TO be LET, for a term of three years, the villa of Secheron, with six acres of Land annexed, laid out in paddocks, gardens, and pleasure grounds.—Apply to Mr. Frankland.
> September 26, 1837. (2526

Colonial Times, 26 September 1837.

Failing to find a tenant, a month later the Franklands listed Secheron for sale.

> **To be Sold,**
> THAT valuable and beautiful Estate 'SE-CHERON,' the property of George Frankland, esq. Surveyor General, consisting of a commodious and elegant villa, with other buildings, and nearly eight acres of building ground in the heart of a rapidly improving neighbourhood.
> The property possesses a frontage of nearly 1000 feet on the harbour, admirably adapted, in every part, for shipping purposes.
> The proprietor will dispose of the estate either in one lot or in several, according to the nature of the applications that may be made to him.
> Title, a new grant, *free from quit rent and from every species of reservation.*
> Apply to the owner.
> Oct. 24.

The Hobart Town Courier, 27 October 1837.

---

[435] *The Tasmanian*, 28 April 1837.
[436] *The True Colonist Van Diemen's Land Political Despatch, and Agricultural and Commercial*, 12 May 1837; *The Tasmanian*, 13 October 1837.
[437] www.thelist.tas.gov.au (Historical Deed 02/0854).

Partial map (top) of the colony of Van Diemen's Land by George Frankland (April 1837).
Tasmanian Archives (AF395/1/4).

Partial map (bottom) of the colony of Van Diemen's Land by George Frankland (April 1837).
Tasmanian Archives (AF 395/1/4)

With preparations well underway for the Frankland family's return to England, including the sale of a '*nearly new*' horse-drawn carriage, George continued his involvement with Hobart Town's society.[438] Finding a kindred spirit in the pursuit of natural science, in late 1837 he was elected to the committee of the newly-established Natural History Society of Van Diemen's Land; Sir John Franklin was appointed President.[439] A few weeks later George Frankland joined Lady Jane Franklin, her step-daughter Eleanor and others on an excursion to the top of Mount Wellington where they stayed the night before returning to Hobart Town the next day.[440]

Certainly enjoying the company of Van Diemen's Lands' new Lieutenant Governor and his wife Lady Jane, the Franklands were in an awkward position: they desperately needed money. Likely to their embarrassment, a substantial newspaper advertisement appeared in the Hobart Town press in early January 1838 advertising Secheron and its grounds to be sold at auction.

The True Colonist Van Diemen's Land Political Despatch, and Agricultural and Commercial, 5 January 1838.

---

[438] *The Hobart Town Courier*, 1 December 1837.
[439] *The True Colonist Van Diemen's Land Political Despatch, and Agricultural and Commercial*, 17 November 1837.
[440] *The Hobart Town Courier*, 15 December 1837.

Meanwhile, George Frankland continued to undertake his duties as head of the Survey Department. In late February 1838, for example, he accompanied Lieutenant Governor Sir John Franklin on a trip to the island's interior, travelling through New Norfolk.[441] George was also, albeit very slowly, proceeding with the trigonometrical survey of the island, in April 1838 requesting a *'decked vessel to be placed at his disposal'* to aid in the process of completing the work associated with Bass Strait's islands.[442]

With Secheron still failing to sell, however, that same month George and Anne Frankland remortgaged the property, this time borrowing a staggering amount of money from George's eldest brother Frederick who at this time resided at Muntham Park in Sussex, England. Signing the property over to Frederick, should they default on payment, they used the money to repay the Derwent Bank whom by now they owed £2,100. Considering the actual amount borrowed from Frederick Frankland was £4,312, it is not known how the couple had come to be so much in debt and where all their assets had gone.[443] Had the money been used towards building and furnishing the residence itself? George's salary was supposedly in the realm of £1,000 per annum. Surely this was enough money to run their household, feed and clothe themselves and their family, educate their three children and host social events in their home.

From this point in time there was no discussion in the press regarding the Frankland family's return to England. Instead, George continued his work with the Survey Department which, by a Government Notice issued on 4 July 1838, was reduced in staff with those remaining having their roles and responsibilities clearly defined and streamlined.[444] He also continued to travel with the Franklins, in September 1838 escorting Lady Jane Franklin on a trip to the D'Entrecasteaux Channel and Huon region.[445]

Not thwarted by their lack of resources the Franklands remained at Secheron, in mid-July 1838 entertaining a large party at their home.[446] George Frankland also sought to lease out a portion of the property that was suitable for shipbuilding.[447]

[441] *The Austral-Asiatic Review, Tasmanian and Australian Advertiser,* 27 February 1838.
[442] *The Austral-Asiatic Review, Tasmanian and Australian Advertiser,* 3 April 1838.
[443] www.thelist.tas.gov.au (Historical Deed 02/1565).
[444] *The Cornwall Chronicle,* 14 July 1838.
[445] *Colonial Times,* 18 September 1838.
[446] *The True Colonist Van Diemen's Land Political Despatch, and Agricultural and Commercial,* 13 July 1838.
[447] *The Austral-Asiatic Review, Tasmanian and Australian Advertiser,* 21 August 1838.

Despite their reduced economy the couple additionally sought the services of a housemaid in September 1838.[448] A few weeks later it was announced that Secheron had been leased to Chief Justice Sir John Pedder for a period of eight years at an annual sum of £300.[449] In turn the Franklands moved to '*Mr. Clarke's tasteful villa near the Wind-mill, while Mr. Clarke, himself, retires to his farm*'.[450] The 'Mr. Clarke' referred to was George Carr Clarke who had moved to Ellinthorp Hall in Van Diemen's Lands' Midlands region. The house in question was Royston Cottage located at 10 Francis Street, just along from James Luckman's windmill which had recently been erected on Cromwell Street.

Following the move, while Anne Frankland and their three children settled into their new home, George found time to serve as Secretary of the committee organising the inaugural Tasmanian Anniversary Regatta. With Lieutenant Governor Sir John Franklin as patron, it was notably the first government-backed Anniversary Regatta held in the colony.[451] George's exuberance for the event and its staging at Pavilion Point was such that he was absent from the Survey Department over the course of several days.

Held on 1 December 1838 with over 12,000 people said to be in attendance, including Sir John Franklin and his wife Lady Jane, the Tasmanian Anniversary Regatta was a resounding success. In fact one newspaper reported, '*We never saw so many people collected in any place in this colony*'.[452] Another article exulted, '*We never witnessed so gay and thorough a holiday in this Colony, as was enjoyed on Saturday. Young, and old, grave and gay, even the tottering Valetudinarian participated in the agreeable recreations of the day, and every one seemed determined to be happy, and few, we suspect, were disappointed. We were highly gratified at the exertions displayed by several gentlemen of high Colonial rank, to render the accommodations for the public as complete as possible; this was as it should have been, and has tended greatly, by the earnestness of the performance, to soften down and assuage many of those bitter asperities of feeling and of temper, which have, of late, so torn and distracted our little community*'.[453] It was an apology of sorts from the press, which had been buoyed by criticism in the lead up

---

[448] *The True Colonist Van Diemen's Land Political Despatch, and Agricultural and Commercial*, 31 August 1838.
[449] *Bent's News and Tasmanian Register*, 21 September 1838.
[450] *Bent's News and Tasmanian Register*, 21 September 1838.
[451] *The Austral-Asiatic Review, Tasmanian and Australian Advertiser*, 20 November 1838.
[452] *The True Colonist Van Diemen's Land Political Despatch, and Agricultural and Commercial*, 7 December 1838.
[453] *Colonial Times*, 4 December 1838.

to the event. George Frankland was likely grateful for the nod of approval, regardless of how subtle.

With on-shore entertainment and boundless refreshments and food provided by local publicans, attendees were bolstered by the fine weather as well as a series of aquatic races featuring gigs, whaleboats, sailing boats and dinghies; all attracting their fair share of shore-side bets. It was the start of a day ingrained in the colony's history with the legacy of the Hobart Town Regatta now formulated as the Royal Hobart Regatta still being staged over 185 years later.

Heavily involved in orchestrating the day, officiating and overseeing the program, and creating the wattle decorations, George Frankland found time to also compete in one of the races, taking part in the event for second-class sailing boats, competing in the *Wallace*. His family would have attended the day too, joining Sir John Franklin and Lady Jane in their tent, all told enjoying the spectacle and time spent together.

Unfortunately this joyfulness did not last. George Frankland died a few weeks later.

For much of this period of Anne Frankland's married life to her beloved George, she has been cast in his shadow while he was regularly noted in documents and the press with regards to his professional and personal pursuits and activities. It has been nearly impossible to trace what Anne's daily life was like, how she interacted within the Hobart Town community and society, and how she and George cared for and raised their three children. It is in the next chapter, following George's death, that we re-trace Anne's movements. She re-emerges and we regain sight of the baby born in Coventry in 1793, the young girl that moved to London with her family during the Napoleonic Wars, the 20-something that was forced to find a job because of her family's financial woes, and the woman that ultimately moved to India as a governess in 1820. Let us see how she fares, for the days to come are some of the most testing of her life.

THE FIRST ANNIVERSARY REGATTA.

Established and under the Patronage of Sir John and Lady Franklin.
SATURDAY, 1ST DEC., 1838.

(The first Boat Race will take place at half-past 10 o'clock precisely.)

 The Flotilla will start from the Steam Boat Wharf, at 10 o'clock precisely, where all Boats will assemble.

UMPIRE—CAPTAIN KING, R.N.
Committee of Management—Capt. Forster, Messrs. Jas. Kelly, T. Hewitt, C. M'Lachlan and Edw. Abbott.
Secretary—Mr. G. Frankland. *Director*—Mr. J. Wilson.

FOUR-OARED GIGS.

First Boat, 15 sovs., if four or more start. Second Boat to receive 5 sovs. If not three or more Boats start, to be no race.

Saucy Kate, J. Cameron—Black all over. Four-oared.
Wallaby, G. Watson—All Black. Four-oared.
Polly, W. J. Mansfield—Black, with a white streak.
Lady Franklin, Club Boat—White.

WHALE BOATS.

First Boat to receive the TASMAN PRIZE, presented by His Excellency SIR JOHN FRANKLIN, K.C.H., of 30 sovs. Second Boat, 20 sovs. Third Boat, 10 sovs. Fourth Boat, 6 sovs.

Highlander, R. Gardiner—green bottom, red nose, white streak.
Parrot, R. Griffiths—green bottom, white nose, yellow streak.
Tasman, J. Watson—fresh bottom, white nose, yellow streak.
Snipe, J. Chipman—white bottom, black streak with red and yellow ribbons.
Lady Franklin, J. Harper flesh bottom, yellow nose with a red bridle, painted green with a red streak.
Sir John Franklin, R. Capon—black bottom, red nose, painted black with a red ribbon.
Mary Ann, M. Connor—green bot., red nose, green with white streak
Red Nose, J. Fulton—green bottom, red nose, with a red and yellow ribbon.
Lady of the Lake, H. Wishart—all blue with white ribbon.
Opposition, W. Garth—green bottom, red nose, painted green with black gunwale and yellow streak.
Magpie, J. Sherbett—black bottom, white nose, yellow streak, vermilion ribbon.
Blue Bell, W. Somerville—green bottom, blue nose, a yel. ribbon.
Amity, W. J. Mansfield—dark lead bottom, black nose, black and white streak.
Dandy, A. Imlay—all blue.
Star, A. Imlay—white bottom, green nose, white.
Nancy, A. Imlay—all green.

SAILING BOATS.—FIRST CLASS.

Any description of boat not exceeding 30 feet in length of keel. First Boat, 20 sovs. Second ditto 10 sovs.

Tasman, Hon. H. Elliot, 27 feet keel, copper bottom—all black.
Black Jake, J. Mathews, 29 feet keel, red bottom—black top streak, second plank white, with a red ribbon.
Mary Ann, C. Bastian, 28 feet keel, white bottom—painted black with two white ribbons.
Kate, J. O'Meagher, 19 feet 6 inches keel; flag St. George's ensign at the peak—black all over.
Booth, F. A. Downing, 30 feet keel, copper bottom—black.
Matchless, McArdell and Buchanan, 24 feet keel, black bottom—white and black streak.
Mary, W. Beachcroft, 22 feet keel; flag, white with red cross at gaff end—black all over.

SAILING BOATS.—SECOND CLASS.

Open Boats only, not exceeding 28 feet in length of keel. First Boat, 18 sovs. Second ditto 8 sovs.

Flinders, J. Montagu, 24 feet keel—black all over.
Mary 2nd, W. Beachcroft, 22 feet keel ; flag, white with red cross at gaff end—black all over.
Saucy Kate, J. Cameron, 20 feet keel—black all over.
Eliza, J. Harburgh (for officers of the *Eliza*), 22 feet keel—all black.
Onyx, W. T. Beaumont, 25 feet keel ; red flag at the gaff end, black bottom—painted black with a red ribbon.
Fanny, J. Gilligan, 24 feet 6 inches keel ; a red, white and blue flag, perpendicular at the mast-head, and at the gaff end, black bottom—painted black, with a white and red ribbon.
Matchless, McArdell and Buchanan, 24 feet keel, black bottom—white and black streaks.
Margaret, E. Luttrell, 21 feet keel ; flag, a Union Jack at ford peak, bottom black—yellow streak on starboard side, ans red on larboard.
Tamar (*Little*) W. Willett (for officers of *Tamar*) 20ft. keel—black.
Wallace, J. Frankland, 19 feet 6 inches keel ; a pendent at the peak and St. George's Cross—all black, with a dolphin and anchor on the bow.

[The *Matchless*, built at Kangaroo Point (now Bellerive) by C. R. Johnson, was the winner of the 1st and 2nd Class Sailing Boats Races, the property of F. H. McArdell, and sailed by Mr. Peter Buchanan. The two following years she won 1st and 2nd prizes, after which the Committee would not allow a boat to receive two prizes.]

DINGEYS.

To be square-sterned, not exceeding 10 feet keel, to contain one man, and to be sculled by one oar over the stern. (No entrance money.) First Dingey, 5 sovs. 2nd do. 2 sovs. 3rd do. 1 sov.

Bandicoot, G. Watson.
————, J. Gilligan, black bottom, red and white ribbon, 9 ft. 11½ in. keel.
Son Pon, E. Kelly—lead color.
Little Tom, T. Kelly—black bottom, green streak and white eye.
Step and fetch it, W. J. Mansfield—black.
I wish you may get it, W. J. Mansfield—blue.
Blue Bell, J. M'Gregor.

Committee Room, Port Office, Dec. 30, 1838. [VIVAT REGINA.

Part Three

Royston Cottage, 10 Francis Street, Battery Point (2011).
www.realestate.com.au/property/10-francis-st-battery-point-tas-7004/.

England and Legacy

George Frankland died at Royston Cottage, 10 Francis Street, Battery Point, on Sunday 30 December 1838. He was 38 years of age. A brief note published in the Hobart Town press on 1 January 1839, ironically in one of the newspapers that often lambasted him, provided the details. '*We sincerely regret to announce the death, on Sunday evening, of George Frankland, Esq. Surveyor General of this Colony, nephew of Sir Thomas Frankland, Bart. also of Lord Colville, his mother being sister of that nobleman and of General Sir Charles Colville, G. C. B. late Governor of Mauritius. The premature death of this lamented gentleman is attributed to the breaking of a tumour in his head, originating in an old injury, aggravated by the present distressing disease.*'[454] Another newspaper report let it be known that George had only taken ill the previous day.[455] Meanwhile *The Tasmanian* conceded the following, '*However unpopular Mr. Frankland might have been in his important official capacity, we know, that, in private life, he was highly esteemed. Mr. Frankland was certainly an accomplished man, in the modern acceptation of the term, and, to his family and friends, his loss will be great*'.[456]

Perhaps *The Hobart Town Courier* offered the best summation of George's death. '*It is with feelings of the deepest regret, that we have to announce the death of Mr. George Frankland, the Surveyor General, who expired at his residence on Sunday evening last, in the 42nd [SIC] year of his age. To a mind imbued with the cultivation of a humanity by which it was softened and improved, he added a nature of the purest benevolence.*

---
[454] *The Austral-Asiatic Review, Tasmanian and Australian Advertiser*, 1 January 1839.
[455] *Launceston Advertiser*, 3 January 1839.
[456] *The Tasmanian*, 4 January 1839.

Incapable of animosity he sought rather to allay than incite the petty feuds and squabbles which agitate the political scene of life. His disposition prompted him to the adoption of that sacred lesson, which "tempers the wind to the shorn lamb" and he was never known, out of an affectation of seeming propriety, but which is always the result of insolent pride and selfishness of character, to abandon or avoid those whom fortune did not favour, or who had by accident, or by the design which sometimes guides such proceedings, forfeited her smiles. Amiable and gentle in his domestic circle his affections moved in that sphere, reflected back with lustre by the lights around him. The orb itself is now extinct, and that absorbing gloom has succeeded, which time alone can serve to dissipate.'[457]

Certainly a true statement. Anne Frankland and their three children, Sophia, Georgina and Augustus, were fraught with grief. Their future was also uncertain. The Franklands had only recently moved into a leased residence at Battery Point, they were heavily in debt, predominantly to George's older brother, and they had lost their sole means of financial support. Their plight was also noticeable. In a letter to her father on 3 January 1839 Lady Jane Franklin wrote, '*Poor Mr. Frankland! Only a short month ago he was in his glory, on the Regatta ground, heading up bareheaded to Sir John who stood under a canopy of flags, the winning boat crews to receive their prizes, the Military Band playing "Rule Britannia" and the crowd of spectators forming a large circle round an arena of green sward in the midst of the wattle trees to which was hemmed in by the squatting boys and girls of the orphan schools with their silken banners. Mr. Frankland's exertions on that day and the preceding ones were more I think than his strength could bear - he fell ill immediately after - but recovered - again became indisposed and was suddenly carried off by inflammation of the brain*'.[458]

In a letter to her sister, Mary Simpkinson, written by Lady Jane Franklin a few days later she divulged further information regarding George Frankland's death, obviously rocked by the news. '*In my letter to my Father, I mentioned the appalling shock we have all received by the death of Mr. Frankland. This is only a week ago, and I scarcely yet realise the afflicting fact. He has left his family more than destitute so that the expenses of their passage will be defrayed by their friends. In John, I have no doubt, will give £50 if necessary*'.[459]

[457] *The Hobart Town Courier*, 4 January 1839.
[458] Jane Franklin (4 January 1839). Letter to her father John Griffin, University of Tasmania Library Special and Rare Materials Collection.
[459] Jane Franklin (December 1838). Letter to her sister Mary Simpkinson, University of Tasmania Library

Lady Jane's letter continued. '*Poor man, he seemed the very essence of vitality, such constant playfulness, wit, humour, and apparent enjoyment of life. Yet he must have had some unhappy moments. We have been lately brought together in the much intimate manner, by our magnificent Regatta. The night previous, it rained, and he was* [at] *the ground* [a] *great part of the night, looking I believe chiefly to the placing of the mottoes on the trees.*'[460] After detailing George's involvement with designing and procuring the wattle flowers used to create the mottoes Lady Jane opined, '*Mr. Frankland seems to have been absolutely adored in his own family. He educated his children entirely himself. Their grief, and their mother's, has been, I am told, something dreadful to witness*'[461].

Part of Lady Jane Franklin's letter to her sister Mary Simpkinson, January 1839.
University of Tasmania Library Special and Rare Materials Collection.

George Frankland was buried at St David's Burial Ground a few days after his death.[462] Realising that she and the children must immediately return to England, Anne Frankland operated quickly. George's will was proved in the Supreme Court of Van Diemen's Land on 4 January 1839. Anne was bequeathed all of his goods, chattels, rights, credits and effects.[463] She was also appointed sole executor with the provision that an inventory of all accounts associated with George's estate be finalised by 4 July 1839. Instead of taking months, this process took a matter of weeks.

Special and Rare Materials Collection.
[460] Jane Franklin (21 June 1838). Letter to her sister Mary Simpkinson, University of Tasmania Library Special and Rare Materials Collection.
[461] Jane Franklin (21 June 1838). Letter to her sister Mary Simpkinson, University of Tasmania Library Special and Rare Materials Collection.
[462] Australia Cemetery Index, 1808-2007 for George Frankland.
[463] Tasmanian Archives (AD960-1-1 Will No. 153).

Five days after George Frankland's death, a request for claims on his estate was posted in *The Hobart Town Courier* by Robert Pitcairn, Solicitor.[464] On 8 January 1839 various pieces of household furniture and other effects of the Franklands were advertised for sale by auction. The listing included a carriage for one or two horses, a piano forte, two boats, a pair of globes, books and maps, six cows, four horses and one filly.[465]

On 15 February 1839 Anne Frankland gave power of attorney with regards to the management and administration of Secheron to Alfred Stephen and her brother Thomas Mason.[466] That night she boarded the barque *Derwent* and sailed from Hobart Town, not only a penniless widow but a 45-year-old woman in debt to her brother-in-law for thousands of pounds.[467] She was also the mother of three teenagers: Sophia, aged 15, Georgina, aged 14, and Augustus, aged 12. Anne would have been extremely grateful for the gift of money provided to her by close friends and associates such that they could all return to England so quickly, along with one of their servants.[468] She was likely glad that the *Derwent* departed Hobart Town at night so she could not see Secheron, the house she had once called home, in all of its beauty. She could also not see the burial ground, the last resting place of George and their beloved infant daughter Matilda.

What a shock the past months had been, not only having to vacate Secheron but also losing George. Anne would have mourned; her husband, her home, her life all gone. What was to become of her and her children? She had no plans other than returning to London. Though in the days immediately following George's death she would have sent rushed letters back to England notifying their families of the tragedy, as well as their intended arrival, it was possible that Anne would outrun the letters to their destination given she had commenced her passage only seven weeks later.

With Anne and her children on board, the *Derwent* slipped out of the river for which it was named and made its way slowly towards Africa. Rounding the Cape of Good Hope, Anne undoubtedly remembered the months her and George had spent

---

[464] *The Hobart Town Courier*, 4 January 1839.
[465] *Colonial Times*, 8 January 1839.
[466] *The Tasmanian*, 15 February 1839.
[467] www.thelist.tas.gov.au (Historical Deed 02/2347).
[468] *Colonial Times*, 19 February 1839.

in Stellenbosch coinciding with the birth of Georgina. There were so many memories tied up in so many different countries.

After a voyage of nearly four months, the *Derwent* passed by Falmouth in Cornwall on 10 June 1839 and docked in London four days later.[469] For Anne, who had last stepped foot in the city 13 years prior, the change in London would have been evident. First, there was a new monarch. 18-year-old Queen Victoria had ascended the thrown on 20 June 1837 following the death of King William IV. Several months after the Franklands' arrival, Queen Victoria would become engaged to her first cousin Albert. Second, with a population of over 2 million people, London had grown significantly, with new buildings and developments spurring a growing and affluent upper and middle class. This growth, however, was contrasted with the development of overcrowded and unsanitary slums housing the poor. Traffic and transportation had also changed significantly with the development of railway lines from London to Birmingham, Liverpool, Portsmouth, Manchester, Nottingham, Leeds and other major cities, as well as horse-drawn cabs and omnibuses operating within London itself.

While Sophia, Georgina and Augustus were likely excited about seeing the city, a place they had heard so much about, as well as meeting new relatives, Anne determined their next steps. Finding sanctuary with her brother Nathaniel, his wife Harriet and their children at 17 Compton Terrace in Islington, on 25 June 1839 Anne applied to the government for a widow's pension, based on the fact that George Frankland had not only served in the military but had also been on half-pay at the time of his death. Though her petition was successful, she was to receive only £40 per year, while her three children were each to receive £6.[470] It was barely enough to live off.[471] Still, Anne was no doubt appreciative for Nathaniel's assistance with the application, his clerkship to become a solicitor was one of the last good things that the Mason family's legacy money had paid for and Nathaniel had proudly made his own way in the profession.

With Augustus nearing 13 years of age, Anne's next priority became finding him a school. He was soon enrolled at Blackheath Proprietary School in Greenwich, moving in as a boarder with the

---

[469] *Lloyd's List*, 12 June 1839; *Morning Herald*, 15 June 1839.
[470] British Army Service Records WO 22 & WO 23 for Anne, Sophia, Georgina and Augustus Frankland.
[471] British Army Service Records WO 22 & WO 23 for Anne, Sophia, Georgina and Augustus Frankland.

Nº ~~2980~~   FORM No. 3.   F. 216
                                                                D. 30/12/38

Registered for placing on the Pension List, the Widow of an Officer who died on Half-Pay.

I *Anne Frankland* do solemnly and sincerely declare, that I was lawfully married at* *Bombay in the East Indies* on the *eighteenth* day of *June 1822* to *George Frankland* late a *Lieutenant* on Half-Pay of the *67th* Regiment of *Foot* who died, at *Hobarton* on the *thirtieth* day of *December last* aged *thirty eight* years;—that ever since his decease I have continued a Widow, and am so at this present time;—and that I have no Pension, Allowance, or Provision from Government. And I make this solemn declaration, conscientiously believing the same to be true, and by virtue of the provisions of the Act 5 and 6 William IV., Cap. 62.

Signature of the Widow } *Anne Frankland*

Her Place of Residence } *17 Compton Terrace Islington*

Declared and Subscribed before me at *17 Compton Terrace Islington* this *Twenty-fifth* day of *June 1839*

Signature of the Magistrate. } *Edw. Chapman JP*

Place or County for which he Acts } *for the County of Middlesex*

N. B. If the Marriage of the parties took place *before the Officer was placed on Half-Pay,* the following Certificate must be filled up and signed in the manner pointed out below; but if the Marriage took place after the Officer was placed on Half-Pay, the Certificate is not required.

We do hereby certify to the best of our knowledge and belief, that *Anne Frankland* now residing at *17 Compton Terrace Islington* was the lawful wife of *George Frankland* who formerly served on Full Pay as a *Lieutenant* in the *67th* Regiment of *Foot* and died at *Hobarton* on Half-Pay of the *same* Regiment of ——— on the *30 December 1838* wherefore we do humbly recommend her as a deserving object of Her Majesty's Royal Bounty. Given under our hands this *25th* day of *June 1839*

To be signed by the Colonel and Agent of the Corps in which the Officer last served. } † *J. Macdonald*
                                      Thomas Frankland Lewis
                                      Cox & Co.

4—625.   500.   May, 1839.

Application by Anne Frankland for widow's pension (1839).
UK, Officers' Birth Certificates, Wills and Personal Papers, 1755-1908.

Tennant family in Lee Terrace.[472] It was a convenient location, the house was situated only one mile from the school. Settling in to a new environment and a new routine, Augustus took up sports, including playing in the school's cricket team.[473]

With regards to the continuing education of Sophia and Georgina, Anne likely initially took on the role herself. Remaining with her brother in Islington, in addition to their scholarship, the trio would have spent their days visiting with Anne's mother Dorothea, who lived six miles away in Ladbroke Square, Notting Hill.[474] Visits with the Frankland side of the family, however, may have been limited. George's oldest brother Frederick, who had loaned them money and taken out a mortgage on Secheron, was stationed in Caen, France, at the time.[475] While George's third oldest brother, Charles, may have been initially helpful to Anne and her children, in February 1840 he was appointed Commander of the Royal Navy corvette *Pearl* and began preparing to leave on a voyage to North and South America.[476] George's youngest brother Arthur was still about, though considering he was living in Park Place, Cheltenham, he may have only visited with Anne, Sophia and Georgina on occasional trips to London, unless the trio travelled the 100 miles to visit him.[477] It was Edward Frankland, George's second oldest brother, however, that appears to have helped the family out the most, likely providing monetary support. Unmarried, Edward was a retired Vice Commander of the Royal Navy who had spent time acting as Private Secretary to his cousin Sir William Bowles, a Commodore of the Royal Navy.[478] In 1837 Edward had retired from service and by the early 1840s he was living in Cheltenham, most likely with Arthur, having achieved the rank of Rear-Admiral.[479]

Replacing Bath as the go-to destination for England's well-to-do families, particularly those associated with or serving in the military, by the late 1820s Cheltenham had become a popular spa

---

[472] 1841 England Census for Augustus Frankland; British India Office Births & Baptisms for Augustus Charles Frankland.
[473] *Bell's Life In London and Sporting Chronicle*, 12 September 1841.
[474] *Saint James's Chronicle*, 5 January 1847.
[475] Calvadose, France Births, Marriages and Deaths, 1450-1930 for Colville Frankland.
[476] *The Standard*, 15 February 1840; *Hampshire/Portsmouth Telegraph*, 13 April 1840.
[477] Gloucestershire, England, Electoral Registers, 1832-1974 for Arthur Frankland.
[478] W. R. O'Byrne (1849). *A Naval Biographical Dictionary: Comprising the Life and Services of Every Living Officer in Her Majesty's Navy.*
[479] W. R. O'Byrne (1849). *A Naval Biographical Dictionary: Comprising the Life and Services of Every Living Officer in Her Majesty's Navy;* Gloucestershire, England, Electoral Registers, 1832-1974 for Edward Frankland.

and resort-like town for members of the Frankland family to spend most of the year, including its matriarch, the Hon Catharine.[480] Situated in the county of Gloucestershire on the fringe of the Cotswolds, it was the presence of mineral springs that initially drew members of the upper-class to the town. By the late 1830s Cheltenham was home to more than 35,000 residents with services including a new railway station, opera house, library, theatre and art gallery as well as numerous parks and gardens attracting more and more residents to the area.

Unfortunately it is not known if Anne Frankland travelled to Cheltenham to visit with George's family during the early stages of her return from Van Diemen's Land or if they met up in London. However, she would have been grateful for any support received from members of the family. It is also not known how long Anne and her two daughters, both now 15 and 14 years of age, stayed with her brother Nathaniel in London. However, after several weeks of his hospitality, she would have realised that they could not stay in London with him permanently. Anne made more plans. With the new school year about to start, the trio moved to Reading in the county of Berkshire, some 40 miles from London, where the girls were enrolled in a school in Castle Street operated by sisters Margaret and Julia Puddicomb.[481] Offering a more economical place to live and receive an education, Reading at the time had a population of just under 20,000 residents.

Conceivably sensing that she needed to make plans for her own succession, possibly due to ill-health, on 8 February 1840 Anne returned to her brother's office in Red Lion Square, London, to sign her last will and testament. The following month the first passenger railway service was established between Reading and London, making the trip between the two locations much more efficient. Leaving the girls as boarders with the Puddicomb sisters, in early June 1841 Anne relocated to Cheltenham, 70 miles northwest of Reading, taking a lease on a villa in Ormond Place.[482] The 1841 Census for England, the first modern census held in Great Britain, was taken on the night of Sunday 6 June 1841 and lists Anne as living off independent means, though she had either intentionally or inadvertently reduced her age. With her villa

---

[480] *Morning Post*, 8 September 1829.
[481] 1841 England Census for Julia Puddicomb, Margaret Puddicomb and Sophia Frankland.
[482] *Cheltenham Examiner*, 2 June 1841.

centrally located in the heart of Cheltenham, with easy access to its shops, gardens and promenades, it was also just under a mile from the Franklands' residence in Park Place. Thus Anne no doubt spent time with George's brothers as well as his mother, the Hon Catharine, who was by now approaching 70 years of age and an occasional visitor to the area. Anne would have also kept up to date on news from her children and other members of the family in England, as well as those in Van Diemen's Land, receiving letters from various family members, friends and associates.

While it is at this point in time that it seemed Anne Frankland and her three children were settled in England, sadly grief and life-changing events followed them across the seas.

Anne Frankland died in London on 29 May 1842, likely at the residence of her brother Nathaniel in Compton Terrace.[483] She was 49 years of age. It is not known where she was buried.

Perhaps due to the complexities over the Secheron estate, it was not until 7 November 1843 that probate was granted on Anne's will. While Secheron is not mentioned by name, it is still an interesting document, providing a window into Anne's mind at the time she wrote it in February 1840.[484]

With no money to convey, first and foremost Anne gave her plate, trinkets and ornaments to her two daughters, Sophia and Georgina, to be divided equally between them. She then gave a small gold watch with a silver chain, a writing set and dressing case that belonged to her late husband George to their son Augustus. Next, a gold repeater watch was bequeathed to George's brother Charles *'as a mark of my esteem and affection for his benevolent exertions on behalf of my children'*. The remainder of her estate was then transferred to her brothers-in-law Edward and Charles Frankland, as well as her own brother Nathaniel Mason, as executors, to sell with the money to be held in trust and then divided equally between her three children and be paid to them upon obtaining the age of 21, with any interest generated during the interim to be used towards their maintenance. With regards to the care of Sophia, aged 18 years, Georgina, now 17, and Augustus, now 15, the three executors were appointed guardians, along with Anne's sister Mrs Frances Williams.[485]

[483] *Launceston Examiner*, 12 October 1842.
[484] England & Wales, Prerogative Court of Canterbury Wills, 1384–1858 for Anne Frankland.
[485] England & Wales, Prerogative Court of Canterbury Wills, 1384–1858 for Anne Frankland.

Following the death of their mother, the three Frankland children appear to have come under the guardianship of their uncle Nathaniel Mason as opposed to the other three executors listed in Anne Frankland's will. Sophia and Georgina remained in the Reading area, finishing school in the years immediately after her death, while Augustus continued his education in Blackheath.

Sadly, there are two more deaths to report associated with the greater Frankland family that were to have an impact on Sophia, Georgina and Augustus. On 19 September 1843, at Clifton in the county of Bristol, their grandmother the Hon Catharine Frankland died.[486] She was 71 years of age. Just over three months later, on 22 December, at 49 Montpellier Terrace, Cheltenham, their uncle Arthur Frankland died.[487] He was 35 years of age.

In addition to his brothers and sisters, Arthur's will specifically mentioned his nieces, nephew and Anne Frankland's brothers whom he referred to as friends.[488] In particular, to Sophia he gave a calf bound music book containing quadrilles and waltzes, as well as an olive wood pen case and a small yard measure in a glass case. To Georgina he gave a brooch representing a Swiss peasant, a gold finger ring and a purse. To Nathaniel Mason he gave a Genova watch and to Thomas Mason he gave a telescope. Other items and objects were bequeathed to various friends he had made in Van Diemen's Land, including Sir John Pedder and his wife, as well as Alfred Stephen.

The next part of Arthur Frankland's will is fascinating. Though it is not stated how much wealth he had at the time of his death, Arthur bequeathed the remainder of his estate, including his real and personal property and money, to his nephew Augustus Frankland, with the assets to be placed in a trust and invested such that Augustus was to receive an annual payment from the interest generated upon reaching the age of 21.[489] Up until this point in time, however, the annual payment from the trust was to go to his older sisters, Sophia and Georgina, equally. This was a unique, gracious and extremely altruistic gift from Arthur to his orphaned nieces and nephew. Not only did it provide much needed funds to Sophia and Georgina at a period when they most needed it, but it

---

[486] *Morning Herald*, 22 September 1843.
[487] *Cheltenham Looker-On*, 23 December 1843.
[488] England & Wales, Prerogative Court of Canterbury Wills, 1384–1858 for Arthur Frankland.
[489] England & Wales, Prerogative Court of Canterbury Wills, 1384–1858 for Arthur Frankland.

also allowed Augustus to receive the bulk of the estate and thereby take care of his older sisters, upon him reaching the age of 21. Arthur Frankland signed his will on 2 November 1843, i.e., less than two months following the death of his mother.

Albeit not equal to the financial generosity shown by her son Arthur, the Hon Catharine Frankland bequeathed several items to her granddaughters Sophia and Georgina, including earrings, brooches and other jewels, as well as silk, satin and velvet dresses. Though it would nowadays seem strange to inherit clothing from one's grandmother, in early Victorian Great Britain it was quite common. Sophia and Georgina would have appreciated the clothing, likely making alterations to the dresses made from expensive fabrics to make them more age-appropriate and modern.

While Augustus is not mentioned by name in the will, he would have benefitted from the fact that the Hon Catharine bequeathed to her son Arthur a property located at 55 Rue des Martyrs in Paris of which she was mortgagee. The asset was stated to be worth £7,000 with a return of investment of 5 per cent.[490]

With both the Frankland and Mason families taking over the care and guardianship of Sophia, Georgina and Augustus, they were well provided for. While Sophia and Georgina initially remained in the Reading area finishing school, by late 1843 they had moved to nearby Malborough in Wiltshire where they established a small school for girls.[491] The establishment was only in operation for a few years before Sophia, following in the footsteps of her mother, sailed for India.[492]

Arriving in Bombay in late November 1845 at the age of 22, Sophia took up residence with one of the local British families, possibly employed as a governess. Less than a year later, on 28 September 1846 in Satara, she married Gore Boland Munbee, at the time a captain in the Bombay Engineering Corps. Though their marriage appears to have been one built on love and mutual affection, with the couple spending time in several different regions of India, as well as returning to England for sojourns, they divorced in 1862 under controversial circumstances following

---

[490] England & Wales, Prerogative Court of Canterbury Wills, 1384–1858 for Catharine Frankland.
[491] *Reading Mercury*, 17 December 1842; *Berkshire Chronicle*, 27 January 1844; *Devizes and Wiltshire Gazette*, 30 January 1845.
[492] search.fibis.org/bin/aps_detail.php?id=2410293.

Sophia's elopement with Charles Payne Barras, a lieutenant in the 29th Infantry and a friend of her husband. The divorce proceedings were played out in both the Indian and British press, including publication of an intimate and revealing letter written by Sophia to her husband on 26 May 1860. It is a bold and striking series of statements from a woman obviously torn between convention and love. In it Sophia confesses, '*What I have now done is done after long and mature consideration, and I have well weighed all the disadvantages attending such a step, and prefer setting every consideration at defiance to continuing to lead a hopeless, aimless, and miserable life*'.[493] She later continued, '*You may choose not to afford me the release which I desire. If so, you will regret it hereafter, and the disgrace of my position will be reflected upon you. Captain Barras; for my sake he cannot and will not give you such satisfaction; duelling too is out of fashion, and redress by law within your reach. If you seek "damages" only you will oblige me to bring forward evidence of a disagreeable nature, to prove that no happy home has been destroyed, and you must fail in gaining them; therefore for your own sake, if not for mine, refrain from such a course*'.[494]

After sending the letter, Sophia then left her sister Georgina's house in Mahableshewar, India, where she had been staying temporarily and made her way to Surat to meet up with Lieutenant Barras, travelling under an assumed name.[495] The couple then eloped to Dohua where they lived together openly. An action for '*criminal conversation*' was then brought against the pair by Sophia's husband Colonel Munbee. He was awarded 3,000 rupees in damages.[496]

The divorce was granted in May 1862 by the House of Lords, the institution having jurisdiction in such cases with regards to British subjects then residing in India.[497] By this time Sophia had returned to England with Lieutenant Barras on medical leave, and was pregnant. The couple married in Great Broughton, Cheshire, two months later with their daughter Alice born shortly thereafter.[498] Sadly, stability failed to find Sophia. Her husband returned to India after several years' absence and retired from service in May

---

[493] *London Evening Standard*, 21 May 1862.
[494] *London Evening Standard*, 21 May 1862.
[495] *Sun*, 21 May 1862.
[496] *Sun*, 21 May 1862.
[497] *Bombay Gazette*, 31 May 1861.
[498] England & Wales, Civil Registration Marriage Index, 1837-1915 for Sophia Catherine Frankland; Cheshire, England, Church of England Baptisms, 1813-1923 for Alice Barras Frankland.

1874.[499] It is not known if he resumed living with Sophia and their daughter Alice who, by this point in time, had relocated to Brighton in Sussex.[500] Lieutenant Colonel Charles Payne Barras died in Hampstead, Middlesex, in February 1886 at the age of 59.[501] Strikingly, his headstone is fixed with the statement '*To Err is Human*'.[502]

Continuing our biography of Sophia and her daughter Alice, on 25 November 1890 at St Thomas' Church on the Isle of Wight the latter married George Massey Watson, son of the late Rev A. E. Watson of Edinburgh.[503] She was 27 years of age, he was 39. Nevertheless, George was from Cheshire which may have been how the couple met. The union, however, may not have been a happy one. George Massey Watson sailed for New Zealand in March 1897 where he remained, often coming into contact with law enforcement officials for numerous offences, including procuring items under false pretences and furnishing valueless cheques.[504] In fact, the epitome of a swindler, he appears to have initially portrayed himself as a '*wealthy gentleman of Montevideo, Uruguay, who* [was] *just passing through the colony*'.[505] Nearly one year later, obviously in need of cash and by now playing the part of an Irishman, he sold his effects, including diamond rings, opal finger ornaments, gold watches and silver spoons, as well as family relics, pictures and clothing.[506] How he had come to have possession of these items remains unknown. What transpired next is even more bizarre, though perhaps indicative of a world without the internet and real-time information.

George Massey Watson placed a notice in the New Zealand press on 1 August 1898 announcing the death of his mother, '*the Honorable Mrs. Massey Watson, at Gad's Hill Park, Shanklin, Isle of Wight*'.[507] The only problem: she was still very much alive and he appears to have taken a leaf out of a Charles Dickens biography with regards to the residence itself. In bankruptcy proceedings a few months later, George divulged that he had '*arrived in the colony*

---

[499] *Times of India*, 2 May 1874.
[500] 1881 England Census for Sophia Barras.
[501] England & Wales, National Probate Calendar (Index of Wills and Administrations), 1858-1995 for Charles Payne Barras.
[502] Colonel Charles Payne Barras in the UK and Ireland, Find a Grave® Index, 1300s-Current.
[503] *Belfast News-Letter*, 28 November 1890.
[504] *Manawatu Standard*, 16 May 1900; *Wanganui Herald*, 10 January 1906.
[505] *Evening Post*, 27 April 1897.
[506] *New Zealand Times*, 19 March 1898; *New Zealand Mail*, 14 April 1898.
[507] *New Zealand Herald*, 1 August 1898.

with about £10,000 in cash, and personal effects to the value of £8,000. For the last three years, since his wife's death in England, [she was also still alive] *I have been addicted to intemperance, and almost constantly under the hands of doctors, who have treated me for brain disturbance'.*[508] Another article relaying statements from the proceedings provided this nugget of information about his mother who '*was the widow of an Episcopalian clergyman of Edinburgh, and was only in receipt of a very small income,* adding "*her son appears to have been living the same fast and precarious life ever since he left this country*"'.[509]

George Massey Watson died in Auckland, New Zealand, in August 1907.[510] In contrast to his antics, his wife Alice remained in England, by the 1920s living in Windsor, Berkshire.[511] She likely died sometime in the 1930s. Meanwhile her mother Sophia had spent the remaining decades of her own life residing in London and Brighton. She died in Brighton on 18 May 1910 at the age of 86.[512] Sophia's estate was valued at £430.

Contrary to her older sister Sophia, Georgina Frankland appears to have lived a more conventional life. At the age of 22, she too left England for India, arriving in Bombay on 27 May 1847 from Aden per the steam frigate *Moozuffer*.[513] Here she was met by her brother-in-law Captain Munbee and then escorted to Dharwar, residing with him and her sister.[514] It was in this couple's house that she married Captain John Thomas Francis of the Native Infantry's Survey, Assessment and Settlement Office on 13 September 1847.[515] The couple had several children born in India in the proceeding years: Edward Augustus (1848), Emily Georgina (1849), George Frankland (1851) and Frederick William (1852).[516] Returning to England, their daughter Clara Maria was born at Brighton in 1853. They then travelled back to India where their son John Cyril was born in 1856 and their daughter Katherine Mary Alexander was born in 1858.[517]

---

[508] *Lyttelton Times*, 3 October 1898.
[509] *New Zealand Times*, 5 October 1898.
[510] Australia and New Zealand, Find a Grave® Index, 1800s–Current
[511] 1921 England Census for Alice Frankland Watson;
England & Wales, Electoral Registers 1910-1932 for Alice Frankland Watson.
[512] British India Office Births & Baptisms for August Charles Frankland.
[513] search.fibis.org/bin/aps_detail.php?id=2397689.
[514] *Bombay Gazette*, 26 February 1861.
[515] *Bombay Gazette*, 26 February 1861; India, Select Marriages, 1792-1948 for Georgina Frankland.
[516] Frankland Family Tree on Ancestry.com.
[517] Frankland Family Tree on Ancestry.com.

Obviously close, Georgina became protector of Sophia during the period that she eloped with Lieutenant Barras, as indicated in the divorce case proceedings. Georgina, her husband John and their children returned to England in the 1870s, establishing themselves in Cornwall and then Hampshire. She died at Bournemouth, Hampshire, on 11 December 1887 at the age of 63.[518] Georgina was survived by all of her children with the exception of her oldest son Edward who died in India in 1873.[519] Her husband John died on 4 August 1896 at Scarborough in Yorkshire.[520]

With regards to Augustus Frankland, there is similarly much to report, though his biography offers up more melancholy. Upon finishing school in Blackheath, with a recommendation from Lord Colville, he gained the position of Cadet with the Bombay Infantry in November 1843. He then left England, travelling to Alexandria by the steamship *Oriental,* arriving in January 1844.[521] Augustus remained with this guard of foot soldiers, being promoted several times and also travelling back to England on furloughs.[522] In particular, he served in a campaign in the Southern Mahratta country in 1844-45, and was present at the storming of Punalla.[523]

Augustus married his cousin Clara Frances Sophia Williams, daughter of Hamerton and Frances Williams (nee Mason), at Poona, India, on 22 September 1851.[524] Tragically she died three months later at Bombay.[525] More tragedy occurred on 8 February 1857 when Augustus was killed in a battle at Kossh-ab in Persia during a calvary charge. His estate was worth £3,200 which was split equally between his two sisters.[526]

In addition to the legacy generated by Anne and George Franklands' three children, Sophia, Georgina and Augustus, there is Secheron, the home that the couple built in the early 1830s in

---

[518] England & Wales, National Probate Calendar (Index of Wills and Administrations), 1858-1995 for Georgina Anne Francis.
[519] India, Select Deaths and Burials, 1719-1948 for Edward Francis.
[520] England & Wales, National Probate Calendar (Index of Wills and Administrations), 1858-1995 for John Thomas Francis.
[521] search.fibis.org/bin/aps_detail.php?id=2397689.
[522] India, Select Deaths and Burials, 1719-1948.
[523] *The Homeward Mail,* 2 April 1857.
[524] *The Morning Advertiser,* 6 November 1851.
[525] search.fibis.org/bin/aps_detail.php?id=2389889.
[526] England & Wales, National Probate Calendar (Index of Wills and Administrations), 1858-1995 for Augustus Charles Frankland.

Map of the Secheron Estate (April 1837).
Tasmanian Archives (NS596/1/1).

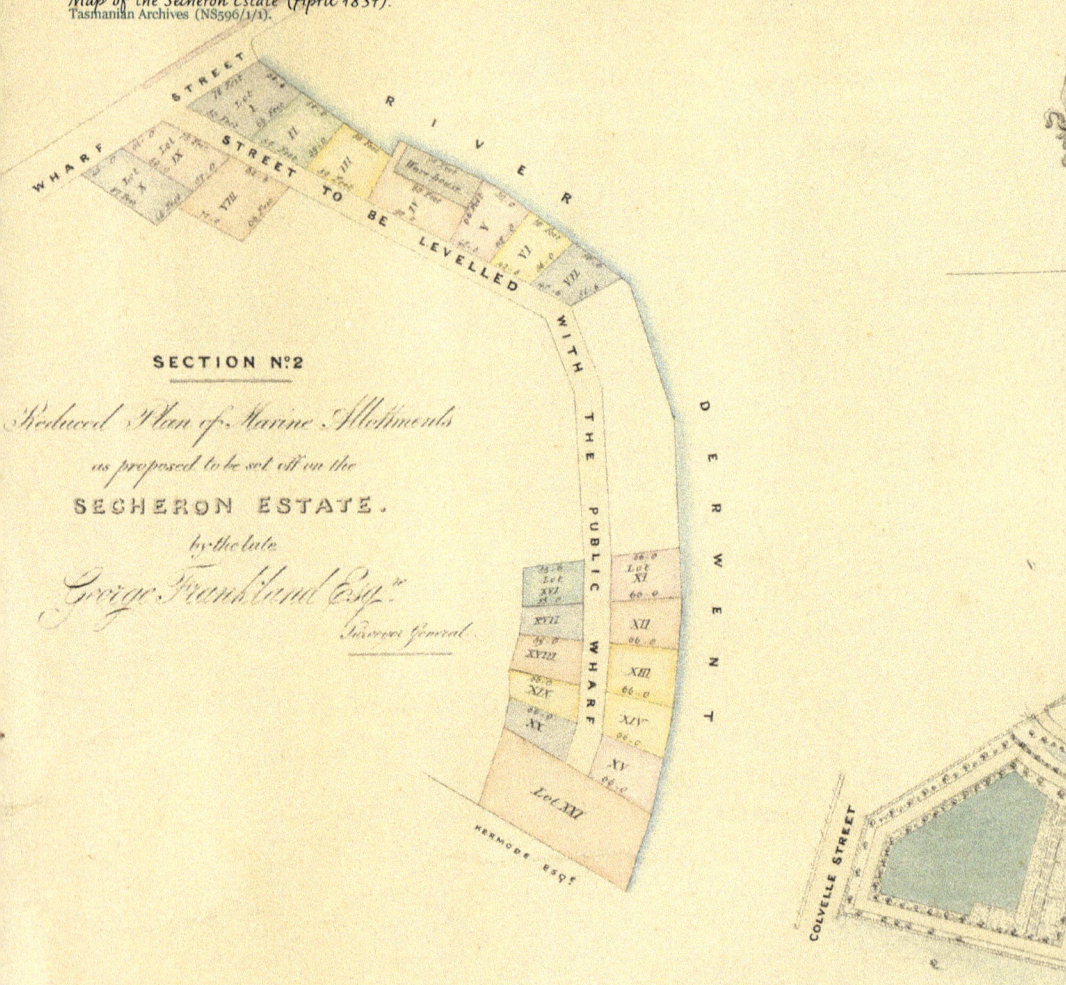

SECTION Nº 2

Reduced Plan of Marine Allotments
as proposed to be set off on the
SECHERON ESTATE.
by the late
George Frankland Esqr.
Surveyor General.

Frontage on the River Derwent
999½ Feet

SECHE

THE ESTATE OF T

Geo. Frankla

Situate on the Banks
RIVER DERWE
& adjoining the Townsh
HOBART T
VAN DIEMEN

Area

Battery Point, Tasmania. There is much to relay with regards to this residence, its history, subdivision, uses and owners. In summary, having borrowed a substantial amount of money from George Frankland's elder brother Frederick, Secheron was transferred to his ownership in February 1838. He in turn mortgaged the property to a firm based in London and leased it to Sir John Pedder.[527] With an interest rate of over 12 per cent, by 1845 Frederick Frankland had defaulted on mortgage payments for Secheron such that it was repossessed by the mortgagees who attempted to sell the property, subdividing it into various allotments.[528] The bulk of the estate was purchased by Hobart Town solicitor Arthur Perry for £900, the aggregate realised from the sale totalling £2,880.[529] The low prices were indicative of the depressed state of the Van Diemen's Land economy at the time.

Sadly, Arthur Perry died suddenly at Secheron in November 1855 leaving a pregnant wife and eight children.[530] His widow Jane remained living at the property, leasing a portion of it to John Ross for use as a shipbuilding yard, incorporating a patent slip. Jane Perry died in July 1870 and Secheron was subsequently put up for lease.[531]

In late 1879 the Secheron estate was purchased by Hannah Clarke, widow of Thomas Biggs Clarke.[532] She then spent over 40 years living in the residence. Following her death in September 1923, the entire estate was purchased by W. A. Finlay and A. J. Nettlefold in June 1924 for the price of £10,000 and subdivided.[533] Secheron House itself was advertised for sale for £2,500 a month later, devoid of most of its land.[534] It failed to sell and was then advertised for lease.[535]

In March 1935 Secheron House was once more advertised for lease, stated to be ideal for conversion into flats.[536] It was next advertised for sale in February 1938 having been renovated and modernised.[537] Another sale occurred in October 1951.[538]

---

[527] www.thelist.tas.gov.au (Historical Deed 02/2857).
[528] www.thelist.tas.gov.au (Historical Deed 03/1485); *The Courier*, 1 February, 29 April 1845.
[529] *Colonial Times*, 18 February 1845.
[530] *The Courier*, 24 November 1855.
[531] *The Mercury*, 12 July 1870.
[532] *The Mercury*, 13 November 1879.
[533] *The Mercury*, 22 September 1923, 20 June 1924.
[534] *The Mercury*, 5 July 1924.
[535] *The Mercury*, 13 January 1925.
[536] *The Mercury*, 20 March 1935.
[537] *The Mercury*, 8 February 1938.
[538] *The Mercury*, 13 October 1951.

The barque Eucalyptus at John Ross' shipyard in front of Secheron House (1852).
Maritime Museum of Tasmania (P_2023-051).

Later purchased by the Government of Tasmania, by the mid 1970s it was used as an art textile centre, and between 1983 and 1999 was home to the Maritime Museum of Tasmania. It subsequently returned to private ownership and in recent years has been lovingly restored.

Independent of Secheron House, there is also the legacy of George Frankland's professional work in Van Diemen's Land. Unfortunately his wife Anne Frankland remains concealed in the shadows of much of this effort, though would have been his primary support mechanism. Of George's professional life, his legacy remains in the maps, paintings and picture boards that are held by several libraries and galleries within Australia, as well as the landmarks which were named after him and the streets which

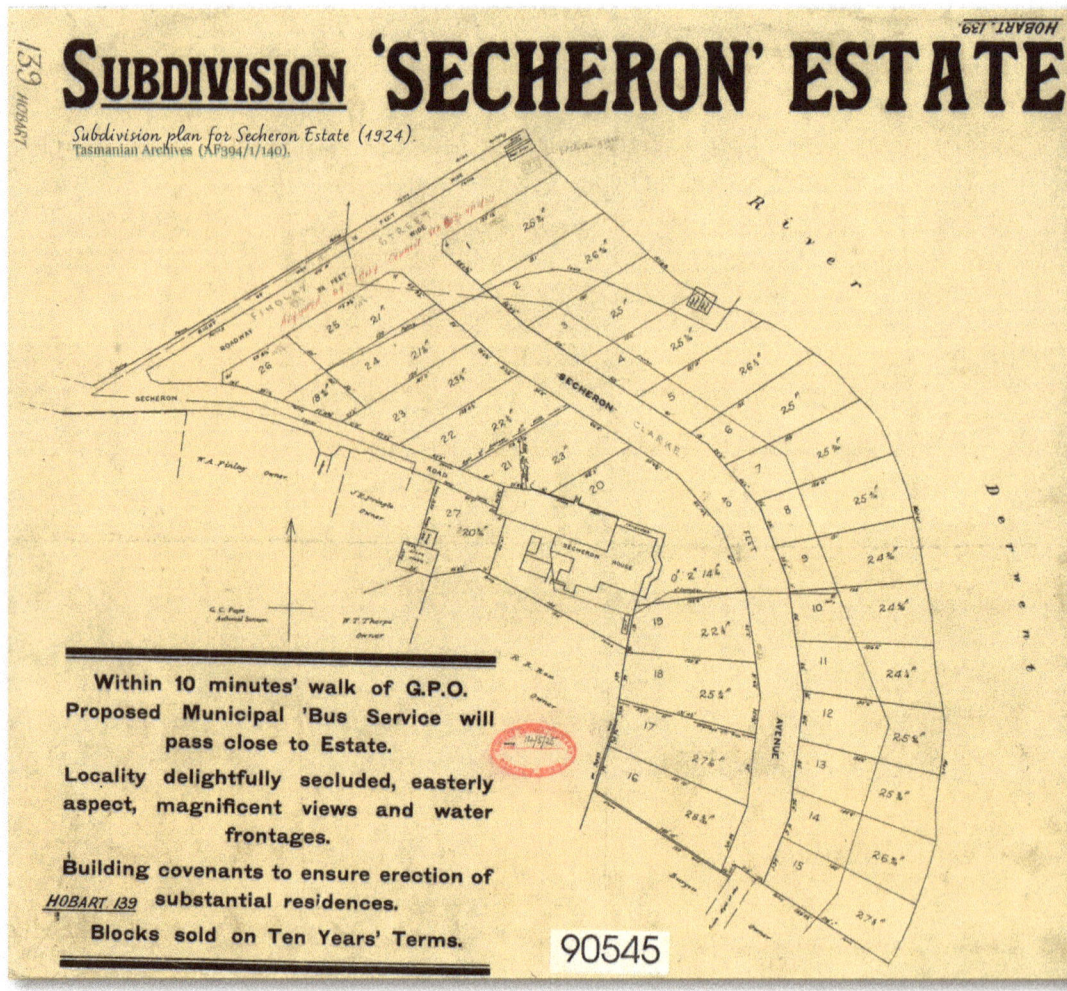

Subdivision plan for Secheron Estate (1924).
Tasmanian Archives (AF394/1/140).

he additionally named. These include the painting of the newly arrived immigrant family that George created in 1827 coinciding with his family's arrival in Hobart Town that is part of the State Library of Tasmania's Allport Library and Museum of Fine Arts. There is also the emblem for the Royal Hobart Regatta that encompasses wattles.

Of the streets he named there were many, including Colville Street which George named for his maternal family. Frankland Street in Launceston was also named after him, as was Mount Frankland in Western Australia, and both the Frankland River and Frankland Range in Tasmania.

Epilogue

Ocean waves had certainly carried Anne Frankland (nee Mason, 1792-1842) around the world. From England to India to South Africa and Australia, and back again several times. It was a life lived within nineteenth-century class conformities and complexities, of love and loss, of financial gain and hardship. It was her life, and hers alone.

Anne could never have imagined what would become of the nearly destitute 26-year-old spinster employed as a governess about to leave London for India in March 1820. Her life had evolved in a series of events, circumstances and opportunities. From a daughter, granddaughter and sister, she had become a teacher, a friend, a wife, a mother, the mistress of a large estate and a member of the upper echelon of society, all within the bounds of an antipodean English colony that was on the other side of the world. She had also been the chief supporter of her husband's career progression, the quiet confidante and counsel with regards to his public portrayal within a brutal Hobart Town press, the host of his many balls, dinners and soirées, and the worried wife when he was away in the remote Van Diemen's Land wilderness. And then she lost it all: her home, her husband, her life as it was. It was never a fairy tale, there was no happy ending.

Like the generations of strong, independent women before her, Anne had made choices and decisions that impacted her family, some with profound consequences. She had also endured the outcome of decisions made by past generations, predominantly the male members of her family, including many prior to her birth.

Of course there were regrets, but she had been adventurous, taken chances and endured the outcomes and persevered, particularly towards the end of her life when the reality of her financial situation became apparent and her health was failing. Seemingly an autonomous and resourceful woman, she had no choice but to rely on her community of friends and family. Thankfully they had lessened her burden, providing well for her, and, moreover, her children. Anne would have been relieved to know that in the years immediately following her death, Sophia, Georgina and Augustus were taken care of by both the Mason and Frankland sides of the family.

Yet, characteristically, this modern generation made their own choices and decisions with the outcome in certain situations pushing proprietary to the limit. Could they be blamed, however? They were the product of generations before yet the shape of the future. They would have heard the stories of wealth, influence,

Secheron House (1970s)
Tasmanian Archives (LPIC1/3/113).

landed gentry and large estates, marriage settlements, sugar plantations, rainbow hair coloured school mistresses who enjoyed appearing in Court, musicians who played with royalty, and meetings with Napoleon and Charles Darwin, and perhaps have been amused at the contrast, not fully believing the anecdotes. Coinciding with the death of Queen Victoria in January 1901 at the age of 81, the grandchildren of Anne and George Frankland were largely considered middle class. Oh what could have been! Yet it was not.

Thankfully, with this book, Anne Frankland's story is no longer hidden in the shadows of history, within the bounds and conventions of a male-dominated Georgian-era England. Her life and memory are intertwined with the women of her family; of her daughters, sisters, mother, grandmothers and great-grandmothers. It it is also associated with the still-extant Secheron House. While she died over 180 years ago, her legacy lives on.

Que Sera, Sera. Complevit.

Family Tree

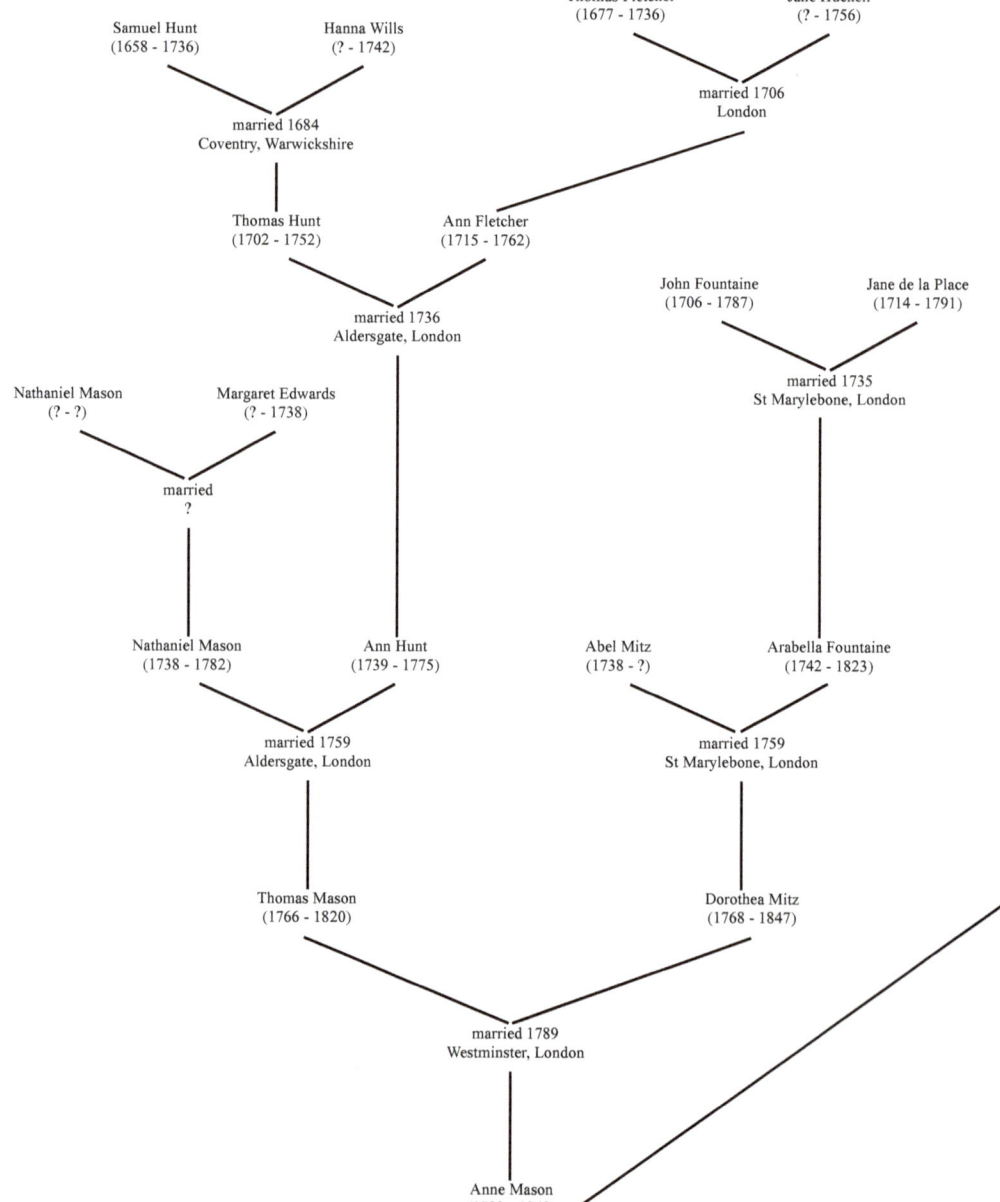

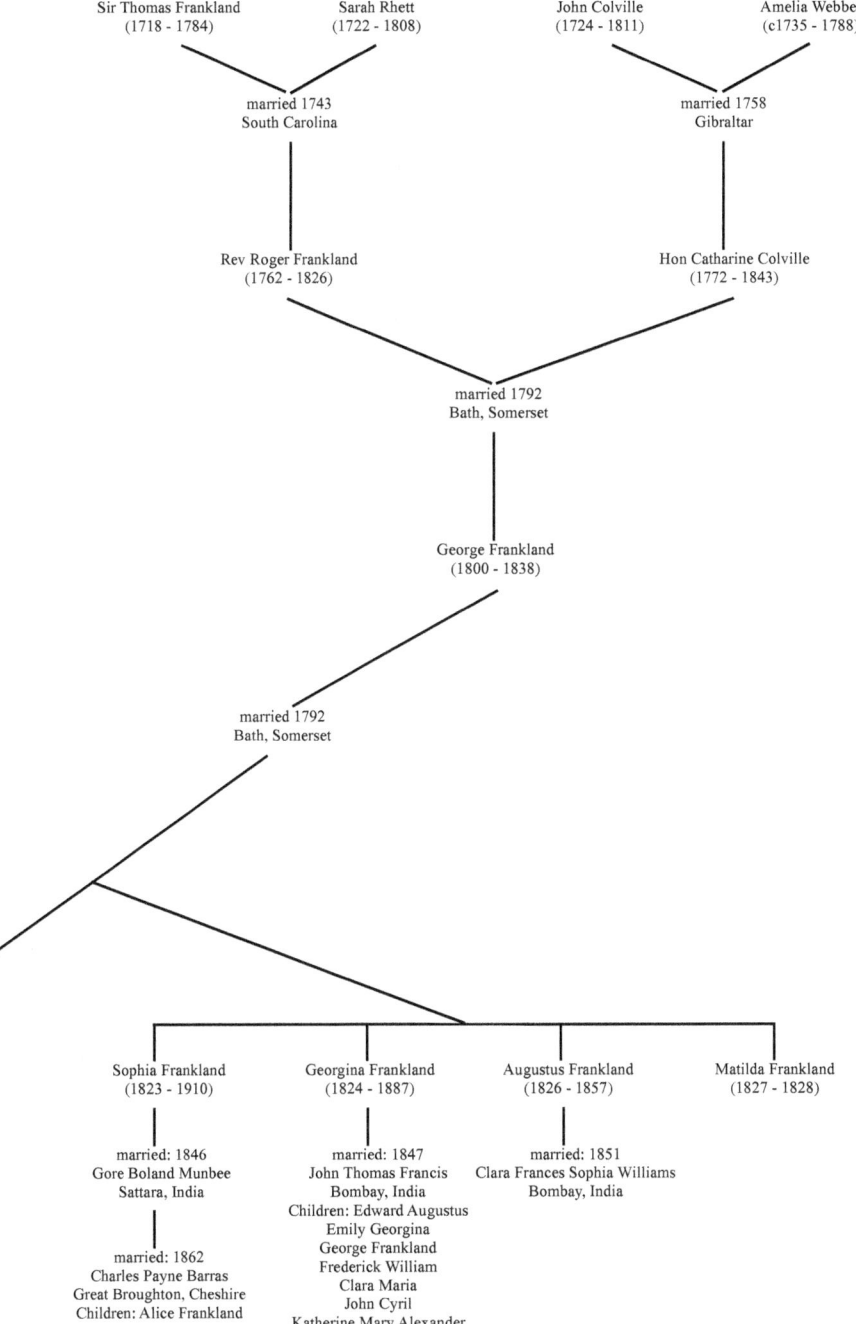

Index

Adams, John 43, 45
Allport Library and Museum of Fine Arts 100, 102, 152, 186
Anderson, W. 81
Archer, John Lee 106
Arthur (family) 142, 147
Arthur, Charles 144
Arthur, George (Lieutenant Governor) 99, 102, 105, 106, 110, 112, 118, 119, 123-125, 130-132, 135, 139-142, 144, 147-150
Austen, Jane 8, 16, 64

Baggs, A. P. 82
Baker's Charity 22, 53
Bank of England 26
Banks, Joseph (Sir) 81
Barras, Alice Frankland 178-180, 191
Barras, Charles Payne 178, 179, 181, 191
Barton, John 26
Bathurst, John (Earl) 96, 97, 103
Becket, Charles 66
Bedford, William (Rev) 106, 140
Bennet (family) 8
Bennet, Elizabeth 8
Bennet, Jane 8
Bennett, Thomas 36
Betts, Mr 112

Billing's Charity 22, 53
Bingley, Mr 8
Blackheath Proprietary School 171, 181
Blakeney, Miss 96
Bock, Thomas 150
Bond's Hospital 14, 53
Bowen, Thomas (Captain) 94
Bowles, William (Sir) 173
Bristow Wilson, H. 35
Brooks, James 66
Brownlow, Thomas 21

Callaghan, Daniel 135
Campbell, Archibald (Captain) 36, 38
Chandler, Sam (Rev) 27
Chaplin, Emma (nee Frankland) 88, 94, 96
Chaplin, William 88
Chapman, Thomas 1, 137
City of Coventry 16, 20, 25, 26
Clake, George Carr 162
Clarke (family) 1
Clarke, Hannah 184
Clarke, Mr 162
Clarke, Thomas Biggs 184
Colburn, H. 50, 83
Coleraine, Lord 48
Collins, David (Lieutenant Governor) 99
Colman, George (the younger) 48

Colville (family) 141, 186
Colville, Amelia (nee Webber) 80
Colville, Catharine (Hon) see Frankland, Catharine (Hon, nee Colville)
Colville, Charles (Jr) 86
Colville, Charles (Sir) 83, 84, 86, 88, 90, 92, 111, 112, 132, 167, 181
Colville, Jane (Lady, nee Mure) 86, 88, 92, 111, 112, 114, 115
Colville, John (Lord) 80, 83, 167, 191
Cromwell, Oliver 81
Crow's Charity 53
Crowther, W. L. 126, 128

d'Urville (Captain) 105
Darcy, Mr 8
Darling, General 104
Darwin, Charles 147, 189
Davies (family) 71-73, 75
Davies, Henry (Rev) 71-75, 90, 93
Davies, Mary Josepha 71, 72
Davies, Sophia Browning 71-75
de la Place, Denis 48
de la Place, Jane see Fountaine, Jane (nee de la Place)
de la Place, Katherine 48

Debrett, J. 80
Derwent Bank 155, 161
Dickens, Charles 179
Drifters, William 24
Dry, Richard 133
Dumaresq, Edward (Captain) 104, 106
Dumaresq, Mrs 107
Dunnington, John 41

Earle, P. 9, 10, 17
East India Company 71, 72, 74-78, 95
Edwards, Margaret 190
Edwards, Thomas 32
Elphinstone, Mountstuart 90
English Copper Company 54
Evans, George 103, 104

Fenton, Elizabeth 68, 71, 111-117
Fenton, Flora 112, 113, 116
Fenton, Michael 111-116
Findley, Captain 98
Finlay, W. A. 184
Fletcher (family) 15, 16
Fletcher, Ann see Hunt, Ann (nee Fletcher)
Fletcher, Jane (died 1766) 53
Fletcher, Jane (nee Huckell) 9, 10, 12, 15, 17, 26-28, 190
Fletcher, Jane see Mount, Jane (nee Fletcher)
Fletcher, Martha (nee Stiles) 53
Fletcher, Mary see Morhall, Mary (nee Fletcher)
Fletcher, Samuel 13
Fletcher, Thomas 8-13, 17, 190
Fletcher, Thomas (Jr) 12, 15, 25, 28-30, 33, 34, 51, 53-54
Flower, Benjamin 59
Forster, Captain 143
Fountaine (family) 48

Fountaine, Arabella see Mitz, Arabella (nee Fountaine)
Fountaine, Diana 50
Fountaine, Elizabeth 49, 50
Fountaine, Frances 50
Fountaine, Jane (Jr) 49, 50
Fountaine, Jane (nee de la Place) 48-51
Fountaine, Rev Dr John 46, 48-51, 190
Fountaine, Thomas 50
Fowler, J. 38
Fox, L. 14
Francis, Clara Maria 180, 191
Francis, Edward Augustus 180, 181, 191
Francis, Emily Georgina 180, 191
Francis, Frederick William 180, 191
Francis, George Frankland 180, 191
Francis, John Cyril 180, 191
Francis, John Thomas 180, 181, 191
Francis, Katherine Mary Alexander 180, 191
Frankland, Arthur 113, 132, 136, 141, 142, 144, 173, 176, 177
Frankland, Augustus Charles 97, 98, 102, 106, 139, 146, 168, 170, 171, 173, 175-177, 180, 181, 188, 191
Frankland, Catharine (Hon, nee Colville) 80, 81, 95, 96, 174, 175-177, 191
Frankland, Catherine 95
Frankland, Charles Colville 83, 84, 173, 175
Frankland, Colville 173
Frankland, Edward 83, 84, 173, 175
Frankland, Emma see Chaplin, Emma
Frankland, Frederick 83, 84, 94, 161, 173, 184

Frankland, George 2, 71, 79-86, 88-98, 100-111, 113, 117-119, 122-137, 139-148, 150, 151, 154-163, 167-171, 173-175, 179, 181-185, 189, 191
Frankland, Georgina Anne 94, 95, 98, 102, 139, 146, 170, 171, 173, 175-178, 180, 181, 188, 191
Frankland, Matilda Roberta 103, 105-107, 170, 191
Frankland, Matilda see Robison, Matilda (nee Frankland)
Frankland, Octavia 95
Frankland, Roger (Rev) 79, 81, 83, 95, 96, 191
Frankland, Sarah (nee Rhett) 79, 191
Frankland, Sophia 95
Frankland, Sophia Catharine 93-95, 98, 102, 110, 139, 146, 168, 170, 171, 173-181, 188, 191
Frankland, Thomas (Sir) 79, 80, 167, 191
Franklin, Eleanor 160
Franklin, Jane (Lady, nee Griffin) 151, 160-163, 168, 169
Franklin, John (Sir, Lieutenant Governor) 148, 150, 151, 154, 155, 160, 161-163, 168
Freeman, Edward 25

Gelebrand, Mr 114
Glennie, F. 85
Godiva 18
Government of Great Britain 15, 56, 78
Government of Tasmania 185
Government of Van Diemen's Land 104, 106, 118, 119, 122, 132, 133, 135, 136, 139, 140, 142, 144, 146, 148
Graham, Henry 144
Grant, John 25

Gribble, C. B. (Captain) 85
Griffin, John 168
Grimm Brothers 64

Hall-Moxey, William (Captain) 143
Hamerton, Major 96
Hamerton, Mrs 96
Hamilton College 37, 38
Hangar, George 48
Harris, John 28
Harrison, Elizabeth 28
Hay, R. W. 97
Heath, John Benjamin 72
Heath, Son & Furze 66
Henkell, Abraham 30
Hill, Lieutenant 112
Hobart Town Grammar School 146
Hobart, Lord 99
House of Commons 63
Huckell, Ann 18
Huckell, Jane see Fletcher, Jane (nee Huckell)
Huckell, Sarah 18
Huckell, Thomas 9
Hughes, Mrs 112
Hunt, Ann (nee Fletcher) 8-18, 19-29, 32, 33, 53, 190
Hunt, Ann see Oldham, Ann (nee Hunt)
Hunt, Charles Henry 67
Hunt, family 27, 29, 33, 51
Hunt, Hanna (nee Wills) 15, 16, 21-23, 190
Hunt, Hannah see Porter, Hannah (nee Hunt)
Hunt, Samuel 13, 14, 16, 23, 190
Hunt, Susanna 38, 43
Hunt, Thomas 8, 12-18, 20-26, 190
Hunt, Thomas (Jr) 21, 24-26, 33-38, 41-43, 45, 51, 55

Kassler, M. 50
Kemp (family) 142
Kermode, William 117, 130, 133
King George II 27, 51

King George III (HRH) 86
King George IV (HRH) 86
King William IV (HRH) 130, 171

Langford, P. 10
Langham (family) 42
Lawrence, H. 68, 71, 111-117
Lewis, Frances Maria Sewell 50
Lewis, M. G. 50
Lewis, Matthew 50
Library of Congress 19, 58, 87
Littell, E. 30
London Assurances 54
Long, Robert 44, 45
Louis XVI 56
Lowfield, Miss 21
Luckman, James 162

Macquarie Hotel 113
Manning, Anne 39, 40
Maritime Museum of Tasmania 185
Marsh, George (Jr) 65
Marsh, George Walker 64, 65
Marsh, Harriet Helen (nee Mason) 53, 64, 65
Marshall, J. 83, 84
Marylebone School 48, 49
Mason, Abigail 154
Mason, Ann (nee Hunt) 3, 21, 23-26, 28-30, 32-35, 28-40, 42, 45, 190
Mason, Ann Harriet 32, 42, 43, 54, 55, 64
Mason, Arabella Jane 4, 68, 94, 115, 116
Mason, Dorothea (nee Mitz) 3, 46, 47, 50-53, 55, 56, 59, 60, 67, 68, 72, 173, 190
Mason, Emily 154
Mason, Frances see Williams, Frances (nee Mason)

Mason, Harriett Helen see Marsh, Harriet Helen (nee Mason)
Mason, Jane 34, 42, 43, 54, 55, 64
Mason, Joseph 35, 42, 43, 52, 54, 55, 64
Mason, Langham 35, 42, 43, 54, 55
Mason, Nathaniel 3, 29, 30, 32-38, 40-43, 45, 190
Mason, Nathaniel (born 1798) 55, 61, 65-67, 171, 174-176
Mason, Nathaniel (Jr) 3, 32, 33, 42, 43, 54, 55, 57
Mason, Peter 35, 42
Mason, Sophia 55, 56, 64
Mason, Thomas 34, 42, 43, 45-47, 51-57, 59-61, 64-68, 90, 190
Mason, Thomas (Jr, born 1794) 55
Mason, Thomas (Jr, born 1799) 56, 61, 66, 67, 72, 73, 130, 132, 140, 142, 154, 170, 176
Mason, William 90
McMahon, Thomas 95
Mellon, Paul 75, 76
Merchant Taylor's School 61
Milan, Archduke of 50
Milan, Duchess of 50
Miles, A. 48
Milltis, Mary 59
Mitchell Library 130, 131
Mitz, Abel 46, 51, 190
Mitz, Abel (Jr) 51
Mitz, Arabella (nee Fountaine) 3, 46, 49-52, 61, 67, 68, 72, 95, 190
Mitz, Dorothea see Mason, Dorothea (nee Mitz)
Mitz, Lucas 51
Montagu, Captain 110, 143
Morhall, Mary (nee Fletcher) 10, 12, 15, 18, 28, 53

195

Morhall, Richard 10, 12, 15, 16, 28
Morhall, Richard (Jr) 18
Morhall, Thomas 16
Mount, Harry 27
Mount, Jane (nee Fletcher) 10, 12, 15, 17, 26-28, 53
Mount, John 27
Mount, John (Jr) 27
Mount, William 27
Munbee, Gore Boland 177, 178, 180, 191

Napoleon 61, 63, 65, 69, 189
National Archives UK 10, 12, 22, 23, 51, 52, 55, 61, 67
Nettlefold, A. J. 184
Nichols, J. 81

O'Byrne, W. R. 173
Old South Sea Annuity Stock 25
Oldham, Ann (nee Hunt) 22
Oldham, Hannah 23
Oldham, Samuel 23, 25
Oldham, Thomas 22
Oldham, Thomas (Jr) 23, 24
Oxford University 66, 84

Paice, Joseph 29-32, 34-42, 51, 64
Paton, G. 85
Pedder (family) 142
Pedder, John (Sir) 162, 176, 184
Pedder, Mrs 176
Penn Symons, W. 85
Perry (family) 1, 184
Perry, Arthur 184
Perry, Jane 184
Pitcairn, Robert 170
Porter, Ann 23
Porter, Elizabeth 23
Porter, George 22
Porter, Hannah (Jr) 23
Porter, Hannah (nee Hunt) 22
Powers, N. 48

Prince Albert of Saxe-Coburg and Gotha (HRH) 171
Princep, A.
Puddicomb, Julia 174
Puddicomb, Margaret 174

Queen Victoria (HRH) 171, 189

Rhett, William 79
Robinson, C. J. 61
Robison, Matilda (nee Frankland) 85
Robison, William 85
Rooker, Michael Angelo 49
Ross, John 184, 185
Roth, H. L. 110
Royal and Sun Alliance Insurance Group 51
Royal British Army 81, 84, 88, 90, 91, 96, 111, 133, 171
Royal British Navy 83, 90, 173
Royal Exchange Assurance Office 30, 54
Royal Military College 83
Royal Society of Arts 34, 35
Ryan (child) 143
Ryan, Major 143

Scott, Thomas 103, 104, 108
Shakespeare 64
Sharland, Mr 103
Shelley, Mary 64
Sheridan, R. B. 36
Simpkinson, Mary (nee Griffin) 84, 102, 117, 168, 169
Siraut, M. C. 82
Smith, William 124
Snodgras, Kenneth (Colonel) 150
Society for Promoting Christian Knowledge 107, 108
Sorell (family) 142

Southern and Craner's Charity 53
St Michael's Collegiate School 136
St Thomas' Hospital 34, 53
State Library of New South Wales 121, 130, 131
State Library of Tasmania 100, 102, 126, 128, 152, 186
Stephen (family) 142, 147
Stephen, Alfred 117, 136, 140, 144, 146, 147, 148, 154, 170, 176
Stephen, Emily 154
Stephen, George 144
Stephen, Virginia 117, 147, 154
Stephens, W. B. 20
Steward, Nathan 41

Tasmanian Archives 103, 106, 109, 122, 130, 134, 138, 145, 146, 149, 154, 156, 159, 164, 169, 182, 186, 188
Tatlock, George 72
Tennant (family) 173
Theatre Royal 150
Troughton, James 55
Trusler, John (Rev Dr) 48

University of Cambridge 49
University of Tasmania 84, 102, 117, 137, 151, 154, 168, 169
Van Diemen's Land Company 110, 133
Van Diemen's Land Society 118, 122, 123

Warwick County Asylum 67
Watson, A. E. (Rev) 179
Watson, George Massey 179, 180
Watson, Sophia 180
Waylen, J. 79, 81
Webb, Richard 116

196

Webber, Amelia see Colville, Amelia (nee Webber)
Wedge, Mr 103
Wellington, Lord 84
Wesley, Charles 50
Wesley, John 50
Wesley, Samuel 50
Whessell, John 31
White, Sir Thomas 22
Wikimedia Commons 13, 31, 80, 84
Williams, Clara Frances Sophia 181, 191
Williams, Frances (nee Mason) 59, 175, 181
Williams, Hamerton 181
Wills, Hanna see Hunt, Hanna (nee Wills)
Wilmot, A. 94
Wren, Christopher 12
Wroe-Brown, R. 48

Yale Center for British Art 75, 76

www.ingramcontent.com/pod-product-compliance
Lightning Source LLC
Chambersburg PA
CBHW061735070526
44585CB00024B/2680